Sir Sidney Eardley-Wilmot

The development of navies during the last half-century

Sir Sidney Eardley-Wilmot

The development of navies during the last half-century

ISBN/EAN: 9783337109028

Printed in Europe, USA, Canada, Australia, Japan

Cover: Foto ©ninafisch / pixelio.de

More available books at **www.hansebooks.com**

Her Majesty leading the Battle Fleet to sea in H.M. Royal Yacht *Fairy*, 1854.
From a picture in the possession of the Hon. Mrs. Denman.

THE DEVELOPMENT OF NAVIES

DURING THE LAST HALF-CENTURY

BY

CAPTAIN S. EARDLEY-WILMOT, R.N.

With many Illustrations

LONDON
SEELEY AND CO., LIMITED
ESSEX STREET, STRAND
1892.

TO
HER MOST GRACIOUS MAJESTY
QUEEN VICTORIA
IN WHOSE REIGN
THE CHANGES HEREIN DESCRIBED
HAVE TAKEN PLACE
THIS BOOK
IS, BY PERMISSION,
DEDICATED

PREFACE

It has been said that nations, like individuals, have their times for self-examination, when they pause, survey their positions, glance back upon the past, study the lessons of experience, and gird themselves up for the future.

The present year, memorable for the opening of an Exhibition devoted to a display of objects connected with the Naval Service, and signalised by the launch of two noble warships by Her Majesty on the same day, seems a fitting period when we may review the changes which half a century has produced in the fleets of the world, and strive to draw some lesson for future guidance.

In tracing the development of modern ships

of war, and their equipment, it was natural to me to describe mainly what has been done in this country; but the progress abroad is also dealt with, as showing the great advance made by other nations. The principal operations in which squadrons and single ships have engaged during this period are briefly described, to demonstrate certain phases of naval warfare connected with modern armaments.

It was difficult to compress such a vast subject into a single volume of moderate dimensions, and I am conscious of many defects in the accomplishment of the task, for which indulgence is pleaded. No effort has been made to give minute technical details, but rather to place before the reader a general review of the whole subject.

I have received cordial assistance from many quarters. For the chapter on steam propulsion I am indebted to Mr R. C. Oldknow, late Fleet Engineer, Royal Navy, whose ability to deal with the subject will be fully recognised. In this portion Messrs Maudslay, Sons & Field afforded valuable information, with drawings of past and present marine engines.

To Lord Brassey my thanks are due for permitting me to reproduce some of the illustrations in Volume I. of his *British Navy*. Sir William Armstrong, Mitchell & Co. placed at my disposal several interesting pictures connected with the vessels and armament constructed at Elswick.

I desire also to thank the Proprietors of the *Engineer* for allowing me to utilise matter which has appeared in the pages of that journal.

Messrs Thornycroft, Yarrow, J. & G. Thomson, and Mr Mackrow of the Thames Iron Works and Shipbuilding Company, have most liberally aided my efforts.

Many of the illustrations are from photographs taken by Mr West of Southsea, whose skill in marine photography is well known.

In dealing with the navy prior to the general adoption of steam propulsion, I have received valuable assistance from distinguished officers who were serving at that period, and to whom my best thanks are now tendered.

S. EARDLEY-WILMOT.

23 CRANLEY GARDENS, S.W.
October 1891.

CONTENTS

CHAPTER I

THE NAVY IN 1840

Reduction in Naval Estimates after 1832—Change in Construction of **Ships by Sir W. Symonds**—The 'Vernon,' 'Pique,' and 'Vanguard'—Ordnance **afloat at that** Period—Defective System of manning Ships—Steamers then in the **Navy**—Bombardment of **Acre**—**Advantages** of Numerous Guns and Rapidity **of Fire** attacking Fortifications, ... 1

CHAPTER II

CREATION OF A STEAM FLEET

Changes in Ship Construction after 1840—Reluctance to recognise **Advantages of Screw** Propulsion—Gradual Conversion of Sailing Fleet to Steam—Armament practically remains unaltered—The Crimean War—Operations in Black Sea and Baltic—Assistance rendered by the Navy—Expedition to Sea of Azof, . 23

CHAPTER III

BROADSIDE IRONCLADS

Prejudice against Iron in Shipbuilding—First Ironclads built in France and England—Increase in size of Ships—Advance in Ordnance—Commencement of Struggle between Guns and Armour—Action between 'Alabama' and 'Kearsage,' showing advantages of Armour, ... 43

CHAPTER IV

EARLY TURRET SHIPS

Introduction of the 'Monitor'—Claims of Ericsson and Captain Cowper Coles—'Merrimac' and 'Monitor' in America—'Royal Sovereign' converted in England—Further development of the Turret System—'Devastation' to 'Inflexible,' . 71

CHAPTER V

BARBETTE SYSTEM COMBINED WITH BROADSIDE

Battle of Lissa—Lessons to be derived from this Action—Introduction of the Barbette System of Mounting Guns—First applied in the 'Temeraire'—The 'Admiral' Class—Increase in dimensions of Battle Ships to 14,000 tons—New Vessels, 'Royal Sovereign,' 'Empress of India,' 'Ramillies,' 'Repulse,' 'Resolution,' and 'Royal Oak'—Disadvantages of Monster Ships, ... 93

CHAPTER VI

COAST DEFENCE—THE RAM

Coast Defence Vessels—Such Constructions of Modern Growth—Erroneous Ideas of Defence—The 'Glatton' and other Coast Service Vessels—Russian Circular Ironclads—Development of the Ram as a Weapon—The 'Rupert' and 'Polyphemus'—Disadvantages of a Vessel for ramming only—Examples of difficulty in ramming, ... 115

CHAPTER VII

ARMOUR—LATER TURRET SHIPS

Early Iron Plates—Increased Thickness—Competition of Guns and Armour—Steel and Compound Plates supersede Iron—Deck and Coal Protection—Progress of Turret Ships 'Nile,' 'Trafalgar' and 'Hood,' 'Victoria' and 'Sanspareil'—Second-Class Battle Ships—Early Types—Latest Development—'Centurion' and 'Barfleur,' 136

CHAPTER VIII

CRUISERS

Frigates in Old Time—Speed an Essential—Early Steam Cruisers—'Inconstant' and others—Action between 'Shah' and 'Huascar'—Armoured Cruisers—'Imperieuse' and 'Warspite'—Development of Internally Protected Vessels—'Blake' and 'Blenheim'—'Royal Arthur' Class—Smaller Types—Scouting Duties—Necessity for High Speed, ... 148

CHAPTER IX

ORDNANCE

Old Smooth Bore Guns and their Manipulation—Mr Lancaster's System—Introduction of Rifled Guns—Early Inventors—Breech-Loaders introduced and discarded—Woolwich Muzzle-Loaders—Growth of Ordnance to 80-ton Guns—Breech-Loaders again introduced—Increase of Length and Power—Advance to 110-ton Guns—Ammunition—Quick-Firing Guns, ... 166

CHAPTER X

TORPEDO WARFARE

Early Application of the Torpedo in America—The Fish Torpedo—Development by Mr Whitehead—Introduction of Torpedo Boats, and their Progress—Submarine Boats—Protection against Torpedoes—Nets—Electric Search Lights—Torpedo Boat Destroyers—Sinking of 'Blanco Encalada,' . . . 193

CHAPTER XI

STEAM PROPULSION

Steam Navy in 1840—Machinery at that Date—Paddle-Wheel Frigates and Sloops—Horse Power, Nominal and Indicated—Voyage of 'Inflexible'—'Banshee'—Introduction of the Screw Propeller—'Fairy'—'Duke of Wellington'—'Victoria'—Substitution of Iron for Wood—'Warrior' and 'Black Prince'—'Octavia,' 'Arethusa,' and 'Constance'—Progress made up to 1865—Compound Engines—'Pallas'—Increase of Boiler Pressure—Twin Screws—'Inconstant'—Loss of the 'Captain'—'Iris' and 'Mercury'—Steel Protective Decks—'Polyphemus'—Forced Draught—'Lightning'—Yarrow's Boats—'Rattlesnake'—Triple Expansion—'Barham' and 'Bellona'—Decrease in Weight of Machinery—Difference between Men-of-War and Merchant Ships—'Blake' and 'Blenheim'—Large Number of Auxiliary Engines—Supply of Fresh Water—Evaporators—The 'Yaryan'—Growth of Steam in the Navy—Personnel—Probable Approach of Finality in Marine Engineering, ... 211

CHAPTER XII

FOREIGN NAVIES—EUROPE

Condition of French Navy in 1840—Progress after Franco-German War—Broadside and Barbette Construction—Cruisers—The Russian Fleet—Influence of the 'Monitor'—New Departure—Black Sea and Baltic Squadrons—Belted Cruisers—Italy—Creation of a New Fleet after 1870—Monster Ironclads—Cruisers—Germany—Late development of Navy—New Battle Ships and Cruisers—Austria, Spain, Greece, and Turkey, ... 248

CHAPTER XIII

FOREIGN NAVIES—UNITED STATES AND SOUTH AMERICA

Condition of United States Navy before and after Civil War—Apathy in Naval Matters—Change of Feeling in 1880—New Cruisers constructed—Battle Ships decided on and commenced—Special Fast Cruiser—Torpedoes—The Howell Torpedo—Dynamite Gun—Development of Navies of South American States—Chili—Capture of 'Huascar' by 'Blanco Encalada' and 'Almirante Cochrane'—Peru—The Argentine Republic—Brazil, ... 270

LIST OF ILLUSTRATIONS

	PAGE
THE BALTIC FLEET, 1854,	*Frontispiece*
MODEL OF THE 'VANGUARD,'	6
MODELS OF THE 'VERNON' AND 'ST JEAN D'ACRE,'	24
'LA GLOIRE,'	49
THE 'WARRIOR'S' ARMOUR,	51
THE 'WARRIOR,'	53
THE 'AGINCOURT,'	57
ARMOUR OF THE 'BELLEROPHON' AND 'HERCULES,'	62
THE BATTERIES OF THE 'ALEXANDRA,'	65
CAPTAIN COWPER COLES' GUN RAFT AND CUPOLA SHIP,	73
ERICSSON'S TURRET,	77
THE 'ROYAL SOVEREIGN,'	79
THE 'DEVASTATION,'	82
THE 'INFLEXIBLE,'	85
TURRET OF THE 'INFLEXIBLE,'	86
THE 'TEMERAIRE,'	104
MODEL OF THE 'RAMILLIES,'	110
THE 'GLATTON,'	121
THE DECK OF THE 'NOVGOROD,'	125
THE 'CONQUEROR,'	130
THE 'VICTORIA' FIRING,	144
THE 'VOLAGE' UNDER SAIL,	150
THE 'IMPERIEUSE,'	155
THE 'ALACRITY' DESPATCH VESSEL,	162
NAVAL GUNNERY IN 1840,	167

List of Illustrations.

	PAGE
67-TON GUNS, MOUNTED *EN BARBETTE*, ...	180
THE 'RODNEY' STEAMING AND FIRING, ...	184
TURRET OF THE 'VICTORIA,' WITH 110-TON GUNS, . .	188
6-IN. QUICK-FIRING GUN, ...	190
TORPEDO BOAT, BUILT FOR THE ARGENTINE GOVERNMENT,	**200**
TORPEDO BOAT, 'ARIETE,' BUILT FOR THE SPANISH GOVERNMENT, ...	204
SIDE-LEVER ENGINES, ...	212
ENGINES OF THE 'BLACK EAGLE,'	**214**
ENGINES OF THE 'IRIS,'	**235**
ENGINES OF THE 'BLAKE,'.	**242**
THE 'ADMIRAL DUPERRÉ,'	251
GUN WITH SHIELD ON THE 'REDOUTABLE,' . . .	256
THE 'ITALIA' AND 'LEPANTO,'	261
THE 'PIEMONTE,' ITALIAN CRUISER, ...	264
THE 'CHARLESTOWN,' UNITED STATES CRUISER, . .	275
THE 'INDIANA,' UNITED STATES COAST LINE BATTLE SHIP, .	275

The Development of Navies

CHAPTER I

THE NAVY IN 1840

Reduction in Naval Estimates after 1832—Change in Construction of Ships by Sir W. Symonds—The 'Vernon,' 'Pique,' and 'Vanguard'—Ordnance afloat at that Period—Defective System of manning Ships—Steamers then in the Navy—Bombardment of Acre—Advantages of Numerous Guns and Rapidity of Fire in attacking Fortifications.

AFTER Trafalgar the British navy was at the zenith of its fame, for we had established a complete supremacy on the ocean, and swept from the sea all hostile fleets. Every project of Napoleon for distant conquest had been frustrated by our fleet, and in after years, at St Helena, he frankly recognised the fact. 'You,' he said to O'Meara, in one of those many interesting conversations recorded by the latter, 'are superior in maritime force to all the world united, and while you confine yourself to that arm you will always be dreaded.' On another occasion he remarked: 'Your soldiers are brave, nobody can deny it; but it was bad policy to encourage the military mania instead of sticking to your marine, which is the real force of your country, and one which, while you preserve it, will always render you powerful.' The Peninsular War and the battle of Waterloo, however, diverted the mind of the country from the navy, and for many years after the conclusion of peace, in 1815, we were content to rest upon the glories we had achieved, exhausted by that long continued struggle. Our maritime strength gradually declined, but it was not until the Reform Bill of 1832 was passed that the navy suffered materially from the desire for economy in State expenditure which then prevailed. At that time the naval estimates for the effective service were about £4,250,000. In 1834 this was reduced to £3,000,000, and in 1835-36 to £2,750,000. Our squadrons maintained abroad gradually dwindled in numbers, and it seemed as if a perpetual peace was expected. Not content, however, with reductions in the number of ships employed, the complements of individual vessels were reduced to what was termed a peace establishment, and we even went so far as to send vessels abroad without some of their guns. I believe it is a fact that a line-of-battle ship about this time was sent as flagship to a station without her lower deck guns, in order to give more room for the admiral's staff. During the first half of the century few changes had been made in naval architecture or armaments. Fleets still consisted of sailing line-of-battle ships, frigates, and smaller vessels. Officers were discussing the value of square or round sterns, the latter introduced by Sir Robert Seppings, then Surveyor of the Navy. The square stern was constructively weak, and the guns it carried could not be directed on a certain bearing termed the point of impunity. This had been observed in previous actions, when ships lost their masts and were not under command. The navy was reluctant to give up the square stern, as it afforded more cabin accommodation. But, as one of the most experienced officers of the day said: 'In peace time the circular stern will not be popular, but in the event of a change to hostilities its utility will find innumerable advocates.'

A considerable modification in the form of ships was, however, made when Captain—afterwards Sir William—Symonds was appointed Surveyor of the Navy in 1832. Being a naval officer, there was considerable opposition to this appointment, which had hitherto been held by a member of the School of Naval Architecture. This school had been established in 1806 for the education of a more skilful class of trained shipwrights. There had been many complaints in the old wars that our ships were inferior in design to the French. Charnock observes that 'when the French captured an English ship they either put her on a lower rating or threw her aside. Their foundered or wrecked ships were invariably British built. When we were in chase, the French prizes of the squadron took the lead, and every officer desired to command them.' It was only the splendid handling of any class by our officers which overcame the defects of our designs. Moreover, captured vessels became the models from which we built. Even as late as 1850, out of 150 ships on the *Navy List*, upwards of fifty were from foreign models. Nor were the Spanish types considered unworthy of this honour. Many of them are said to have been the production of an Irishman named Mullens, who went over to Spain and offered his improved plans to that Government after having failed with the English Admiralty. The 'San Josef' and 'San Nicolas,' taken by Nelson in Lord St Vincent's action, were both handsome vessels.

The principle of Sir William Symonds was to give greater beam at the water line and sharpness below. The old school were in favour of less beam. The average length had hitherto been 3.6 to 3.9 times the breadth. In Sir William Symonds's ships it ran from 3.1 to 3.3 times. He adopted the same principle for great and small, so that one would fit inside another like a series of trays. The 'Vernon' was the first large vessel built from his designs. She was a 50-gun frigate, 183 ft. long, with a beam of 53 ft. Hitherto Surveyors of the Navy had been limited in the proportion of guns to tonnage, but Captain Symonds refused to have his hands tied in this respect, and no limitation was enforced on him. He therefore built the 'Vernon' of 2080 tons, a considerable increase over the tonnage of existing frigates. A great success was the result. The 'Vernon' sailed remarkably well, and is still up Portsmouth Harbour, having served for many years as the torpedo school ship.

The 'Pique,' another frigate of his design, of thirty-six guns, launched in 1834, was rendered famous in 1835, when, under the command of Captain the Hon. H. Rous, she came across the Atlantic without a rudder.

She had previously grounded at the mouth of the St Lawrence, and sustained severe damage, but was got off, and her captain determined to proceed to England. Three days after starting she lost her rudder. This was a severe demand even upon the seamanship of those days, but a jury rudder was rigged up by which the ship was steered the rest of the way home. When Captain Rous afterwards stood for Westminster he was met at the hustings with the usual cry, 'Who are you?' He answered, 'Captain Rous of the "Pique," who brought her across the Atlantic without a rudder.' 'Bravo Rous!' shouted everyone, and 'Bravo Rous' became for a time the common cry in London.

Owing to the economical principles then in vogue, it was not until 1835 that the first line-of-battle ship on the designs of Captain Symonds was launched. This was the 'Vanguard,' of 2610 tons and eighty guns. Her dimensions were, length 190 ft., and breadth 57 ft. She was the broadest ship in the navy. Her principal characteristics were speed and handiness under canvas, with great space between decks. A great improvement effected by Captain Symonds in 1836 was in reducing the different lists of ships' stores, which had gradually accumulated to the number of eighty-seven, owing to there being so many classes of vessels in the navy. It is recorded that when Nelson was off Cadiz he had no less than seven classes of 74-gun ships each requiring different spars, so that if one had been disabled the others could not have supplied her wants.

In 1839 the 'Queen,' a three-decker, and the largest

ship built by Sir William Symonds—he was knighted in 1836—was launched at Portsmouth. Her dimensions were, size 3100 tons, length 204 ft., and beam 61 ft. The armament consisted of a hundred 32-pounders and ten 68-pounders. Her total cost was £115,000. The shape of the stern was elliptical, an improvement on Seppings's round stern. The 'Queen' was justly considered a remarkably fine vessel, and formed the model on which many future designs were based. Up to 1830 the want of precision in our ideas as to the best types of line-of-battle ships to adopt had been very apparent. But after that date we discontinued building small three-deckers, and converted some into two-decked ships of eighty guns. In the same way small two-deckers were cut down to 50-gun frigates. These were termed Razées. A certain lot of vessels were known as Jackass frigates, because it was said they could neither fight nor run, while a batch of small two-deckers were called the 'forty thieves.' The general outcome of the old wars had brought home to the minds of all who studied the question that neither the very great nor the very small in ship construction was desirable. Number, not size, was our great requirement, and moderate dimensions had sufficed to maintain the sea against all comers. The next great war will probably lead to the same result in modern naval architecture.

Turning to the armaments of ships of war at that period, we find little advance since the beginning of the century. Cast-iron smooth bore ordnance was universally employed, with spherical projectiles. In 1838 the

H.M.S. Vanguard, launched in 1635. From model in Royal Naval Exhibition.

heaviest solid shot gun was a 32-pounder, 9 ft. 6 in. long, and weighing 56 cwt. A 42-pounder had been used in the old wars, but was now discarded as having no advantages over the lighter piece. But guns for throwing hollow shot and shell had recently been designed, though not at first regarded with great favour. The principle on which guns were constructed in those days was exceedingly simple. The rule of Mr Monk, who then designed ordnance, was to have 1¾ cwt. of metal in the gun to each pound in weight of shot. A great advance, however, was made about 1840 by the introduction of a gun weighing 95 cwt., which threw a solid shot of sixty-eight pounds. It was at first intended as a pivot gun for steamers, but afterwards was almost universally carried by all ships, and remained for many years our heaviest piece of ordnance afloat. Carronades, short guns of large calibre, also formed part of a ship's armament. They were formidable at close range, but no match for long guns at any distance. Consequently only a certain number of these guns were carried, because if the wind failed at a critical moment, before close quarters could be reached, an enemy with a single long gun might do great damage, without her adversary having any power of reply. Instances of this had occurred during the old wars. Loading guns with double shot was still in force, but owing to the inaccuracy of this mode of firing it was only used at very close quarters. As regards penetration of wooden sides, some curious results were obtained, at Gavre in France, about the year 1838. A 32-pounder with double shot was fired against timber, and it was found that the shot nearest the charge penetrated 29 in., while the one furthest from the charge penetrated 42 in. There were three types of mortars then in the sea service, the 13 in. of 100 cwt. and 81 cwt., and the 10 in. of 52 cwt. They had a range of about 4000 yards, with an elevation of 45°, and their object was, in a bombardment, to crush buildings and penetrate magazines. Their transport by sea was not difficult or costly, and it was considered that a fleet should be provided with vessels for this service. The introduction of shells was slow. The old prejudice in favour of solid shot was not easily overcome. The latter were said to be more accurate, and to have greater range and penetration than hollow shell. Objections were also raised to putting too many shell guns in ships, on account of the danger of accidental explosions.

Another argument used against the introduction of these projectiles was their cost. Sir Howard Douglas, in his work on Naval Gunnery, says: 'The expense of shell equipment is enormous. The cost of every 8-inch shell in box is 11s. 6d. Each one fired costs 17s. 4¾d.' The 17s. 4¾d. included the powder, the amount of which was 10 lbs. What would Sir Howard have said if told that fifty years later the cost of a single round from guns mounted in battle ships would range from £150 to £200? How insignificant seems the 68-pound shot, propelled by 16 lbs. of powder, beside the 1800-lb. projectile of to-day. But as regards shell, it required the incident of Sinope a few years later to demonstrate the terrible effect of shell fire upon wooden ships, and the necessity of a change in naval architecture. In other matters connected with ordnance we were also very conservative. Our guns were still fired with flint locks, which had replaced the priming horn and match in 1780. The French had already adopted the percussion lock. In a letter from Commander Milne—now Sir Alexander Milne—to the Surveyor of the Navy, dated May 5th, 1839, when the former was in command of the 'Snake,' at Bermuda, he says: 'The French Squadron have left Vera Cruz. We were nearly three months lying together at that place, and had an opportunity of seeing their new improvements. The chief one was the invariable use of detonating locks, acting on the principle of a hammer falling down on the vent hole, in which a tube is placed of the same material as ours, the top alone being of detonating powder. They say they answer most completely, and never miss fire.' We did not introduce the hammer and percussion tube until 1842. Our powder was enclosed in paper cartridges, but in a few years flannel was substituted, and continued in use until a comparatively recent period.

In gunnery training, however, our seamen had not been neglected. The 'Excellent' had been established at Portsmouth in 1830, by Lord Melville, for training seamen in gunnery. This establishment was extended by Sir James Graham in 1832, and placed under Captain Sir Thomas Hastings. There it has remained until the present time, turning out an admirable corps of naval gunners, which may be truly considered the backbone of the fleet as far as its seamen are concerned. Previously to this there had been no systematic gunnery in the navy, and proficiency in this respect much depended on individual captains. Not long after the 'Excellent' was established at Portsmouth, the 'Edinburgh,' a 58-gun ship, was stationed at Plymouth for the same purpose, and placed under the 'Excellent.' It is now better known as the 'Cambridge,' where equally good work is carried out, and efficiency is ensured by the healthy rivalry maintained between the two depots.

At the time under review there is no doubt that the great defect of our naval system was in the manning of the ships, and the difficulty of procuring seamen without great delay. Ships sometimes had to wait months before the crew was complete. Officers had to visit all the well-known haunts of seamen, and use every sort of persuasion to get men to enter their ships. According to the custom then, men only joined a ship for a commission, and on paying off—if no other ship was being brought forward for commission—a number of men were thus thrown on their own resources. The result was that hundreds of splendid men were lost to the navy, many going over to America, or taking up other avocations. The time required for manning a ship depended much on the captain's reputation in the service. Placards in the seaport of fitting out such as the following were resorted to:—'Wanted active seamen for the "Powerful"—Captain Napier. The "Powerful" is a fine ship, and in the event of a war will be able to take her own part.' 'Wanted seamen for the "Superb." A superb ship, a superb captain, and a superb crew.'

This difficulty of obtaining men was not experienced to the same extent when war was anticipated, because the attraction of prize money was a powerful inducement to join, and there is always the natural love of adventure in the British race. Hence on an emergency the radical defects of our system were not so apparent. In France, on the other hand, where, since Colbert established the Maritime Inscription, all seamen are bound to serve in the navy for a few years, and then pass into the reserve, there has at times been a difficulty in getting them back promptly when required. On one occasion, some years ago, additional ships were ordered to be equipped in France, which necessitated calling out a portion of the naval reserves. These consisted chiefly of coast fishermen, and a number tried to put to sea in their boats to evade the order. Some succeeded, and others were arrested before they could get away. Another example may be cited. When the Crimean War broke out we were far from being prepared, yet the manning of the fleet was comparatively expeditious. Lord Malmesbury records in his memoirs, on February 9th, 1854: 'Sailors are coming in very fast. The rapidity with which our ships are equipped excites the astonishment of the French.' Again, on March 10th, he says: 'The Queen reviewed the fleet at Spithead. The French fleet is not ready, neither are their transport for the troops.' The result was that our squadron was in the Baltic a considerable time before it was joined by our allies.

When we passed from the old irregular method of manning the fleet, and adopted the continuous service system (under which seamen enter for ten years, with the option of continuing at its expiration for a further similar period, followed by a pension), coupled with the entry and training of boys, a complete revolution was effected in this portion of the naval service. The delays of manning in peace time disappeared, and all uncertainty in the matter, when hostilities are apprehended, is removed. For a reserve in time of war we rely on 20,000 merchant seamen, who, though they have never served on board a man-of-war, are annually drilled to guns and small arms at various depots round the coast. How far the comparatively small number of highly trained seamen we maintain, together with this somewhat uncertain reserve, would supply the requirements of a protracted maritime war it is difficult to say. The waste, from many causes, would be very great if the struggle were severe, but seeing the number of men this country possesses who are, or have been, connected in some way with the sea, and who would be of great assistance when acting with trained seamen, I do not think that in this respect our resources will prove inadequate.

A review of the composition of navies half a century ago would be incomplete without a reference to steam propulsion, because the paddle-wheel steamer was then in existence, and a certain number of vessels of this description were in the fleet. Of course, the great step at this period was the introduction of the screw propeller, but of this it is proposed to treat in a subsequent chapter.

Previous to the year 1830 our Government only

possessed a few small steamers, principally employed for the purpose of towing ships in and out of harbour, or for coast service, with an occasional trip to Malta or Gibraltar. They were all paddle-wheel vessels. There does not appear to have been at this time any general idea that the new motive power was about to supersede the propulsion of war ships by sails. Even the most advanced and talented of naval officers could not contemplate steam vessels otherwise than as an auxiliary—more or less important—to the larger fighting vessels of the past. Thus, writing to the Secretary of the Admiralty, in 1827, Captain Charles Napier says: 'In another war steam will become to the navy what cavalry is to the army. It will be the post of honour.' By another distinguised officer it is compared to the horses which draw the artillery in the field. The usefulness of steam was to be found in scouting, in towing the regular fighting ships into action, and afterwards falling upon any of the enemy which might be disabled. Calms would no longer prevent our ships from closing, or light airs enable a faster sailing ship to escape. Hitherto there had been no other way of giving progress to a sailing ship in a calm than by getting the boats out to tow her, a very slow and tedious operation. But it was thought at this time that paddle-wheels might be utilised even though not worked by steam power. Hence the 'Active,' a 46-gun frigate, was fitted with paddles worked by the capstan. A speed of from two to three knots was obtained, but the plan involved so much labour on the part of the crew that it was given up. When, however, Captain Napier, who was then a man of great energy and enterprise, commissioned the 'Galatea,' a 42-gun frigate, in 1829, he was allowed to fit her with paddles actuated by winches inboard. About two-thirds of the crew were required to work them efficiently, and a speed of three knots in a calm could be obtained. It was, of course, hard work for the men, but as the captain said, they did not mind it if they were thus enabled to get into harbour when the wind failed, instead of remaining outside waiting for a breeze. But as we advanced in the application of steam power all such rude mechanical appliances were given up, and in 1830 it was determined to add steam paddle-wheel vessels to the fleet. Five—the 'Dee,' 'Phœnix,' 'Salamander,' 'Rhadamanthus,' and 'Medea'—were then laid down. Taking the 'Medea' as a specimen, her dimensions were :—

Extreme length,	206 ft.
Breadth, outside paddles,	155 ,,
,, inside, ,,	46 ,,
Burthen,	830 tons.
Horse power,	220.
Coal carried,	300 tons.
Speed according to draught,	8 to 10 knots.

They had three masts, and carried sails. With the paddles disconnected, and allowed to revolve freely, they sailed fairly well. They were called steam sloops, and had a few guns on the upper deck for hollow shot and shell. Later on the 68-pounder was employed as a pivot gun at their extremities. A larger class were called steam frigates, and had guns on the main deck.

They varied in size from 1200 to 1800 tons. The amount of coal carried in proportion to their size was large, owing to the great consumption with those early engines. Thus the 'Sidon,' one of these frigates, could stow 600 tons of coal. The general armament for this class consisted of fourteen 32-pounders on the main deck and four 68-pounders on the upper deck. One of this type, the 'Terrible,' of 1830 tons, was considered a very fine vessel, and performed efficient service in the Black Sea during the Crimean War. Paddle-wheel steamers were, moreover, represented in our navy until quite recent years. All the Royal yachts are even now paddle-wheel, as this application of steam power allows of such excellent accommodation and comfort. Another advantage is that it enables a comparatively large vessel to be constructed on a light draught of water.

This review of fleets half a century ago may fitly conclude with a brief notice of an operation carried out by a British naval squadron composed of sailing ships supplemented by paddle steamers. This was the bombardment of Acre in the year 1840. Steam played an unimportant part in the action, and the incident is chiefly valuable as showing the power of the old ships and their armaments when opposed to forts which could be attacked from the sea.

Such an attack must be considered hazardous or the reverse, according to the circumstances of the case. When to Lord Exmouth was entrusted the service of reducing the stronghold of Algiers, in the year 1816, people in England were surprised at the smallness of the force with which he entered upon the task. But his plans were based upon certain information by which he was convinced that the batteries could be destroyed by a squadron of moderate dimensions. The result entirely justified his views, and he gained the greater credit in consequence. In considering the attack of fortifications by the vessels then employed, and the success which attended such operations at Algiers and Acre, the number of guns carried by line-of-battle ships and the rapidity of their fire are important points. As regards the first point, take the armament of one of the largest ships of that day, the 'Nelson.' She carried 120 guns, sixty on each side. Of course, in attacking forts a ship of this type could usually only engage one broadside, but this consisted of sixty guns, and the weight of metal thrown by them was 2750 lbs. When we add to this the rapidity of fire which then prevailed, say a round a minute, which was usually exceeded, an idea can be formed of the overwhelming cannonade to which a dozen line-of-battle ships could subject fortifications mounting probably far fewer guns. The height of the land defences from the sea, also, was material in affecting the result. Batteries placed nearly on a level with the water are far more subject to the fire of ships, and much less formidable to them, than batteries elevated somewhat above the surface of the sea. A practical illustration of this was given in the Crimean War, when our ships attacked the forts on the north side of Sebastopol. To this I shall refer again later on. Let us now see

The Navy in 1840.

how some of these remarks on the attack of fortresses are borne out in the bombardment of Acre.

On July 15th, 1840, a convention was concluded between Great Britain, Austria, Prussia, and Russia and Turkey, whereby the four powers agreed to support the Ottoman Empire against Mehemet Ali, the Pacha of Egypt. In the previous year a strong squadron, sent by the Sultan to act against the Egyptian forces, had deserted to the enemy without striking a blow. This squadron was now in Alexandria, watched by a detachment of our Mediterranean fleet, while the remainder, in conjunction with a Turkish and Austrian Squadron, were operating against Northern Syria, then in the possession of Mehemet Ali. The operations proving successful, the attack on Acre was decided on. The fortifications of this town were considered most formidable, and had been kept in good order since the time when Acre, under Sir Sidney Smith, had resisted the efforts of Napoleon. Mehemet Ali appears to have considerably strengthened the defences on the land side, but not to have done much to the fortifications on the sea front. Nevertheless, the walls were of considerable height and solidity, mounting about 200 smooth bore guns of different dimensions. The garrison consisted of about 5000 men, who had been well trained by the commander of the place. This was a Polish officer, Colonel Schultz, who had taken service with the Egyptians, and by his exertions had brought the troops under his command into a high state of efficiency.

The feasibility of attacking Acre had been discussed

some time previously, and two of our frigates, the 'Pique,' Captain Boxer, and the 'Talbot,' Captain Codrington, had been employed in surveying the water approaches. This work was admirably carried out; the positions of the shoals were ascertained, and buoys placed to mark their positions. No impediment was offered by the garrison to this proceeding, and apparently the officer in command treated such preparations with contempt. But it was not so in reality, for he had the distances to the buoys carefully measured, and detailed the guns so that the vicinity of each buoy was commanded by a portion of the defence. Fortunately the ships, as it happened, did not take up the prearranged positions, and the casualties on our side were much reduced in consequence. The force about to attack Acre consisted of seven line-of-battle ships, the 'Princess Charlotte,' 'Powerful,' 'Bellerophon,' 'Revenge,' 'Thunderer,' 'Edinburgh,' and 'Benbow'; four frigates, the 'Castor,' 'Pique,' 'Carysfort,' and 'Talbot'; two sloops, the 'Wasp' and 'Hazard'; and four paddle steamers, the 'Gorgon,' 'Stromboli,' 'Phœnix,' and 'Vesuvius.' Admiral the Hon. Sir Robert Stopford was Commander-in-Chief, and flew his flag in the 'Princess Charlotte,' and Commodore Charles Napier, in the 'Powerful,' was second in command. There were also three Austrian ships and the Turkish flagship co-operating in the attack. Admiral Stopford was an officer of long and meritorious service. He had entered the navy in 1780, and as captain of the 'Aquilon' participated in Lord Howe's action on the 1st of June 1794. In 1804, when in command of the 'Spencer,' he accompanied Lord Nelson in his chase of the French and Spanish fleet to the West Indies, but did not take part in the battle of Trafalgar, having been detached a few days previously to proceed with a squadron under Rear-Admiral Louis to Gibraltar for provisions. He had also been engaged in numerous other actions, and his record was such as to leave no doubt that any operation undertaken by him would be well performed. Commodore Napier also had seen much service in all parts of the world, and gained considerable reputation for his exploits when in command of the Portuguese fleet some few years previously. He had lately been employed in Northern Syria, in land operations against the forces of Mehemet Ali, and displayed special aptitude for such irregular warfare. His energy was remarkable, but confidence in his own powers tended to make him impatient of control, and hence the position of second in command was not altogether congenial to him. This characteristic led to a misunderstanding as regards the method of attacking Acre, which not only produced unpleasantness between the two chiefs, but also nearly brought about a failure in the intended attack.

The squadron anchored on November 2d, barely out of range of the guns of the fortress, and the plan of attack for the next day was then discussed. Acre stands on an acute angle of the coast, jutting out into the sea. It therefore presented two faces, one running nearly north and south, and facing west, while the other side ran nearly east and west, facing south. Both sides were well defended, though the batteries on the western face were more powerful, but few of the guns were much above the level of the sea. On each side shoals prevented large ships from coming close in. It was decided to divide the squadron into two detachments, the 'Edinburgh,' 'Benbow,' the small ships and foreign vessels were to attack the south side, and the remainder would engage the west face. The steamers were to lay off and use their shell fire to best advantage. At one time it was proposed that they should tow the other vessels to their positions, but there not being enough steam vessels to do this simultaneously, the plan was abandoned. The decision come to was that the vessels should take up their positions under sail, the 'Powerful' to lead, until opposite the further or southern end of the west face, followed by the others, then all to anchor together in their assigned places, according to which each portion of that side would have a ship opposite to it.

The next morning, therefore, when a fair but light breeze sprang up, the ships weighed and sailed down to Acre. Napier, however, anchored before arriving at the extremity of the west face. He for some reason misunderstood the plan, and apparently expected the other ships to pass ahead of him. The result was that a portion of the west face was not covered by an opposing force. Fortunately the 'Revenge' had not anchored, and she was directed by the admiral to fill the gap ahead of the 'Powerful.' This she did. The force to act against the southern side was somewhat put out by these movements, but Captain Stewart, in the 'Benbow,' asked permission to proceed to his station, and went on, followed by the 'Edinburgh.' As the 'Benbow' approached, Captain Stewart found deeper water than he expected, and was thus enabled to pass inside the buoys and get nearer the town. The 'Edinburgh' did the same. Up to this time no sign of life had come from the fortress, and the guns were screened. They had, however, been laid on the buoys, and the instant the ships anchored flags were hoisted on shore, and a heavy fire opened. Owing to the altered positions of the ships on both sides it was not nearly so deadly as it would otherwise have been. On the south side the shot just passed over the ships; and the water beyond was a sheet of foam. It would have been unsafe to hold a hand up above the bulwarks. On the north side, also, the shot struck the water where the buoys had been placed, but as the ships anchored in other positions they escaped much of the fire. The ships began the bombardment about the same time, and for two hours it was returned from the shore with gradually decreasing energy. Then an event took place which decided the fate of Acre. A large magazine blew up, having been ignited by a shell from one of the ships, and destroyed a great portion of the town and defences, and killed over 1000 of the defenders. From this moment the fire of the batteries on shore slackened, and half-an-hour after had virtually ceased. It being now sunset, the ships also discontinued the action, but made preparations to renew the combat next day as no indications of submission were apparent. The place, however, was evacuated in the night, and we took possession of it next morning. On our side the casualties were not numerous, consisting of eighteen killed and forty-one wounded. The damage sustained by the ships was not serious, and soon repaired. The number of the enemy killed and wounded was never ascertained, but it could not have been less than from 2000 to 3000. About the same number were taken prisoners, or gave themselves up when our force landed the following day. Among them was Colonel Schultz, who had been wounded. He said it was impossible to withstand such an incessant stream of fire as was poured from our guns. Even the bravest troops would have been demoralised. The result was due to a heavy cannonade at close quarters, kept up unremittingly from a great number of guns. At the same time the ships had certain fortuitous advantages which might not be conceded on another occasion. The action did not prove that our wooden walls could at all times attack forts with impunity, and indeed the contrary was demonstrated fourteen years later in the Black Sea. But the bombardment of Acre showed in a striking manner the terms upon which the old ships could contend successfully with land defences which at first sight seemed almost impregnable.

CHAPTER II

CREATION OF A STEAM FLEET

Changes in Ship Construction after 1840—Reluctance to recognise Advantages of Screw Propulsion—Gradual Conversion of Sailing Fleet to Steam—Armament practically remains unaltered — The Crimean War—Operations in Black Sea and Baltic—Assistance rendered by the Navy—Expedition to Sea of Azof.

THE discovery that steam could be profitably utilised for the propulsion of ships, and the tardy adoption of the screw, did not for many years materially affect the construction of war vessels. There was a strong prejudice to overcome in the minds of those who retained a vivid recollection of the glories accomplished in the past under sail, and who had a natural love for the art in which we excelled. Sir William Symonds, to whom I have alluded as effecting considerable improvement in the qualities of our sailing ships, had, as his biographer states, no love for steamers in any shape. They were an order of vessels which forbade the application of his favourite principles of construction. When Sir John Franklin left England, in May 1845, for the Arctic, the 'Erebus' and 'Terror' were each fitted with a screw. It is stated that Sir William spoke plainly of the risk to Sir George Cockburn, First Naval Lord of the Admiralty, and foretold their fate. In a letter to Lord Auckland about this time he states: 'I consider steamers of every description in the greatest peril when it is necessary to use broadside guns in close action; not alone from their liability to be disabled from shot striking their steam chest, steam pipe, machinery, etc., but great probability of explosion owing to sparks from funnel.' These views were shared by others; but circumstances were too strong, and slowly we began to convert our sailing navy into a steam fleet. In other respects, while retaining the two and three-decker as the embodiment of naval force, an advance was made by giving them an increased length. Whereas, in 1840, the 'Queen' was 204 ft. long, the 'Howe,' launched in 1860 as a screw three-decker, was given a length of 260 ft. This fine specimen and her sister ship the 'Victoria' were the last of that race of noble structures which we recall with regret. The first two-decker designed for the screw was the 'Agamemnon,' launched in 1852. Her length was 230 ft., while the 'Albion,' launched in 1842, was but 204 ft. long. We see the same modification in the frigates of 1860. From the 'Vernon' of 176 ft., in 1832, we passed to the 'Emerald' of 237 ft., in 1856. The latter was the first ship I served in, and a prettier model it would be hard to find. She was one of a class largely represented in the service as 50-gun screw frigates, and built of wood. We were, however, impelled to a further advance in this type by the action of the United States. That country had lately been producing frigates of large dimensions, and the appearance of the 'Niagara' in the Thames during 1857 created quite a sensation

Sailing frigate, The Vernon, fifty-gun.

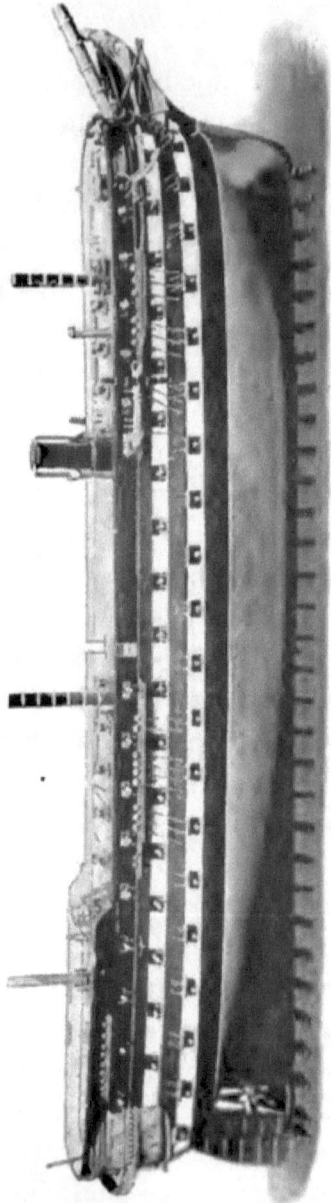

Screw two-decker, St. Jean d'Acre.

in England. Her dimensions were, length 335 ft., breadth 54 ft., and burthen 4750 tons.

This led to the construction over here of the 'Orlando' and 'Mersey,' the largest frigates built entirely of wood, and launched in 1858. Their length was 300 ft., beam 52 ft., and burthen 3750 tons. They were, however, structurally weak, and did not last long. The 68-pounder was still the heaviest gun carried, for we had not yet arrived at rifle guns. Shell equipment was now universally provided, for Sinope had convinced even the strongest adherents of solid shot that whatever might be the advantages of the latter against stone walls in their smashing effect, shell for the attack of ships must prevail. Appliances for the use of red-hot shot were still supplied. These projectiles were formidable to wooden ships. Nelson considered fire the greatest danger of a naval battle. Before going into action it was the custom, as far as possible, to remove everything below which might feed a fire. But there was danger also to the ship using red-hot shot. Guns occasionally burst owing to the expansion of the projectile, for which provision had to be made in the diameter of the bore. There might also be a premature discharge by the ignition of the powder. To prevent this, thick junk wads were supplied for use with hot shot, to be well soaked in water and then rammed down after the powder, thus interposing a screen between the charge and shot.

Rockets were another species of weapon much favoured then, but which have recently ceased to form part of our ships' equipment. They were also for incendiary purposes, and proved very effective against savage races and bodies of men. They were first introduced, early in the century, by Sir William Congreve. Their flight was produced by the escape of the gas to the rear, generated by the ignited explosive, and steadiness was imparted by attaching a wooden rod to the case. The use of the rod was dispensed with by the invention of Mr Hale, who caused the rocket to rotate in its flight. This was effected by the gas in its escape impinging on short iron wings at the end of the case, thus imparting rotatory motion. Rockets, however, for war purposes were not to be depended on, especially after being kept for some time, and occasionally they gave rise to serious accidents.

Before passing on to the great change which the adoption of iron as a material for ship building and as a means of protection produced in our fleet, it seems desirable to review briefly the operations in the Black Sea and Baltic during the Crimean War, when we had for the last time sailing ships combined with screw and paddle steamers. These operations afford an example of the effect of a powerful navy in rendering possible military operations in distant lands, and aiding them in many ways. Our success at Acre is not repeated in a bombardment of land batteries under different conditions in one locality, whereas it is shown elsewhere that if special plant is provided such an operation can be undertaken without great risk. This war, from a naval point of view, has many striking features. It is difficult

Creation of a Steam Fleet.

to realise now how little prepared we were in 1853 for war with a powerful continental nation, and for such an operation as the invasion of its territory. Though the Naval Department has generally been assumed to have emerged from that war with more credit as regards its organisation than the War Office, the term 'mobilisation,' and its meaning, was entirely unknown in reference to any possible naval operation. If success has come in the past, it has been in spite of our system, not in consequence of it.

For instance, previously to the Crimean War there had been a Transport Department at the Admiralty, but a regard for economy had led to its suppression. Nevertheless, when it was reorganised, energy and ability supplied the want of experience. Its operations were on a large scale, for we conveyed to the east 70,000 officers and men, 5600 horses, and 85,000 tons of stores. To the Baltic, also, we transported 13,000 officers and men, with about 10,000 tons of stores. It must be remembered that our allies looked to us in a great measure for transport. Though steam propulsion was in its infancy, we employed over 100 steam transports, and a slightly greater number of sailing ships. Sir Stafford Northcote, in a letter to Mr Disraeli, dated April 19th, 1862, and printed in his life, says: 'We showed in the Crimean War both our weakness and our strength. Our strength consisted in the elasticity of our resources, the temper of our people, the length of our purse, and the power of our endurance. Our weakness was shown in the confusion of our arrangements and the absence of military skill.' But he might have added that the chief evidence of our strength was to be found in our maritime supremacy, which made such an expedition possible. History has not adequately recorded the part played by the navy on this occasion, because there were no fleets to overcome, and it did not repeat the success at Acre; but in other ways the assistance it rendered was of the utmost importance.

In command of the Mediterranean Squadron at that time was Admiral Deans Dundas. He was an officer who had seen much service, but had now reached the age of sixty-eight, and owing to a former wound could not sustain great exertion. When he was appointed to this command, it was not anticipated that we should shortly be involved in war. As second in command of the squadron we had in Sir Edmund Lyons a man of great ability and energy. His early career had been a distinguished one, but in 1835 he was appointed Minister at Athens, a post he filled for several years, so that in 1854 his capacity for naval affairs was not well known in the fleet. Detailed by Admiral Dundas to organise arrangements for transporting the army from Varna to the Crimea, he at once gave proof of his capability. All difficulties disappeared before his energy and gift for organisation. Yet it was no easy task to shift the base of operations from Turkey to Russia. To forward 60,000 troops from England and France had taxed the resources of those countries, but to tranship them on the barren shores of the Black Sea entailed a greater call on those entrusted with the operation. Much had to be created on the spot; yet although the order to invade the Crimea only reached Lord Raglan on July 6th, 1854, the combined armies, with their necessary equipment, embarked on August 24th. Circumstances delayed their sailing till September 7th, when they set forth for the enemy's country. What a splendid sight it must have been, over 150 vessels conveying the troops, guarded and convoyed by a British squadron of ten sail of the line and fifteen smaller vessels. The French men-of-war were filled with troops owing to insufficiency of transports. What a time for an enterprising enemy to make a dash at this armada! Inside the harbour of Sebastopol there was a powerful flotilla, consisting of thirteen sail of the line and sixteen smaller vessels. A determined attack might have scattered that cloud of transports, and, taking into consideration the time of year, indefinitely postponed the expedition. But the opportunity was lost, and 63,000 men, with 128 guns, were landed without opposition, as if for some peaceful autumn manoeuvres. As an operation of war it was hazardous. A night assault on our force after landing might have been disastrous. None took place, and the battle of the Alma strengthened our position in the occupied territory. It was then decided to invest the south side of Sebastopol, while the navy were to occupy the port of Balaclava as a base of operations for the army. From a naval point of view this harbour was well suited to the purpose. Though not of great extent, it contained deep water, and had facilities for landing stores. Moreover, the anchorage was well sheltered from all winds, and as at this time it was not considered that the siege would prove a lengthy operation, I am unable to see that the choice of Balaclava was a bad one.[1]

The arrival of the army at the head of Balaclava Harbour and the entry of our ships took place simultaneously on the 26th of September. To this no resistance was offered by the enemy, and the siege train was landed next day. By the act of the Russians in sinking most of their largest ships across the entrance to Sebastopol our naval force was freed from any thought of having to meet the enemy at sea. What a blow to those gallant Russian sailors, who afterwards took such

---

[1] Sir Edward Hamley, in his interesting volume *The War in the Crimea*, states that the choice of Balaclava as a base brought untold miseries upon the army, and speaks strongly of the influence Sir Edmund Lyons had with Lord Raglan. But the point the admiral had to consider was, whether Balaclava was suitable to receive transports and store ships, and whether the harbour offered facilities for discharging cargo? He could assure the general that no delay should take place in these respects. The proof of this lies in the fact that the siege train was landed the day after the harbour was entered. As to the distance of the harbour from our camp, that was a matter which the general would weigh in deciding whether to accept or reject the admiral's recommendation. It did not affect the suitability of the port for getting the stores on shore; their prompt transport to the camp rested with the Military Department. If the land transport arrangements were faulty, and want of men prevented good roads from the base to the camp being made until after the battle of Inkerman, the difficulties that resulted are not attributable to any deficiency of Balaclava as a naval port. I regret that the gallant author of this work should speak of Sir Edmund Lyons as Lord Raglan's evil genius. The mind of the admiral was wholly absorbed by the desire to render every assistance to his comrades on shore, and he brought to this work an energy, ability, and single-mindedness which, hardly realised in the past, will some day, I am sure, receive ample recognition.

a distinguished part in the siege, to see a fleet it had taken years to construct settling down in the water without a combat. Though the foe was a combination of the two most powerful maritime nations of Europe, they were ready for the fray, and the disappointment could not be otherwise than bitter. England had experienced such a day of humiliation two centuries before when she scuttled her own vessels to bar the passage of the Dutch up the Medway, and then vainly turned to forts as a substitute for an efficient fleet.

But our squadron in the Black Sea was able to afford material assistance in other ways towards the object aimed at, the capture of Sebastopol. Over sixty guns were landed from the ships, and a naval brigade formed of 2000 officers and men. This greatly augmented the resources of the allied armies in preparing for the first bombardment of the Russian works defending the southern side of the town. This took place on the 17th of October, and in order to assist the operation the admirals of the English and French Squadrons were requested to attack simultaneously the sea defences. When I use the word 'requested,' it is perhaps hardly applicable to the French naval commander. He was under the orders of the general in command, and hence to such a direction could only demur on strong grounds. In our case the admiral was acting independently, and though he would naturally afford the general the fullest co-operation, he was at liberty to withhold his consent to any course of action as regards the fleet which might to him seem undesirable. Admiral Dundas was reluctant to expose his ships to damage in an attack which, according to his judgment, would have no direct influence upon the assault by land. It must be remembered, moreover, that he had willingly denuded his vessels of a portion of their armament, and reduced their crews by a considerable number; and he might have insisted that a sea attack should only be undertaken with ships fully equipped. But when his French colleague informed him of his intention to carry out the desire of his general, with or without our assistance, Admiral Dundas felt compelled to join in the attack.

The forts which the combined squadrons were about to bombard defended the approach to the harbour of Sebastopol. On the north side, to which our ships were allotted, they were especially strong. At the entrance was Fort Constantine, a massive stone structure mounting 100 guns. But still more formidable to ships were the batteries on the high ground above, which, though not armed with numerous guns, could sweep the sea beneath with comparative impunity. The southern side was defended by a battery at the mouth of Quarantine Bay, and Fort Alexander further in. The French Squadron was to attack on this side, and with our vessels form a continuous line in front of the harbour. It had been arranged that fire on land and sea should be opened early in the morning; but at the last moment this was altered as regards the ships, and they did not commence until after one o'clock. By this time all idea of a land assault had been given up owing to the discomfiture of the French batteries on shore. More than one explosion had taken place in their lines, and they were not prepared to join us in the intended movement which was to follow a vigorous cannonade. The ships, however, proceeded to carry out their part of the day's work. Sir Edmund Lyons, in the 'Agamemnon,' with the 'Sanspareil,' 'London,' 'Albion,' and 'Arethusa,' formed an inshore squadron, and anchored within 800 yards of the northern batteries, while the rest of our ships were further off, prolonging the French line. Fire was then opened on both sides. Considerable impression was made on Fort Constantine, but the batteries on the cliff, when they got the range of our ships, subjected them to an effective fire to which little return could be made. The 'Rodney,' 'Queen,' and 'Bellerophon' then closed to reinforce the hardly pressed inshore squadron, and the cannonade was continued. Owing to the fact that most of the ships had landed their upper deck guns, and that this portion was comparatively clear of men, our casualties were not so numerous as they otherwise would have been. The Russians used chiefly time fuses with their shell, numbers of which burst over the upper decks, cutting them up like a ploughed field. But, nevertheless, at the close of day, when our vessels withdrew from their positions, we had lost over forty killed, and 250 men wounded. The French had an easier task, and did not suffer so severely. The gain was not commensurate with such a loss, and in fact the whole proceeding was unwise. If the object was to facilitate the assault and entry of our troops on the south side, it is difficult to see what benefit would accrue from shelling batteries in another quarter. When this assault was postponed, there was clearly no reason to attempt the destruction of works intended to resist entry by sea, and which could have little influence upon an army taking the city in rear.

From a naval point of view, however, the principal lesson taught by this episode is the strength exhibited by a few guns on high ground even when opposed by a powerful squadron. Fort Constantine must have succumbed in time, even as the forts at Acre were unable to withstand the heavy and rapid fire of our ships. But a single elevated battery is difficult to silence, and may defy the efforts of a fleet. This was perfectly well understood in the old wars, but the lesson had been forgotten, until it was once more brought home to us on this memorable occasion. Another point demonstrated was the disadvantage attached to joint enterprises under dual command. Of this we had not much previous experience, because in most of our struggles at sea we had fought single-handed. But the Franco-Spanish alliance, which was punished at Trafalgar, is an example of the doubtful strength of such combinations. How bitterly Villeneuve complained of his Spanish colleagues. No plans could be formed that were not liable to be disturbed by their different methods of business and organisation. One supreme chief is necessary to success, and should we ever engage in any maritime alliance again, there must be one head, recognised by both States, and invested with full authority over the whole force.

A more profitable service rendered by the navy in the

Crimea was in cutting off communications with Sebastopol by the Sea of Azof. In February 1855, about six weeks after Sir Edmund Lyons assumed chief command of the Black Sea fleet, Admiral Dundas having gone home, the Admiralty called his attention to the importance of occupying as soon as possible the Sea of Azof, as the Russian army in the Crimea drew largely both reinforcements of men and supplies of provisions conveyed by water between Rostof and Taganrog and the shores of the Crimea bordering on the Sea of Azof. Such an enterprise accorded with the energetic spirit of the admiral, and in conjunction with our allies an expedition was organised for this service. The entrance to this inland sea is commanded by the powerful fort of Kertch, and to take this in rear a strong landing force was provided. This consisted of 7000 French, 3000 English, and 5000 Turkish troops. They were conveyed in nine sail of the line and forty smaller vessels. The expedition started on the 22d of May, and arrived in the vicinity of Kertch the next day. A bay within ten miles of this town was selected, and disembarkation was effected without delay or obstruction. Baron Wrangel, the Russian general in command of this portion of the peninsula, did not oppose the landing. In fact, he could not tell where it might take place, and was unable to move troops as fast as ours could be conveyed by sea. Fearing to be cut off from Sebastopol, he destroyed several batteries on the coast and retired. As Kinglake eloquently says of the incident: 'He (Baron Wrangel) succumbed to the power (of which the world will learn much in times to come) an armada can wield when not only carrying on board a force designed for land service, but enabled to move swiftly, whether this way or that, at the will of the chief.' Kertch was occupied on the 24th of May, and Sir Edmund Lyons, hoisting his flag on board the 'Miranda,' entered the Sea of Azof. He then placed a squadron of light draught vessels under the orders of his son, Captain E. M. Lyons, consisting of fourteen sloops and gun vessels, with five French steamers. Holding commands in this squadron were some of the ablest men our navy possessed. Such names as Commerell, Sherard Osborn, Cowper Coles, Hewett, M'Killop, Burgoyne, and others, were a guarantee that activity in this quarter, at least, would prevail. Events succeeded each other rapidly. On May 26th the squadron appeared off Berdiansk, where the enemy burnt four war steamers of his own and large depots of corn. On the 27th Arabat was bombarded, and in three days 106 merchant vessels were destroyed. The same activity continued until the operations closed in November by reason of approaching winter. A volume might be written of the work done in this region by the navy. It has never been adequately recorded, but the cutting off and destruction of all the sources of supply to the Russian army from the Sea of Azof contributed in no small or unimportant degree to the fall of Sebastopol.

Although, as I have endeavoured to show, the naval operations in the Black Sea afforded invaluable assistance to the Crimean expedition, it was to the Baltic squadron that the nation looked for the greatest triumphs on the sea. These expectations were not destined to be realised by any great feat of arms. For this there were many reasons, the principal one being that the means were not adapted to the end, and that there was no clear conception as to what the fleet could be reasonably expected to perform.

When, in the early part of February 1854, it was seen that war could not be avoided, every exertion was made to fit out a formidable Baltic Squadron. Of the ships detailed to form this squadron some were at Lisbon, while others were laid up in the various home ports. It had been usual to offer a bounty to seamen to ship afloat when required on an emergency, but in this case it was not done, and all sorts and conditions of men were entered to complete the complements of the ships. By this means a squadron was collected with what was considered at that time creditable expedition. Admiral Sir Charles Napier was selected for the command, whose reputation in the country was still high, though he was now sixty-eight years of age. The squadron, having assembled at Portsmouth, left on the 12th of March, Her Majesty leading it to sea in her screw yacht the 'Fairy.' On that day the force consisted of eight ships of the line, four frigates, and three paddle steamers. Other ships not yet complete with crews had to be left behind, and joined afterwards. Bound for the Baltic, where the water all round the coast is very shallow, vessels of light draught for certain operations were an essential adjunct to such a force; but no gunboats had been provided. This omission strongly influenced the course of events.

On March 27th the fleet anchored in what was then the Danish port of Kiel. Our first object was to confine the enemy's vessels to the Baltic, so that their power of offensive action against our coasts and commerce might be neutralised. A blockade was therefore essential. A trial of strength between the two fleets was also desirable, as success in such an action would secure the same end more effectually. Attack on strong fortresses was deprecated as likely to damage the fleet without an adequate return. The nation, however, expected an attack on Cronstádt, no doubt with the recollection of Acre in its mind. But the conditions were very different. Not that the sea defences of Cronstadt at the declaration of war were of the formidable nature attributed to them, but because the neighbouring water was so shallow that the approach of large ships was a difficult matter. The want of gunboats capable of taking up advantageous positions within range of the forts was the reason given by Sir Charles Napier for abstaining from an attack on Cronstadt. He was unwilling to risk injury to his own squadron by such an operation while the Russian fleet was intact. It was no secret at Acre that he opposed the bombardment as most hazardous, but orders from England were imperative on that occasion. In the Baltic many of the ships were most indifferently manned, and kept the sea with difficulty. We were unable to prevent a junction between the Russian Squadrons at Sveaborg and

Cronstadt, the former getting out when a gale of wind had driven our squadron of observation from the port. But a younger and more energetic commander would probably not have been so much impressed with the risks incurred; and Nelson in his daring exploit at Copenhagen undertook a task of equal magnitude without hesitation.

Sir Charles Napier having set his face against a direct attack on Cronstadt or Sveaborg — another place where powerful land batteries guarded the sea approaches — turned his attention to Bomarsund, the stronghold of the Aland Islands. It was guarded by forts mounting numerous heavy guns, with a garrison of 2500 men. No reinforcement was possible while our ships commanded the water intervening between these islands and the mainland. Hence the safest and most certain form of attack was to land a sufficient force at a convenient spot and take the forts in rear. This was decided upon, and the British admiral desired to effect it with the resources of the combined squadron alone, but the French commander considered them insufficient, and a body of 9000 French troops was sent out arriving early in August. When all was ready, guns and men were landed without opposition. Besides the regular troops, a large contingent of sailors and a battery of 32-pounders from the ships formed part of the force. Works were then thrown up within range of the forts, and between the 13th and 15th the forts were bombarded. One after another surrendered, until the whole of Bomarsund was ours. In default of relief from the sea, capitulation was inevitable. This incident is an excellent example of the power conferred by command of the sea when at the same time there is a sufficient land force judiciously employed.

No other operation of any magnitude was attempted that year, and when the Baltic Squadron returned to England for the winter it was not considered to have put forth its full strength. There was much criticism on the decision not to attack Sveaborg, so a new commander-in-chief, Rear-Admiral the Hon. R. Dundas, with a stronger squadron, was sent up the following year. By this time gunboats and mortar vessels had been prepared, and the crews of the squadron had much improved, so that the new admiral started under fair auspices, Her Majesty again leading the squadron to sea and wishing it success. In the beginning of August the whole flotilla approached Sveaborg. The gun vessels and mortar boats were to perform the principal part in the bombardment. The fortress consisted of five islands, on which were batteries with numerous heavy guns. On the 9th of August the attack took place. Carefully assigned positions were taken up by our small vessels—the remainder of the fleet being in rear—and a heavy fire opened on the defences. The gun and mortar boats offered so small a mark and were at such a range that the return fire from the shore did comparatively little damage. After some hours our shells blew up more than one magazine and set fire to several buildings. At sunset the gunboats were withdrawn, but the place was plied with rockets during the night. During the next day the attack was continued. The whole place now seemed a sheet of flame, and on the morning of the 11th, the enemy's batteries having ceased to reply to our guns, the action was discontinued. On our side only a few men were wounded, but the Russians lost considerably. Though the fortress was much knocked about, a few days would have put it in a condition to sustain another bombardment; and whether it surrendered or not, we were unable to land a sufficient force for its occupation. We had, however, shown that a powerful fortress could be attacked from the sea, and without great loss, if undertaken with plant adapted to the purpose. It was simply a question of providing sufficient material, and keeping up the supply until the object was attained. Success would rest with that side which possessed the longest purse and the greater resources. With an absolute command of the sea, the impregnability of a fortress becomes a comparative term, and another year of war would doubtless have seen a similar attack on Cronstadt. But Sebastopol now fell, and peace was made.

This war produced no naval actions or single combats between ships, but maritime strength had in other ways brought about a result even greater than could have been secured by a great naval victory. The voluntary sinking of a large portion of the enemy's fleet, the inaction of another part, the invasion of territory, the reduction of some fortresses, and the total stoppage of sea commerce, were directly or indirectly owing to naval supremacy tacitly acknowledged. Steam had materially assisted the attack, while it conferred no advantage on the defence. As Kinglake eloquently says of the result of the Kertch expedition: 'The simple truth is that, in regions where land and sea much intertwine, an armada having on board it no more than a few thousand troops, and propelled by steam power, can use its amphibious strength with a wondrously cogent effect.'

CHAPTER III

BROADSIDE IRONCLADS

Prejudice against Iron in Shipbuilding—First Ironclads built in France and England—Increase in Size of Ships—Advance in Ordnance—Commencement of Struggle between Guns and Armour—Action between 'Alabama' and 'Kearsage,' showing advantages of Armour.

THE same reasons which operated on the minds of the naval officers in respect to the application of steam propulsion retarded the use of iron for the construction of war vessels. That material was first employed for canal boats about the year 1812, and afterwards for steamers of the mercantile marine. About 1834 the Admiralty were urged to institute experiments to ascertain whether iron might not be utilised for ships of war, but they moved so slowly that the first iron war steamer built in this country was the 'Birkenhead,' by Messrs Laird, in 1845. For reasons to be mentioned presently she was turned into a troopship. She was lost in 1852 at the Cape, under the circumstances well known from the heroic conduct of the soldiers and seamen on the occasion. To test the behaviour of iron under the effects of shot, and to compare it with wood, some experiments were carried out at Portsmouth from 1849 to 1851. Iron plates, ⅝ in. thick, placed 35 ft. apart, to represent a section of the 'Simoom,' a vessel then under construction, were fired at from a 32-pounder. The effect was most ominous. Not only were the iron splinters produced by the shot passing through the side of a destructive nature, but it was found that the shot broke up in perforating the plate, and became an additional cloud of splinters too numerous to be counted. The experiment was repeated with the addition that the iron was backed with 5 in. of oak. A similar result ensued, but wooden splinters mingled with the iron. When wood alone was tried, the splinters were trifling as compared with those from the iron. Other experiments were then carried out to see if these effects could be mitigated, but without success. The deduction was that the destructive effects of shot on iron ships could not be prevented. If the iron sides were of the thickness required to give adequate strength to the ship—as ⅝ or, at least, half-an-inch—the shot was broken up. If the plates were thinner, the ships would be deficient in strength, and though the shot might pass through without breaking up, the disc of iron driven in was broken into numerous small pieces.

These results created a great sensation. A verdict was given that iron vessels, however convenient and advantageous in other respects, were utterly unfit for purposes of war, and a committee of naval and military officers, which had been directed to report how far it might be possible to arm vessels of the packet service in case of war, rejected all constructed of iron. Many years were to elapse before this material was taken into favour again. It was even a question then whether iron steamers were fit to be employed as transports for the conveyance of troops and stores during war. However, the Admiralty decided to employ those which were being built as troop ships. In one or two others which were completed the armament was removed from the main deck, and timber substituted for iron in the upper works, behind which a few light guns were placed. Considering the present almost universal adoption of iron and steel for naval architecture, the foregoing events appear to me to have no little interest. I have not dwelt upon the defects of the substances employed, such as cast-iron shot, and probably the inferior nature of the plates. No doubt both had an important bearing on the results obtained, but I will pass on to the revival of iron for warship construction. As practically in England this occurred simultaneously with the introduction of armour, I shall deal with them together in reference to the creation of our modern navy. With many inventions it is difficult to assign to any country or individual either actual discovery or practical application. In most cases the two operations are distinct, and separated by a considerable interval of time. This is certainly true as regards both the idea of protecting ships with an external casting of iron and its actual use. The first idea is, I think, due to Colonel Paixhans, the French officer who was mainly instrumental in substituting horizontal shell fire in place of shot. In 1825 he expressed an opinion that line-of-battle ships might be cuirassed against cannon shot by sacrificing a tier of guns, and that seven or eight inches of iron would effect it. In this we see a complete foreshadowing of what was to come thirty years later. He recognised at once the revolution his own invention would effect in naval armaments, and that provision must be made against it. Though no sailor or naval architect, he saw that his new idea was incompatible with the lofty sides of the old liner; but still more strangely, considering the date of his opinion, he indicated an amount of protection which was not reached for some years after the introduction of armour, as though he had an inkling of the later development of ordnance now so familiar to us.

But this conception of the future battle ship remained unheeded until the Crimean War, when the Emperor Napoleon, who in matters of war material often showed considerable ability, proposed the construction of floating batteries, or ships protected on the exterior by thick plates of iron, and shortly after five such batteries were commenced in France. All were of the same dimensions, 172 ft. long and 44 ft. broad. The side above the water line, which was only a few feet high, had a covering of $4\frac{1}{2}$ in. of iron, a thickness determined after experiments with existing guns and projectiles. Behind the armour was a backing of 17 in. of timber. This added to the protection, besides being useful for supporting the heavy weight of iron with bolts. The first was launched in March 1855, and the others in July. We followed suit with three similar vessels, the 'Thunderbolt,' 'Erebus,' and 'Terror.' They were at first intended for an attack on Cronstadt, but this idea being abandoned, they were sent to the

Black Sea, and arrived in October 1855. Three of the French batteries had been previously despatched to the same locality, and took part in the bombardment of Kinburn. Our vessels were armed with thirty 60-pounders, the largest piece of ordnance then in use. Having a flat bottom, they only drew 9 ft. of water. They were, in fact, ships from which a thick slice had been removed from their hulls above and below the water. They were well suited, from their light draught, for the shallow waters of the Baltic, and with their powerful armament could have attacked the forts at Cronstadt with advantage, because these were all low down, and not of the formidable nature asserted at the time.

The defence of Kinburn in the Black Sea consisted of a strong casemated fort armed with over sixty guns, and supported by earthworks with a few additional guns. These batteries were on a narrow spit of land at the entrance to the River Boug, about forty miles east of Odessa. A combined English and French force was sent to attack them early in October 1855. It consisted of ships of the line, steamers, gunboats, mortar vessels, and the three French floating batteries lately arrived. On the 17th the assault took place. The mortar boats first opened fire, and then the floating batteries. Curiosity was excited as to the behaviour of the new constructions, and it was soon evident, after the forts commenced returning the fire, that the iron plates afforded efficient protection. The floating batteries were repeatedly struck by shot, which hardly indented the sides, and the shells burst harmlessly against them. Damage, of course, they received as, having numerous port holes, all the projectiles and pieces of shell could not be excluded, but the injuries received were small in comparison to what they would have been had the sides been without the armour. To have been completely effectual there should have been at least a dozen of these batteries. The number of guns three could bring into action was relatively small. After a two hours' cannonade the line-of-battle and other ships advanced and poured in a heavy fire. In less than half-an-hour the batteries were silenced, and the appearance of a white flag showed that all resistance was at an end.

The success attending the employment of these floating batteries in the Black Sea indicated that in some such direction was to be found the solution of a problem now exercising men's minds, namely, how to resist the destructive effects of shell. In England we were disposed to rely on what had in former years admirably answered the purpose, and given us a supremacy on the sea by which the security of the country was ensured. Had our fleet suffered defeat, we might have been more ready to adopt new inventions, indeed, to initiate them, rather than wait until their utility was proved by others. But the weapons to hand not having failed, the natural tendency was to let them go with reluctance. In France, on the other hand, no such sentiment prevailed; and the skill she had always shown in naval construction was at once displayed when an entirely new departure for the designs of battle ships was taken. She had, moreover, in the head of the naval constructive department at that time, a man of genius and originality. M. Dupuy de Lôme had already given proof of both these qualities, and now he determined to boldly transform a wooden line-of-battle ship into an armour-clad which should be a seaworthy as well as a formidable fighting structure. To this end he took the 'Napoleon,' a fine two-decker, removed the upper portion, lengthened her by 24 ft., and placed 5-in. armour plates on the side, with 26 in. of wood backing. This work was commenced in 1857, but not completed till the autumn of 1859. The vessel thus changed was renamed 'La Gloire,' and is now historically famous as the first seagoing ironclad. Her armament was placed along the main deck,

'LA GLOIRE.'

as in a frigate. With a length of 235 ft., and breadth of 55 ft., she had a displacement of 5000 tons, and her speed under steam was about 12 knots. Her completion created even more excitement than the appearance of the 'Niagara' but two years previously.

In the meantime we had been watching with curiosity the experiment of our neighbours, unable to recognise that the day had arrived when a new system of naval architecture for war purposes must be adopted. But public opinion was roused, and the Admiralty saw that change could not be resisted. Designs were invited from various quarters, but the plan prepared by the Chief Constructor of the Navy, Mr Isaac Watts, in conjunction with the eminent naval architect Mr Scott Russell, was decided upon. This produced the 'Warrior,' ordered in 1859, and completed in 1861. She embodied some remarkable characteristics. In the first place, her hull was of iron, and considering what had taken place ten years previously, the boldness of this step can be appreciated. But as any project of adding iron to the lofty sides of a line-of-battle ship was impracticable, the necessity of limiting the principal armament to one deck was apparent. To compensate for such a reduction, the single deck should carry a number of the most powerful guns then in use, with greater space between them than had usually been accorded, so as to reduce the injury that the entrance of a shell would inflict. Though the sides might be impregnable, the port holes were so many weak points which must not be lost sight of. In 'La Gloire' they were very close together, and hence much of the value of the armour was lost. Such considerations involved a length of ship which previous experience with the 'Mersey' and 'Orlando' had shown to be impossible in vessels built of wood and carrying powerful machinery. Another point urged was that iron would be less subject to fire than wood, so the former material was adopted. The result was an iron frigate 382 ft. long at the water line, which was increased to 420 ft. over all when the old graceful form of bow was added. All former associations could not be given up at a swoop, and as the ram was not then considered an important weapon, it only received partial recognition. This was effected by the stem at the water line being made to project slightly in the form of a spur, but the bow added to the upper part hid the ram thus disposed and gave the 'Warrior' the appearance forward of a

THE 'WARRIOR.'

sailing clipper. In the event of ramming, the overhanging portion would be knocked away, and the spur be brought in contact. On the ship's side, for a length of 212 ft., plates of iron $4\frac{1}{2}$ in. thick were secured to teak backing 18 in. thick. This wood is durable, and had other advantages for such service. The side armour left off a little over 80 ft. from bow and stern, as it was not considered desirable to load the ends of the ship with such weights.

The main armament consisted of thirty-eight 68-pounders. Of these thirty-six were on the main deck, eighteen on each side, forming a battery extending nearly the whole length of the ship, but only thirteen on each side were behind the armour. Two 68-pounders were placed on the upper deck, one forward and the other aft. As these guns weighed 95 cwt., only a few hitherto had been mounted in battle ships, in conjunction with numerous 8-in. and 32-pounder guns. The principle of concentrating the armament in a small number of heavy guns was thus introduced, and we had sprung from a three-decked ship 260 ft. long to an armoured frigate of 400 ft. As regards speed, the dimensions of the 'Warrior,' and the machinery given her, enabled her to steam over 14 knots an hour, an advance of more than 2 knots over her rival 'La Gloire' and the wooden screw ships of that day. I have heard officers express an opinion that 'La Gloire' was the better conception, because she was armoured from stem to stern. In an important locality the 'Warrior' was undoubtedly weak. The rudder head and steering apparatus were neither below the water nor behind armour, and consequently the directive power was liable to be disabled early in an action. This defect was aggravated by the ship having a large aperture in the stern, which enabled the screw to be raised, when required, out of the water. This operation was only carried out when the vessel was under sail, to add to her capability in this respect, and prevent the screw dragging in the water. When, even now, many question the expediency of relying only on steam, it can be understood that thirty years ago a seagoing battle ship without masts and yards could find no favour. Yet such a radical view had been put forward. In a work by the late Lord Dunsany—*Our Naval Position and Policy*, published in 1859, he says: 'Old sailors will laugh at the idea of ships without masts, but we shall surely see them. As steamers themselves and railways were at first scoffed at, so will be the idea of mastless ships. In runs across the Atlantic the masts are mere encum-

THE 'WARRIOR.'

brances, as in action they are sources of great danger.' Two years previously the First Lord of the Admiralty had defended the sending of troops to India in sailing ships, on the ground that if the screw ships ran short of fuel they would be helpless.

The 'Warrior' was thus given extensive sail power, and to all appearance she was a long, graceful frigate. The transition was thereby rendered more palatable to the old navy, whereas if we had gone at once to those structures irreverently—but not inaptly—termed 'flat-irons,' now so familiar in the later turret ships, the exasperated feelings of the ancient mariners would have been pitiable to contemplate.

The 'Warrior' was built at the Thames Iron Works, and a proof of the excellence of her construction is to be found in the fact that after an interval of thirty years her hull is as sound as the day on which she was launched. That day was a memorable occasion. All the world had been interested in the 'bold experiment,' as Sir John Pakington truly described it on her trial trip. No ship ever had so many visitors from all parts during her construction. In France, though first in the field, they had simply cut down a wooden ship and plated her with iron. It was a great advance on the floating batteries, but in England an entirely new departure had been taken, and in my opinion there is no question as to which was the best fighting ship. I should infinitely have preferred to command the 'Warrior,' taking into consideration her higher speed and greater dispersion of armament. The gun ports were 15 ft. apart, in 'La Gloire' they were much closer. Hence shell entering the battery of the latter would have taken much greater effect.

It is not my intention to detail at length the changes made in successive designs after the 'Warrior.' Already rifled ordnance was imposing a fresh advance, and the struggle between guns and armour had begun. The 'Warrior' had one sister, the 'Black Prince'; and that the second-class battle ship, corresponding to the two-decker, should be represented under the new order, two smaller armour-clads, the 'Defence' and 'Resistance,' were begun. The disposition of their armour was similar to that of the 'Warrior,' but they were only 280 ft. long, and the displacement 6150 tons. The 'Hector' and 'Valiant' were two other ships of the same type, with slight modifications. In the next designs it was determined to remedy the defect already alluded to, namely, the unprotected ends. This was first done in the 'Achilles.' Her length was the same as that of the 'Warrior,' but she was 600 tons larger, to allow of the armour being carried completely to the ends. This ship may be considered the first example of the armoured belt, with gun battery in the centre, though this battery before long became even more contracted.

We come now to three more ships of the 'Warrior' type, the 'Minotaur,' 'Northumberland,' and 'Agincourt.' To have the advantages of their model, without the defects, the length was increased to 400 ft., and the armour taken completely round. Its thickness was increased to $5\frac{1}{2}$ in., but secured to only 9 in. of wood

THE 'AGINCOURT.'

backing. This was not found to have greater resisting power against shot than the 4½-in. plates and 18-in. backing. The armament of this class was improved by the introduction of rifled guns of greater weight than the 68-pounder. Such modifications involved a larger vessel, and the 'Minotaur' and her sisters reached 10,600 tons, a considerable advance on the 'Warrior.' While the weight of the 'Warrior's' armour and backing amounted to 1350 tons, the 'Minotaur's' protection weighed 2100 tons. As sail power was still considered necessary, these vessels were given five masts. Thus equipped they presented a curious appearance, and puzzled the nautical world. It is related that a merchant vessel on one occasion approached inconveniently near one of the 'Minotaur' class at night, her great length and the five masts leading those in charge of the other to believe that there were two ships, and that their own might pass between!

It may be imagined that the change from wood to iron in construction did not find us—in our dock yards, at least—with a body of men accustomed to work with the new material, and when it was decided to build an iron ship of the 'Warrior' type at Chatham it had to be carried out by shipwrights whose previous experience had been limited to wooden shipbuilding. I have heard it said they used the same tools for the harder substance, but whether so or not the ship was completed in less time than the others, and the workmanship was excellent. All the previous vessels had been built in private yards.

Though we had thus by 1862 made a good start with armoured ships, the fleet contained a great many wooden ships at that time, either completed or building. It was then determined to convert several of them into ironclads. A certain number were selected for this purpose, cut down, lengthened, and armoured similarly to the iron ships with $4\frac{1}{2}$-in. plates secured to 30 in. of teak backing. These measures produced the 'Prince Consort,' 'Ocean,' 'Caledonia,' 'Royal Alfred,' and 'Royal Oak.' In the two last the armour was 6 in. thick. Two others, the 'Lord Clyde' and 'Lord Warden,' were also built of wood and armoured. Iron was still considered to have disadvantages, which are expressed in a memorandum by Sir Spencer Robinson, then Controller of the Navy, and dated March 2d, 1863. These were, liability of the bottom to injury and to becoming coated with marine growth; small quantity of good iron in the market and uncertainty of quality; greater cost of iron ships. If they were more durable, there was the probability of their becoming obsolete, and thus a cheaper and less durable vessel might prove best in the end. For some such reasons the French preferred wood. There is good sense in these arguments, though much might be said on the other side. The danger of durable ships is the temptation to resist building new ones, and to be content with patching up what has rendered good service. Ten years ago we were under this influence, and our naval strength was thereby impaired. The recent Naval Defence Act broke the spell.

I must, however, now pass on to a change which took place when the present Sir E. Reed was appointed Chief Constructor of the Navy. He was an advocate for iron, shorter ships, complete armour belts, and the concentration of the armament into a smaller number of heavier guns in a central battery or citadel. In 1752 a French naval architect had written: ' Il est certain que ce sont toujours les gros canons qui sont les plus avantageux dans un combat, et ainsi il est préférable de mettre sur un vaisseau un petit nombre de gros canons qu'un grand nombre de petits,' and yet in the old wars we had found number not size most influential in deciding a combat. This was owing to the fact that the issue depended more on the disablement of the crew than of the ship itself. Injury to the masts assisted this result, because it enabled the other ship to attain a position from which the opposing crew could be decimated with impunity. The greater the number of guns (provided their projectiles could penetrate the sides of the enemy's ships) the more chances of disabling men and guns, until submission followed inability to resist. Ships were seldom sunk in action. Such an incident was a matter for regret, because, though diminishing the force of the enemy, it added nothing to your own, whereas a capture counted, to use a parliamentary phrase, two on a division. The prize under another flag was speedily utilised by the conqueror. Of late years sinking appears to be the object aimed at in action, and greater care is taken to avert this than to protect the crew.

The ideas of Mr Reed in reference to construction were adopted, and in one respect it could not be otherwise. The size and power of guns were being increased to overcome the resistance of armour, and this necessitated a smaller number, unless ships were to be much larger. At this time, however, a displacement of 10,000 tons was considered an outside limit. The 'Bellerophon,' begun in 1863, was the first vessel under the new *régime*.

THE 'BELLEROPHON.'

With a length of 300 ft., and a displacement of 7500 tons, she carried a 6-in. belt of armour, which in the centre was carried up to form a central battery to contain ten guns, each weighing 12 tons. Two more guns were placed forward to give bow fire.

It was soon seen that a further advance must be made to meet the growing power of the gun. This led to the design of the 'Hercules,' in which the displacement was increased to 8700 tons, the armoured belt to

THE 'HERCULES.'

9 in., and the principal armament to 18-ton guns. To add to the fire right ahead and astern the ends of the

battery at the sides were recessed. This enabled two of the battery guns to point ahead and two astern. The length of the ship did not exceed 325 ft.

From this brief description it is evident how rapid had been the advance in most of the fighting elements of the new warship. Speed alone had not increased, but this had been maintained with a shorter and handier ship. The great length of the 'Warrior' and 'Minotaur' was inconvenient, to say the least of it, owing to the space they required to turn in. The 'Hercules' was universally recognised as a splendid specimen of construction, and remains to this day a great favourite with naval officers. She was, however, eclipsed by the 'Alexandra,' launched a few years after—the last representative of the broadside system. Her length was the same as that of the 'Hercules,' but the displacement was increased to 9500 tons, by which she was enabled to carry armour 12 in. thick at the water line opposite the machinery, and tapering to 6 in. at the bow and stern. The importance of protecting the motive power more completely than other portions of the hull had for some time been recognised, and, moreover, the extremities would be overburdened with such heavy weights as 12-in. plates. The disposition of the armament differed somewhat from that of the 'Hercules.' There was the same central battery, containing ten 18-ton guns, but above this was another battery, in which was placed two 25-ton guns. Both batteries had recessed ports, by which a powerful bow fire was obtained. It may be observed here that the mounting and working of such heavy guns on the broadside was only possible from their comparative shortness, so that when required they could be withdrawn or housed inside the ship. Guns of the present day, and of the same diameter of bore, are twice the length. We had already adopted the twin screw, and the 'Alexandra' was so fitted. This, added to improved machinery, gave her a speed of 15 knots. The climax in broadside ironclads had now been reached. Few were found to dispute the merits of our latest production as an engine of war. Though never yet opposed to a hostile vessel, the 'Alexandra' took part in the bombardment of the Egyptian forts at Alexandria in 1882, and rendered good service on that occasion. She was struck about thirty times, but sustained no serious injury.

Space has not permitted me to allude to a number of other vessels built between the production of the 'Warrior' and 'Alexandra.' They partook more or less of the character of those described, though varying in size. The second-class ironclad was well represented by several of moderate dimensions, so that the old gradation of two and three-deckers was preserved in the new fleet. Moreover, the Suez Canal was completed, and its depth was such that the heaviest ironclads could not pass through. It was desirable that some of our battle ships should be able to utilise this route to the East, instead of taking the longer passage by the Cape of Good Hope. We should never neglect this consideration whatever the temptation to add to the dimensions of warships.

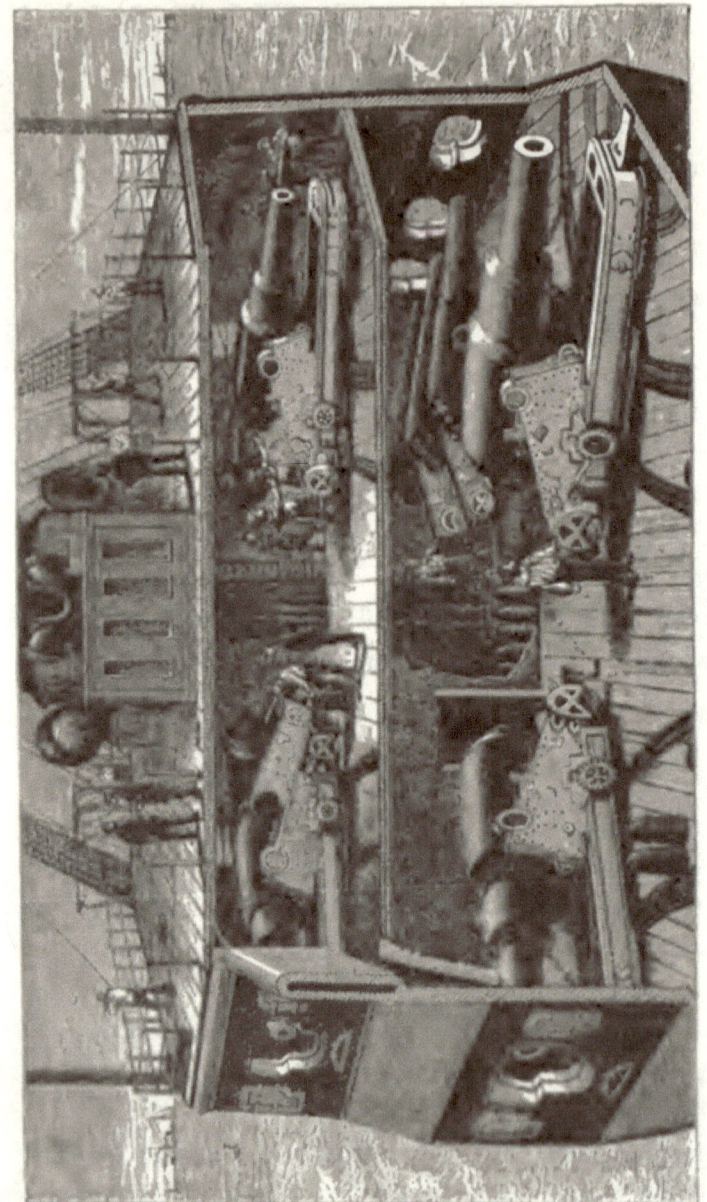

THE BATTERIES OF THE 'ALEXANDRA.'

Broadside Ironclads.

In this brief review of progress between 1861 and 1877 I have confined myself to the development of the broadside system of armoured vessels, and, looking back, how wonderful that progress seems. The 'Warrior' carried only 1350 tons weight of iron and wood for protection out of a total 9000 tons displacement. The 'Alexandra,' only 500 tons larger, is enabled to sustain 2300 tons employed for protection, and is a knot faster. Rolling iron plates of any thickness was practically a new industry in 1860; but in sixteen years, commencing with $4\frac{1}{2}$-in. plates, the demand for a thickness of 12 in. had been as promptly met.

While we, in common with other nations, were thus encasing our ships in coats of mail, the advantage conferred by this system was to my mind strikingly illustrated by an episode in the American Civil War. After a cruise of two years the celebrated 'Alabama' put into Cherbourg to be docked and repaired. Her commander, Captain Semmes, in his interesting account of her career, says of this period: 'The poor old "Alabama" was not now what she had been. She was like the wearied foxhound limping back after a long chase, footsore, and longing for quiet and repose. Her commander, like herself, was well-nigh worn down.' Three days after her arrival the United States sloop 'Kearsage' turned up off the port, and Semmes sent a message to her commander that if he would wait until the 'Alabama' had completed with coal he would come out to meet him. The two vessels were not unequally matched in dimensions and armament. The 'Kearsage,' Captain Winslow, was a wooden sloop of 1030 tons. She carried two 11-in. smooth bore guns, four 32-pounders, and one rifled 30-pounder. Her crew numbered 160. The 'Alabama' was also a wooden vessel of 1040 tons. Her armament consisted of one 8-in. smooth bore, one 7-in. rifled gun, and six 32-pounders. She carried 150 men. Beyond stowing away her top hamper and making the preparations for action common to rigged vessels she took no special precautions. The 'Kearsage,' on the other hand, had suspended her spare chain cables up and down the side, opposite the boilers and machinery, thus giving armour protection to that important locality and a large portion of the hull at the water line. The chain was covered over with a thin casing of wood, which effectually concealed what was beneath. This method of adding to the defence of wooden ships had been first adopted by Admiral Farragut when passing hostile forts in the Mississippi the same year. As against the guns and projectiles of that time, and especially as a preventive to the penetration of shells, by causing them to burst outside, the plan was ingenious and effectual. The same procedure was open to Captain Semmes, but for some reason he did not adopt it, nor does he appear to have been aware of this move of his opponent. Though Semmes afterwards sneered at an enemy 'who went out chivalrously armoured to encounter a ship whose wooden sides were entirely without protection,' such utilisation of the resources of a ship to improve her defensive capability was not only perfectly justifiable but the plain duty of a commander desirous of ensuring the victory with as little injury as possible to his own vessel.

On the morning of June 19th, 1864, the 'Alabama' steamed out of Cherbourg Harbour, and steered for the 'Kearsage,' then awaiting her about six miles off the port. When the distance between them had been reduced to a mile, the 'Alabama' opened fire, but it was not returned until the two ships were 900 yards from each other. The 'Kearsage' then steered to close with her antagonist, but the 'Alabama' kept on at full speed, and the two ships steamed round in a circle at a distance from each other of about 800 yards. The firing now became very hot. The 'Alabama' was hulled several times, and a number of men were disabled. Her own fire, on the other hand, had little effect on the 'Kearsage,' the chain cables affording protection to the hull, and her principal damage was aloft. After an hour's action a shell from one of the 11-in. guns of the 'Kearsage' struck the 'Alabama' near the water line and burst, making a large hole, through which the water poured into the ship. Semmes turned his vessel towards the French shore, and endeavoured to reach it under sail and steam. But the 'Alabama' was filling fast, and further effort being useless, her flag was hauled down. She sank soon afterwards, the officers and crew being picked up by boats from an English yacht, a French pilot vessel, and the 'Kearsage.' Semmes complained that his adversary was dilatory in this matter, but after an action boats are not often in a condition to be despatched at a moment's notice, and the captain of the 'Kearsage' was not a man to disregard the claims of humanity. The casualties to the crew of the 'Alabama' were nine killed and twenty-one wounded, while the 'Kearsage' had only three wounded. This vessel was struck thirty times, of which thirteen only were in the hull. The firing of the 'Alabama' was wild, but she suffered under another great disadvantage, that she had previously little shot or shell practice against a target, being unable to replenish her ammunition. Mere drill with guns unloaded can never render men efficient in action. Frequent target practice is essential to give confidence and proficiency before the enemy. Lack of this and the improvised armour of her antagonist told against the 'Alabama,' and two valuable lessons were thus afforded by this action. They should not be forgotten at a time when the principle of protecting ships with armoured decks only is being so much extended, and when there is a tendency to curtail practice with full charges of powder owing to their effect upon the guns.

CHAPTER IV

EARLY TURRET SHIPS

Introduction of the 'Monitor'—Claims of Ericsson and Captain Cowper Coles—'Merrimac' and 'Monitor' in America —'Royal Sovereign' converted in England — Further development of the Turret System—'Devastation' to 'Inflexible.'

ERICSSON is generally credited with the first idea of mounting a gun in a revolving turret and placing it in a low iron-plated vessel, as practically applied in his celebrated 'Monitor' of the American Civil War. But Captain Cowper Coles, some years before, had been urging the adoption of the same system, and many of his original ideas are to be seen embodied in the ships of to-day. The plan with him seems to have originated in 1855, when during the Crimean War he mounted a 32-pounder on a raft, for service in the shallow waters of the Sea of Azof. This proving useful, he next thought of protecting the gun, and proposed an improved raft, formed of empty casks planked over, to carry a 68-pounder, pointing through an aperture in a hemispherical iron shield placed over it. He proposed a number of these rafts for an attack on Cronstadt. A committee of naval officers serving in the Black Sea reported favourably on the scheme, and Captain Coles was ordered home to lay his plans before the Admiralty. Peace, however, intervened, and nothing further was done. Captain Coles continued working out his ideas, and in June 1860 read a paper at the United Service Institution, in which he proposed a low freeboard vessel, on which were to be a number of cupolas or turrets, such as he had devised for the improved raft, each containing two guns; the space required for a pair of guns being little more than that necessary for a single piece. But now follows the principal feature of his system. Hitherto changing the direction of a gun was effected roughly and laboriously by tackles and handspikes. Captain Coles' proposal is thus described in his own words: 'The horizontal motion or training is effected by turning the shield itself, with the gun, crew, and the platform on which they stand. The whole apparatus thus becomes, as it were, the gun carriage, and being placed on a common turntable, can be revolved to the greatest nicety of adjustment by means of a winch.' The idea of a turntable he no doubt took from the arrangement of the railway system. As all heavy guns are now mounted on turntables, and revolve either with the shield, as in case of turrets, or independently, as in the case of ship barbettes, we must recognise the claim of Captain Coles to be the inventor of the modern system. The 'Monitor' was not built until two years afterwards.

Our Government, however, had decided upon the 'Warrior' type, and were not disposed to try an experiment in quite a different direction. Nor were the continental powers so inclined. The broadsid

GUN OR MORTAR CASK RAFT WITH SHOT PROOF SHIELD.
By Commander Cowper P. Coles R.N
August 1855.

Longitudinal Section

Transverse Section

CAPTAIN COWPER COLES' PROPOSED CUPOLA SHIP, 1860.

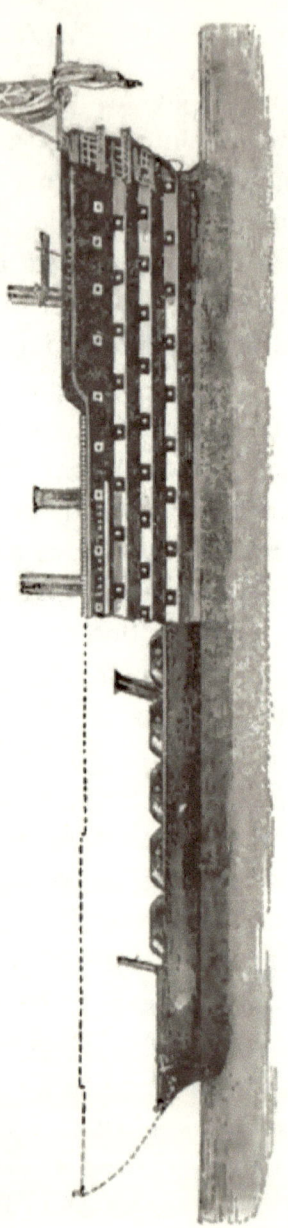

Early Turret Ships.

armour-clad for sea service, and the broadside floating battery for coast defence, had been generally adopted. But the Civil War in America broke out, and certain naval operations had an immense influence on the course of naval construction. The Southern Confederacy was the first to appreciate the value of armour-clad vessels. In July 1861 it was decided to raise and convert into an ironclad the wooden frigate 'Merrimac,' of 3400 tons and forty guns, which had been sunk at the Norfolk navy yard when it was abandoned two months previously. When raised, the upper portion of the vessel was cut down to within 2 ft. of the water line, and on this reduced hull was constructed a casemate with slanting sides. Two layers of railway iron formed the protection of this casemate, in which the guns were placed, and worked in ports on the broadside system. Dearth of plant in the South for such work, at the beginning of hostilities, caused considerable delay, so that it was not until March 8th, 1862, that she proceeded to Hampton Roads, where the Federal fleet was at anchor. This consisted of wooden vessels. Among them were the 'Cumberland,' of thirty guns, and the 'Congress,' of fifty guns. No attack appears to have been anticipated, and presumably no information of the 'Merrimac's' completion had reached the Northern commander. Though fire was opened on the 'Merrimac,' it had no effect on her protected sides. She made straight for the 'Cumberland,' and struck her forward on the starboard side. The 'Cumberland' sank shortly after. The 'Congress' in the meantime had slipped her anchor and got into shallow water, where the 'Merrimac,' owing to her deeper draught, could not follow. Her guns could reach, however, and the 'Congress' was set on fire, when she hauled her flag down. The 'Merrimac' then withdrew, intending to return the next day and destroy the rest of the squadron.

There was great consternation in the North at this event, but the means were at hand to arrest the Southern vessel in her triumphant career.

In August 1861 the Northern States had determined to obtain ironclad steam vessels, and at the end of that month Ericsson offered to construct in a few months a vessel which would destroy the rebel squadron. A board of officers was appointed to consider plans proposed, and in September it recommended that a vessel on Ericsson's design should be built. She was commenced in October, launched on January 30th, 1862, and completed on February 15th, 1862. The design provided for a hull not more than 2 ft. above the water, and with a flat bottom, that the draught might not exceed 10 ft. The sides, to a short distance below the water line, were protected with 4-in. plates. In the centre of the deck was built a circular turret, revolving on a central spindle, and protected with 8 in. of iron. Inside the turret were mounted two 11-in. smooth bore guns, pointing through port holes. They could thus fire in any direction without turning the vessel, an obvious advantage not only on the open sea but especially in narrow waters, for which she was more intended. Such was the famous

Early Turret Ships.

'Monitor,' a name given by Ericsson to his creation to admonish the leaders of the Southern Rebellion, and to be also a monitor to the Lords of the Admiralty in England, suggesting to them doubts as to the propriety of their building four broadside ironclads at three and

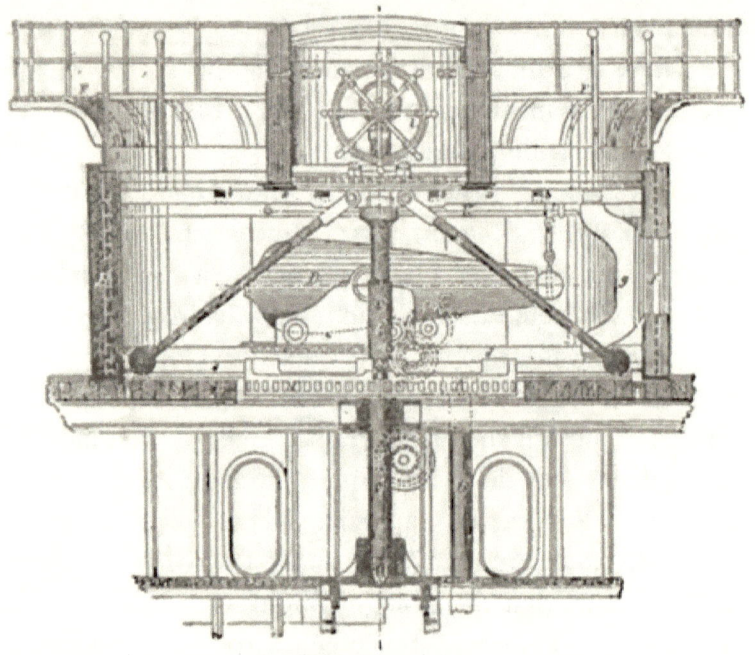

ERICSSON'S TURRET.

a half million dollars each. Such were the reasons given by Ericsson himself for the choice of this name. He had not forgotten his unsuccessful attempts to favourably impress their lordships with his screw propeller twenty-four years previously.

We have seen that on March 8th, 1862, the 'Merrimac' had sunk the 'Cumberland.' On March 2d the 'Monitor' left New York under the command of Lieutenant Worden, and after a somewhat stormy passage she arrived at Hampton Roads on the evening of the 8th. The next morning when the 'Merrimac' appeared again, bent on destruction, those on board descried a strange-looking object, an iron tower, apparently, on the surface of the water. Then the low hull was made out, and a dash made for this new opponent. The battle then began, but it was soon apparent that the 'Merrimac's' ordnance could make no impression on the turret of the 'Monitor,' and there was little else to hit. The casemate of the 'Merrimac,' however, offered a good mark, and almost every shot of the other took effect somewhere. After two hours' pounding the 'Merrimac' hauled out of action, having sustained considerable injury, and, owing to orders previously given, the 'Monitor' allowed her to depart. But the principal object had been gained, and the 'Merrimac' gave no further trouble. The 'Monitor' was struck twenty times, of which nine hits were on the turret, but the injury done was trifling. Great rejoicings took place throughout the North at this event, and it was believed this new method of naval construction would supersede all others. It certainly exercised a powerful influence in more than one country.

But an essential quality was lacking in the 'Monitor,'—seaworthiness. Steaming against a moderate wind and sea, the water swept over her like a deluge, and found its way down the funnels and any aperture leading to the interior. A few months after

Early Turret Ships.

her encounter with the 'Merrimac' she foundered in a gale off Cape Hatteras. In England it was evident that a type of vessel unfit for distant service could not serve as a model for general adoption. But as coast defence was then prominently before the country, owing to the views expressed by Lord Palmerston when proposing in 1860 a large outlay on sea forts, it was decided to construct two turret ships on Captain Coles' plans. A wooden three-decker, the 'Royal Sovereign,' was accordingly cut down and armoured with 5½-in. iron

THE 'ROYAL SOVEREIGN.'

plates. She carried four turrets, the foremost one containing two guns, and the others a single gun each. To give more freeboard at sea there were hinged light iron bulwarks, 3 ft. 6 in. high, which were thrown down when it was desired to fight the guns. The turrets, instead of revolving on a central spindle as in the 'Monitor,' rotated on rollers fixed on the lower circumference of the turret, thus giving greater rigidity to resist impact of shot. A similar vessel, the 'Prince Albert,' was specially built of iron by Messrs Samuda for the same equipment. The 'Royal Sovereign' was completed in 1864, and underwent successful trials. Having a low freeboard, and being without masts, she was not considered a ship capable of service on foreign stations.

Captain Coles, however, considered that a seagoing turret ship was perfectly feasible, and persistently advocated the principle. As he was supported by the press, the Admiralty decided to build a masted turret ship, and the 'Monarch' was commenced. As she did not embody the views of Captain Coles, he was at length permitted to build a vessel of his own design, and he entrusted the work to Messrs Laird of Liverpool. Guns having increased so much in weight it became necessary to limit the number of turrets to a pair placed on the centre line of the ship, 120 ft. apart, each containing a pair of guns. There were three masts, on the tripod principle, by which the necessity for rigging is dispensed with, and she was given full sail power. It is unnecessary to go into further details, because this unfortunate vessel, which was named the 'Captain,' was lost, with nearly all hands, on September 6th, 1870. She capsized in a heavy squall off Cape Finisterre when under sail. Captain Burgoyne was in command of her, while Captain Coles was his guest, desirous of observing the behaviour of his design at sea. The loss of two such men, with the remaining officers and crew, was a national disaster not likely to be forgotten. Errors of construction caused the catastrophe, combined with the great leverage exerted by the sails when struck by a heavy squall.

Loss of the 'Captain' and the principal advocate of masted turret ships led the Admiralty to abandon this type, but the 'Monarch' was completed, and remains the solitary specimen in our navy. She was similar in general design to the 'Captain,' but in many important respects the two ships differed widely. The sides of the 'Monarch' were 14 ft. above the water, whereas in the 'Captain' they were only 6 ft. In the original design of the latter they were to have been 8 ft., but additional weights placed in the ship reduced this by 2 ft. The two turrets of the 'Monarch' were closer together, the lower portion of them being protected by the side armour above the belt, which was carried up for this purpose. The thickness here was 7 in., while the turrets were given 10 in. of armour. In each was mounted a pair of 25-ton guns, the largest ordnance then in use. As the masts obstructed the right ahead and astern fire smaller guns were placed at the ends of the vessel. All this was accomplished on a displacement of 8350 tons, and produced a powerful fighting machine, but the sailing capacity was indifferent. In fact it was becoming recognised that the gain in one respect was a loss in another, and that the turret system suffered if combined with a large spread of canvas. The advantage of turrets was the large arc of training they enabled guns to cover on either side of the ship, and that the whole of the armament was brought into play instead of only half, as in the case of a broadside ship. But if masts and their rigging were given to such ships, as in the case of the 'Monarch,' this arc was much circumscribed, and the full benefit of the system was not reaped.

It was therefore determined to build turret ships for extended sea service without this objectionable feature. Locomotion was to depend wholly on steam and two screws with separate engines gave a double chance against a total breakdown. To make up for the absence of sail power, the supply of fuel must be increased. This led to the design of the 'Devastation,' and as she was the first mastless seagoing turret ship we built, her construction excited considerable interest. The leading features were a low freeboard hull, carrying two turrets, on the middle line of the ship. To protect the base of the turrets an armoured breastwork or citadel was built round them. This did not extend right across

THE 'DEVASTATION.'

the vessel, so that there was a space between the walls of the breastwork and the ship's side. At the instance of a committee appointed after the loss of the 'Captain' to consider designs, this space was enclosed by carrying up the side of the vessel to the height of the breastwork and extending the deck over the latter to meet the raised portion. This addition to the side, though not armoured, increased the freeboard of the ship in the central portion to over 10 ft., while right aft it was only 4 ft., and forward there was a low forecastle 8 ft. above the water. The armour on the side extended right round, and was 12 in. thick amidships, tapering to 10 in. at bow and stern. On the turrets it was 14 in. It was at first intended to mount in these

Early Turret Ships.

four 25-ton guns similar to those of the 'Monarch,' but we had now reached ordnance of 35 tons, and a pair of these 'infants,' as they had been ironically termed, were allotted to each of the 'Devastation's' turrets. She was given twin screws, worked by separate engines, and a coal stowage provided for 1300 tons. This capacity was largely in excess of that of all previous ships, and forms one of the most valuable features of this class. When it is considered what was done with dimensions—9350 tons—just under those of the 'Alexandra,' that the total weight of protection carried was 2950 tons of iron and wood, or an increase of 600 tons over the broadside ship, and that she could present on either side a concentrated fire of four 35-ton guns, while the range ahead or astern was covered by two such pieces, all efficiently protected, it may be conceded that the success of the turret system had been proved. But what a change from the three-decker of 120 guns to the 'Warrior' of forty, and thence to the 'Devastation,' with only four heavy guns. Could the principle of concentration of armament be extended further? The limits were not yet reached. The 'Devastation' was completed in 1873, and any doubts that may have been felt as to her seaworthy qualities were speedily set at rest. She proved able to encounter severe weather, and wonderfully steady in a heavy sea. The sea washed over her like a half-tide rock, but with apertures closed it could not find its way below. There was, of course, discomfort to the crew, who were dependent on artificial ventilation, but for service in the Mediterranean, where bad weather is of short duration, this class of ship has proved well suited.

The 'Dreadnought' was the next improvement. A slight increase in the thickness of the armour and weight of the armament involved an additional displacement of 1500 tons. There were also structural differences of some importance, which entailed extra weight. The armoured breastwork extended right across the ship, and was 186 ft. long, instead of 154 ft. in the 'Devastation.' A higher freeboard throughout was also given. She had four 38-ton guns, which, owing to improvements in ammunition, were considerably more effective than the 35-ton guns. With these modifications the 'Dreadnought' was, and is to this day, regarded as an excellent type of fighting ship. After a departure of some years, we again returned to the general principle of her construction in the 'Nile' and 'Trafalgar,' to which allusion will be made later on.

Though we had, without unduly increasing the size of the battle ship, passed from $4\frac{1}{2}$ in. to 14 in. of protective armour, the power of the gun had more than kept pace, and it was evident that if armour capable of resisting the heaviest ordnance was applied to a ship the area covered by it must be contracted, or we should be compelled to resort to enormous ships. At that time it was considered undesirable to exceed 12,000 tons. Not only had the resistance of the structure to hostile shot to be considered, but the power to strike heavy blows in return was even more important. Artillerists were, with improved plant, constructing heavier guns than the 38-ton, and we were not prepared to view with equanimity foreign vessels with an advantage over ours in this respect. The outcome of such views was the 'Inflexible,' designed by Mr Barnaby, then Chief Constructor of the Navy. In her the armour at the side only extended for a length of 110 ft., in the centre of the vessel, so that the complete armoured belt was abandoned. This was the principal innovation, which led to

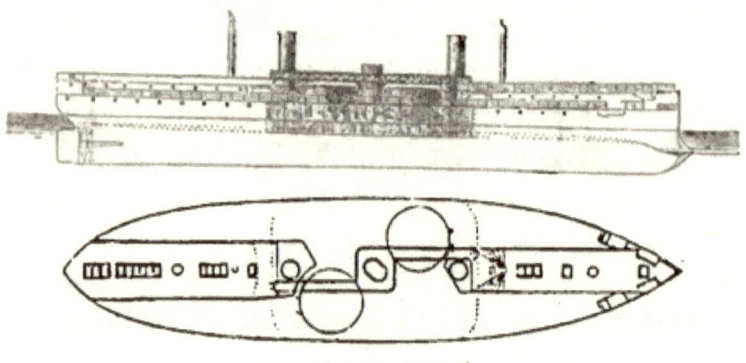

THE 'INFLEXIBLE.'

much controversy at the time. There was a breastwork or citadel, as in the 'Dreadnought,' the whole breadth of the ship, which was increased to 74 ft., a remarkable amount of beam for a length of 320 ft. In the 'Monarch' the proportions were 330 by 58. By thus contracting the citadel of the 'Inflexible' to 110 ft. it was possible to protect the sides with 24 in. of iron, disposed in two thicknesses of 12 in. each, with a layer of wood backing between. Diagonally across the citadel, and within its walls, were placed two turrets, each armed with a pair of 80-ton guns, such a bound had ordnance made since the days of the 'infants.' This arrangement of the turrets was to allow all four guns to point directly ahead or astern, whereas if placed on the fore and aft line, as in previous ships, only half the armament could be so utilised. The turrets were protected with 16 in. of armour, consisting of a wrought-iron plate of 7 in., and

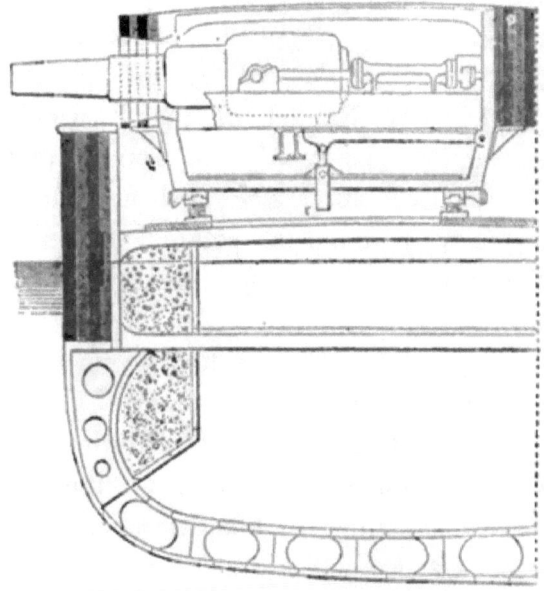

SECTION THROUGH TURRET OF THE 'INFLEXIBLE.'

outside that what is termed a 'compound' plate of 9 in. This was simply a plate of wrought-iron of $5\frac{1}{2}$ in. thick, to which a hard steel face, $3\frac{1}{2}$ in. thick, had been added and the two plates welded together. Wrought-iron was too soft, and allowed the projectiles to penetrate, but the hard steel face broke them up. Hence a reduced thickness of the new material could be used with a corresponding saving of weight.

Early Turret Ships.

When turrets were first introduced steam was employed to rotate them, and also, as the guns increased in weight, for many of the operations connected with their manipulation. But steam has the disadvantage of condensation in pipes when transmitted, and for such a delicate manœuvre as keeping the sights of a gun on a mark, which was effected by small movements of the turret, steam power has defects. Hydraulic power was therefore devised by Sir William Armstrong and Mr G. Rendel, of the Elswick firm, to perform all these operations, and applied in the 'Inflexible' with great success. The heavy turrets could be rapidly swung round or rotated with almost imperceptible motion, and stopped dead at any required moment.

From the day on which we had begun to construct warships of iron it became necessary to guard against injury in the event of such a vessel striking the ground or rock. A wooden ship might do this and suffer little damage or danger of foundering, as the material, being more elastic, had a tendency to close in over the fractured part, and swell as it became sodden with water. Iron did not possess this advantage, and, moreover, to give the requisite buoyancy the submerged portion of the hull must necessarily be thin, so that injury was easily inflicted in this part. Even at the slowest speed the momentum of a weight of 9000 tons coming in contact with a rock would crush in the fragile shell like matchwood. To meet this the double bottom was devised, which consisted in having an inner iron skin a short distance from the outer bottom. In case of the latter being punctured, the inner skin would prevent an influx of water to the interior of the ship. This was first carried out in the 'Warrior,' but the dual portion only extended 11 ft. on each side of the keel. In succeeding ships this principle was developed, and the inner skin became a veritable second hull under water, the space between the two being increased and sub-divided into a number of cells. This cellular sub-division was adopted with the view not only of giving strength in case of striking the ground, but also of reducing the effect of a torpedo explosion under water. As it was impossible to place armour here, the double bottom was a substitute, the hope being that the inner skin would be intact after the outer hull had been driven in by the explosion. As against the blow delivered by a ram such a protection would be insufficient. The only safeguard is to divide the interior of the vessel into watertight compartments, so as to confine the water which would rush in when both skins were fractured to that particular locality. This principle had been carried out in greater degree with succeeding ships, so that the 'Inflexible' had 127 of these compartments. Each is provided with a watertight door, to allow free access to all parts at ordinary times, and these, of course, must be a source of weakness to the principle. They may not be closed at the proper time, and are liable to get out of order unless continually worked.

Although the difference in weight between four 38-ton

guns and the same number of 80-ton guns, including the carriages on which they are mounted, does not exceed 200 or 300 tons, it is in the ammunition that a heavier armament makes so much difference. We had arrived at projectiles weighing nearly a ton each, with a charge of some hundreds of pounds of powder. To provide, therefore, say a hundred rounds for each gun, or even a smaller number, involved a great addition of weight. Hence the dimensions of the 'Inflexible' and her equipment increased the displacement to 11,600 tons —the largest warship we had constructed. The design was not to pass unchallenged. Grave doubts were expressed by a high authority as to the wisdom of leaving the ends unprotected, and as to the stability of the vessel when these had been subjected to a heavy shell fire. The extremities were guarded only by an armoured deck 3 in. thick just below the water line, and at the sides by spaces filled with cork, to give buoyancy when this part was perforated by shot and water gained admittance. A committee, however, of distinguished men appointed to investigate the design did not consider that the ship would be specially liable to such a disaster. The question really hinged upon the amount of fire a ship is likely to receive in action in any particular part, and experience teaches us that, under such conditions, no one portion is more liable than another. The 'Inflexible,' therefore, was completed, and in 1882 assisted in the bombardment of the Egyptian forts with the 'Alexandra,' each representing a system and its development in twenty years. A brief review of this important operation as the first serious bombardment by an ironclad squadron may be of interest.

There has been rather a tendency to depreciate this engagement by dwelling on the weakness of the defence. Much is made of the fact that no submarine mines were used to keep the ships at a distance, that the guns on shore were weak and badly served, and that under totally different conditions the fleet could not have succeeded. It seems unnecessary to discuss what might have been, or we could reply that no special arrangements had been made on the side of the attack, no mortars provided, and the ships that took part were not all the most powerful we possessed. The fact, however, remains that the batteries were silenced, and the guns deserted, showing that the admiral in command had accurately estimated the force necessary to produce this result. But these batteries may well have been considered as formidable. About twelve in number, they were distributed along the coast commanding the approach to Alexandria Harbour. They mounted over 200 guns, of which about forty were rifled, while the remainder were smooth bores. Except for the penetration of armour, the latter were capable of inflicting heavy damage on the assailants.

The attack was to be made by eight armoured ships, carrying less than 100 guns so arranged that in many cases only one side could be brought to bear at a time. That some of the guns threw projectiles infinitely larger than could be returned from the shore did not give a corresponding advantage to the ships, because it has usually been found that number, rapidity of fire, and moderate size tells most against fortifications. Every hole and cranny is then found out, to the discomfiture of the garrison.

The ships opened fire early on the morning of July 11th, 1882, at ranges varying from 1500 to 4000 yards. The fire was returned from the forts, but the ships being mostly under weigh were difficult to hit. This also affected the accuracy of their own fire, so that eventually they anchored and continued a heavy cannonade upon such forts as were still working their guns. Some were silenced about half-past ten, and this released some of the ships to devote their fire to other forts. At three o'clock fire had ceased from the shore. No great damage had been inflicted on the ships. The 'Alexandra' had suffered most. She was hit about thirty times, but mostly by round shot. About forty more hits were distributed among the remaining ships, and the total number of casualties was six killed and twenty-five wounded. The casualties on shore could not be ascertained, but they were probably heavy. The fire of the ships was accurate on the whole, but the fuses being defective, many of the shell did not burst. Several of the guns on shore were dismounted or disabled, but the works behind which they fought were not greatly damaged. This was owing to the small number of guns that could be opposed to them. The guns were silenced chiefly by projectiles entering the embrasures. In such operations vessels carrying a large number of moderate sized guns will be more effective than ships carrying monster ordnance few in number. For the attack of forts high angle fire from mortars and howitzers is very effective, but no provision for vessels so equipped is made in our fleet. To do the same work with direct fire would necessitate a numerical superiority in guns, such as existed in the days of 100-gun ships.

CHAPTER V

BARBETTE SYSTEM COMBINED WITH BROADSIDE

Battle of Lissa—Lessons to be derived from this Action—Introduction of the Barbette System of Mounting Guns—First applied in the 'Temeraire'—The 'Admiral' Class—Increase in Dimensions of Battle Ships to 14,000 tons—New Vessels, 'Royal Sovereign,' 'Empress of India,' 'Ramillies,' 'Repulse,' 'Resolution,' and 'Royal Oak'—Disadvantages of Monster Ships.

HAVING thus detailed the changes by which the stately three-decker of 1850 was transformed into the massive ironclad structure of twenty years later, it is desirable here to give an account of the first action between two fleets containing this new type of battle ship. In the short but decisive war between the combined forces of Prussia and Italy against Austria, in 1866, the issue could not depend upon any naval operations that might be undertaken, and the decisive victory of Sadowa overshadowed to a great extent the sea fight off Lissa and the many lessons to be derived from it. Even in naval circles there was not that keen scrutiny into cause and effect which might have been anticipated when constructions based largely upon theoretical considerations had thus been brought to the test of actual conflict. Yet no naval incident of such importance had occurred since the battle of Trafalgar. The American Civil War had been signalised by gallant encounters between single ships, and interesting as well as instructive assaults upon land defences. The Crimean War had shown that even when denied the opportunity of meeting an enemy at sea a powerful navy can enable operations on land to be undertaken and sustained which otherwise were impracticable. But since 1805 no hostile fleets had met, and when we consider the nature of the naval forces engaged at Lissa, the strategy displayed, and the tactics adopted, this action is worthy of the closest attention. I shall deal very briefly with the composition of the forces engaged. Nearly all nations had followed the example of France and this country in reconstituting their fleets, so that in 1866 Italy was able to muster twelve ironclads, varying in size from 5800 tons to 2000 tons. According to dimensions, they were protected with $5\frac{1}{2}$, $4\frac{1}{2}$, or 4-in. iron plates. The armament was in most cases a combination of rifled and smooth bore ordnance, mounted on the broadside system. Besides these ironclads there were several wooden frigates and smaller vessels. In command was Admiral Persano, a man who had seen much service, though without war experience.

The Austrian fleet was less powerful in ironclads, of which there were only seven, varying from 5200 tons to 3000 tons. Their armour ranged from $4\frac{1}{4}$ to 5-in. plates. The guns of this squadron were decidedly inferior to their opponents, consisting for the most part of smooth bore 48-pounders, though five of the ironclads had rifled ordnance in addition. Besides these

Barbette System combined with Broadside.

there was a wooden screw line-of-battle ship, the 'Kaiser,' with several other wooden frigates and smaller vessels. In command was Admiral Tegethoff, an officer of distinction, who had commanded an Austrian Squadron in the Danish War of 1864, and taken part in an action off Heligoland, between two small squadrons, which was without decisive result.

The following is a list of the vessels that were to meet in the Adriatic:—

ITALIAN.		AUSTRIAN.	
Ships.	Tonnage.	Ships.	Tonnage.
Armoured.		*Armoured.*	
'Ré d'Italia,'	5800	'Ferdinand Max,'	5200
'Ré di Portogallo,'	5600	'Hapsburg,'	5200
'Maria Pia,'	4300	'Don Juan d'Austria,'	3600
'Castelfidardo,'	4300	'Kaiser Max,'	3600
'Ancona,'	4200	'Prinz Eugen,'	3600
'San Martino,'	4200	'Drache,'	3000
'Affondatore,'	4000	'Salamander,'	3000
'Carignano,'	4000		
'Formidabile,'	2800	*Unarmoured.*	
'Terribile,'	2800		
'Varese,'	2000	'Kaiser,'	5000
'Palestro,' 12	2000	18 Frigates and smaller Vessels.	
Unarmoured.			
22 Frigates and smaller Vessels.			

When hostilities commenced, Tegethoff made a demonstration on the Italian coast, but was unable to meet any portion of the Italian fleet, and returned to

Fasano. This appears to have caused considerable excitement in Italy. The navy recently created was held in great esteem, and known to be, both in the number and equipment of its vessels, superior to that of the enemy. It was doubted whether an Austrian Squadron would venture to encounter it at sea under such disadvantages. This only can account, to my mind, for the course taken. Persano was urged to some striking feat of arms, and the attack on Lissa was organised. What can be thought of such strategy? No indication had been given that he had such a command of the sea as to permit him to take no account of the enemy's squadron. Proof had been afforded that the Austrian commander was a man who would be troublesome if not disposed of. His force must be sought out and fought, or blockaded. Persano's first duty was to follow the Austrian fleet. Such was his numerical superiority that he might have detailed a portion of his force for this duty while the remainder carried out some other operation. But he disregarded all the experience which has shown that naval supremacy must first be obtained before territorial attack is justifiable, and he embarked upon an undertaking which only added one more lesson to the many history affords on this head.

Persano left Ancona, on the 16th of July 1866, with nearly thirty vessels, of which eleven were ironclads, and steered for the small island of Lissa on the Austrian coast. The principal port was San Giorgio, where fairly strong batteries skilfully handled might be expected to give hostile ships a warm reception. A short distance off was another harbour, Carobert, and on the other side of the island were the bay and town of Comissa. Neither of these places had any defences to speak of. The plan of Admiral Persano was to attack the batteries of San Giorgio, and when these had been silenced to land a body of troops sufficient to overcome the garrison and occupy the island. An alternative plan would have been to land his own force at any convenient place, under cover of his ships, and take San Giorgio in rear—as we had done at Bomarsund—keeping his squadron ready and uninjured to meet the enemy at sea. But he started without his troops, which were to follow the next day, convoyed by an ironclad and three wooden vessels— another error, as they were thus liable to be cut off by an Austrian Squadron before reaching their destination. Arriving at San Giorgio, on the morning of the 18th, the ships shortly after opened a heavy fire on the batteries, which was returned, and the action continued throughout that day. Night brought about a cessation of the cannonade, but the land defence was not overcome. The next day the troops arrived to the number of about 2000, and preparations to land were then made. The disembarkation was to be at Carobert. Two ironclads were sent to make a diversion at Comissa, four others were to endeavour to enter the harbour of San Giorgio while the remaining ships covered the landing. This was on the 19th. But the naval attack on San Giorgio did not succeed, and the detachment detailed for it withdrew, having sustained considerable injury and loss. The disembarkation was postponed for that day.

G

In the meantime where was Tegethoff? He had heard of the intended attack on Lissa while at Fasano, but distrusted its reality until, on the 19th, he received news which cleared away his doubt on the matter. He therefore sailed with his whole squadron that afternoon, bent on attacking the enemy and frustrating his purpose. Whether Persano heard that night of his departure I do not know, but on the morning of the 20th he prepared to renew the attack and land his troops, as if deeming no interference possible. At eight A.M., however, one of his look-out vessels signalled 'suspicious fleet in sight.' And what a condition he was in to meet even a less powerful squadron than his own. He had materially contributed to put the two fleets on an equality. One of his ironclads had been so knocked about the day before that she was practically useless, two others were out of reach, making a diversion elsewhere, and his un-armoured vessels were encumbered with the landing appliances, and unable to cope effectively with the Austrian vessels of the same nature. Persano hastily collected his uninjured ironclads and advanced to meet Tegethoff, whose squadron was now plainly visible. The fighting formation he adopted was single line ahead, so that his squadron presented a long line extending over 2 miles. The Austrian squadron bore down in three divisions, each forming an obtuse angle and composed of seven ships. The divisions were about 1000 yards astern of each other. Tegethoff led in the 'Ferdinand Max.' This formation was more compact than the single line, but one difficult to maintain when the opposing forces came in contact. To bring this about, however, was the first aim of the leader, and after that the result must mainly depend on his subordinates. At about half-past ten Persano, who was in the 'Ré d'Italia,' stopped her and went on board the 'Affondatore.' To do this at such a moment indicates a sudden decision not made known to his followers. The 'Ré d'Italia' was fourth ship in the line, consequently those in rear had to reduce speed, thus increasing the distance between them and the three leading ships. Tegethoff's order to his squadron was to rush at and sink the enemy. He was then bearing down on the port bow of the Italian line. When about 1000 yards distant the leading vessels of the Italian Squadron opened fire, which was not returned until Tegethoff's leading division had arrived within about 300 yards; but little damage was done on either side. Whether smoke now obscured both squadrons or an alteration of course was inadvisable at the last moment is uncertain, but it happened that the whole of the Austrian vessels passed through the gap between the third and fourth ships of the Italian line without contact. The fight now became a *mêlée*. The Austrian division of wooden ships bore down to attack the Italian unarmoured vessels that had remained behind, but was intercepted and engaged by the rear Italian ironclads. The 'Kaiser' was attacked by the 'Affondatore,' who tried to ram, but failed. Then another ironclad, the 'Portogallo,' made for the 'Kaiser,' whose captain, to cover his smaller wooden consorts, decided to ram the newcomer. He succeeded in striking her on the port side, sustaining severe injury to his own ship without greatly damaging the 'Portogallo.' Being now almost disabled, the 'Kaiser,' followed by most of the Austrian wooden ships, made for San Giorgio. Though all had suffered more or less severely, they had held their own against a portion of the Italian ironclads, leaving the remainder to be dealt with by their own.

Tegethoff had meanwhile attacked the Italian centre, and a hot engagement ensued. The 'Ré d'Italia' had her rudder damaged, and being observed by Tegethoff in this condition, he directed the 'Ferdinand Max' to be steered at her. The 'Ré d'Italia' endeavoured to avoid the assault, but did an unwise thing by first going ahead and then astern. She thus had little movement at the instant the 'Ferdinand Max' struck her on the port side at full speed. The shock was tremendous on board the 'Max,' but by going astern with the engines she extricated her stem from the hole made in the ill-fated 'Ré d'Italia.' That vessel had heeled over to the blow, then rolled to port, and almost immediately sank, taking down most of her crew. Another Italian ironclad, the 'Palestro,' had been set on fire by a shell, and blew up afterwards. Several single fights had taken place between other ships, but without decisive result. One is struck by the opportunities for ramming this action afforded, the many instances in which it was attempted, and the number of failures to strike that took place. The battle was practically over soon after noon. The Italian Squadron withdrew, and Tegethoff went

Barbette System combined with Broadside. 101

into San Giorgio, which he had thus saved. The number of killed and wounded in his ships was about 200, while the Italians lost over 700 men, principally by the sinking of the 'Ré d'Italia.' Besides this vessel they had lost another ironclad, the 'Palestro,' while the Austrian Squadron was intact. The 'Kaiser' was most injured, but forty-eight hours sufficed to put her in a seaworthy condition. Whatever errors he may have committed previously, when once the action began, Persano fought gallantly. His ship, the 'Affondatore,' was in the thickest of the fight, though he failed to ram any of his opponents. Even when his squadron was much scattered, Persano signalled to attack again, and made for the Austrian vessels. But his ships were in some cases too distant to join in time, the opportunity passed away, and the attack was not made. Though his force was reduced by two ironclads, he was still superior in numbers. The preceding attack on Lissa, coupled with this action at sea, had so told on the crews that the Italian commander molested his adversary no further. Tegethoff having gained his object was not likely to assume the offensive.

On the Austrian side only the wooden vessels suffered to any considerable extent from the enormous quantity of shell and shot discharged during that day. This was due to inaccuracy, in the first place, and, secondly, to the protection of $4\frac{1}{2}$-in. iron plating. The Italian fire was exceedingly wild; broadsides at close quarters missed their object, and I have heard it stated that often guns were fired without projectiles. This showed a most inefficient control of the fire on the part of the officers, and it is a matter which should receive the greatest attention in all navies. Much is written about the fire discipline of armies in the field, but no less important is this supervision in a naval action.

One thing is wanting to complete the valuable experience gained on that day and make it applicable to the present time. No locomotive torpedoes were used, this arm as a naval weapon not having been then introduced. Whether, after the line was broken and the ships were all mixed up together, it would not have been as dangerous to friend as to foe may well be questioned; but small vessels specially armed in this way would have had good opportunities of gliding in under cover of the smoke and dealing deadly blows to partially disabled ships. Time was everything to Tegethoff, and hence it is difficult to say what effect torpedoes would have had upon his tactics. We can only deal with matters as they were; and we have sufficient material for reflection both in the strategy preceding the action and the manner in which two modern fleets first met in war.

While we were thus developing side by side the broadside and turret systems of mounting guns behind armour our neighbours the French had proceeded on somewhat different lines. At first, like ourselves, they had adopted the broadside system, and then the central battery, but with the latter and above it they usually placed a few guns *en barbette* on each side. This prin-

Barbette System combined with Broadside. 103

ciple was continued as guns increased in weight until the combination became impossible. Then, rejecting the turret except for coast defence vessels, they mounted all the heavy guns *en barbette*. Even now considerable difference of opinion exists as to the relative advantages of the two systems, as may be observed from the fact that one of the new 14,000-ton battle ships we are building is a turret vessel. This is one of the problems that only such a practical test as war can solve. The barbette system consists of a thick inclined wall of armour, usually pear-shaped, built into the ship, enclosing a turntable, which carries the gun, and is high enough to permit the latter to fire freely over the wall in any direction as the turntable revolves. Therefore only the apparatus for manipulating the gun is protected, and the piece itself is exposed throughout its length to hostile fire. With the revolving turret protection is afforded to a greater portion of the gun, because the height of the wall is greater, and the gun points through an embrasure. With short ordnance there was little exposed even at the moment of firing, and after discharge rotation of the turret took the guns out of danger. It was this peculiarity of the turret system which gave the 'Monitor' such an advantage over the 'Merrimac.' As the officers of the latter said, the 'Monitor's' guns were fired and the turret revolved so quickly that they had not a chance of getting a fair shot at them. But when guns were given great length, and slender muzzles which might be disabled by small projectiles, the advantage in this respect was lessened. Moreover, the turret involved additional weight, while the barbette permitted a higher position for the gun, which at sea is a considerable advantage. When a gun is not many feet above the water there is a liability of projectiles striking crests of waves near the ship and being deflected from the path required. This has been observed at target practice from some of our turret ships in rough weather.

Though circumstances inclined us to the turret, we tentatively gave one ship—the 'Temeraire'—a barbette at each end. These were pear-shaped redoubts, but differed from those now constructed, because their dimensions were such as to allow the gun mounted within to recoil down after firing behind the walls, and thus disappear during the process of reloading. This

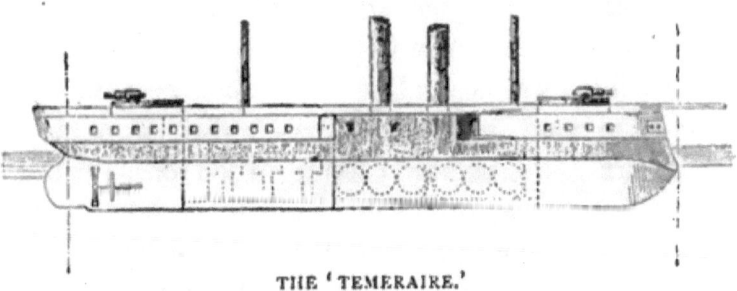

THE 'TEMERAIRE.'

necessitated a larger enclosure, and the gain was considered so small as against the extra weight entailed that this disappearing principle has not been repeated in ships, though it is coming into greater favour for land defences.

But a further consideration brought about a modification not only in the method of carrying the heavy guns which the genius and enthusiasm of artillerists had pressed upon us, but also in the composition of the armament itself. The inevitable result of contracting the thickest armour to a comparatively small area on the side of a ship was that the remainder of a hull could be effectually penetrated by less powerful ordnance. Much damage could be done by light shells to the unprotected parts. It might be more profitable to disregard the 24-in. armour of the ' Inflexible ' and endeavour to disable the ship by attacking the much larger portion without protection. Numerous light guns would be useful for this purpose, and the French for some time had been in the habit of associating with the heaviest guns an auxiliary armament of lighter ordnance, mounted on the broadside. The latest phase was to be a combination of the barbette and broadside systems. A series of vessels were constructed, now well known as the 'Admiral' class, because each bears the name of a distinguished British admiral, which varied in size from 9200 to 10,000 tons. All are constructed with a pear-shaped barbette at each end, for one or two heavy guns, and between the barbettes a broadside battery of 6-in. guns. The armour at the water line is 18 in. extreme thickness, and of compound manufacture. This armour does not extend to the ends, which are protected with a steel deck. The absence of a complete belt gives an opportunity for critics to deny that such vessels are efficient as battle ships. On the other hand, their speed is higher considerably—17 knots—than any previous vessels, and they carry a large supply of coal. They differ chiefly in the heavy armament. The smallest, the 'Collingwood,' carries four 45-ton guns, the 'Howe' four 67-ton, and the 'Benbow' two 110-ton guns. Probably naval opinion would incline to the 'Collingwood's' armament for all ships of this size, with perhaps an addition to the auxiliary ordnance. There might also be a preference for a reduction in thickness of armour, and a corresponding increase in the extent of water line covered by it. But of vessels that can steam fast and hit hard it is easy to be hypercritical.

Another inducement to supplement the necessarily few heavy guns with an auxiliary armament had gradually been assuming great importance, and that was the necessity of meeting the attack of torpedo boats. It was evident that neither an 80-ton nor a 6-in. gun would be the best weapon to stop the advance of a small craft capable of covering a mile of water in three minutes. One round from a heavy gun at such a mark was as much as could be anticipated, while under cover of the cloud of smoke the boat, if intact, had an excellent opportunity for effecting her purpose. Numerous guns of just sufficient power to penetrate the boiler, or smash the machinery of a torpedo boat, would therefore be most effectual in neutralising such an attack. Hence the development of machine and quick-firing guns throwing projectiles of from 1 to 6 lbs. The armament, therefore, of the modern ship is composed of a few heavy guns, a secondary battery of ordnance of moderate calibre, and numerous machine and quick-firing guns. All this entails a great weight of ammunition, so that if required to be combined with extensive

Barbette System combined with Broadside.

armour protection, great speed, and a large coal supply, we are forced into a ship of huge dimensions. Confining our attention at present to the barbette system, let us see the latest development of this type of battle ship, though there was an interval when we returned to our early love the turret.

In the 'Benbow' we have a ship of 10,600 tons, in which the principal armament is a single gun of 110 tons at each end, and ten guns of 5 tons on the broadside. She has 18 in. of compound armour covering the central portion of the water line, but the broadside guns, as well as the ends of the vessel, are unprotected with armour on the side. It was freely asserted that for this reason such vessels were liable to be disabled by vessels with numerous light guns before perhaps their own ponderous ordnance could neutralise the attack. The explosion of a number of even small shell at the water line would, it was urged, admit sufficient water to impair the speed and manœuvring qualities of the ship, though not necessarily to overcome her buoyancy. Again, all nations were seeking some more powerful explosive than powder as a bursting charge for shells. To get these projectiles through iron without breaking, their walls must be thick. Consequently the interior capacity is reduced, and the amount of powder such shells can contain is only sufficient to just open the iron case, or may not even do that. We want, however, the shell to be fractured with violence into numerous pieces, each acting as a separate projectile, and for this a more energetic explosive is required. Many exist, but the difficulty hitherto has been to obtain one which with great power, will combine safety in handling and withstand the great concussion of the enormous powder charges now fired in guns. Experiments in different countries seem to show that this difficulty can be overcome, and that such shells are terribly destructive when exploded inside a ship. Thus the old idea of protecting crews from such effects again came to the front. All these moderate sized guns and their workers must fight behind armour of some sort, and not be left entirely unprotected. There was also a demand for more of such guns to supplement the principal armament. Nothing was to be given up, but a good deal more was asked for.

The naval architect was willing to provide it, but said that all this could not be done under a displacement of 14,000 tons. Thus when a large increase to the navy was sanctioned in 1889, and it was decided to at once lay down ten battle ships, of which eight were to be of the first class, it was perhaps not unnatural that we should endeavour to embody in these all the varied demands for powerful armament, extended protection, great speed, and prolonged endurance at sea, only to be given in mastless ships by a large coal supply. As regards the first item, a feeling that we had exceeded the limit of usefulness in guns of such weight as 110 tons, and the restriction thereby imposed as to number, led to a more moderate calibre being adopted for the principal armament. The 67-ton gun had been tried, and found satisfactory in some ships of the 'Admiral' class, so it was selected for the new vessels. All of them are to have

Barbette System combined with Broadside. 109

four of these guns, mounted in pairs, at each end of the ship. In seven out of eight of these first-class battle ships, to be named the 'Royal Sovereign,' 'Empress of India,' 'Ramillies,' 'Repulse,' 'Resolution,' 'Revenge,' and 'Royal Oak,' this part of the armament is to be *en barbette*. This system would therefore appear, according to present opinion, to offer the greatest number of advantages. The two barbettes form separate protected positions, so that no injury to one could affect the other. Where two such stations are placed in a single central citadel, and hence necessarily in somewhat close proximity to each other, there must be a risk of both being disabled at the same time.

The auxiliary or secondary armament is to consist of ten 6-in. guns, five on each side, in a central battery between the barbettes. To obtain greater distribution of these guns, and so reduce the effect of hostile fire in this part of the ship, they will be mounted on two decks, one above the other. As to protect them by external armour on the side of the ship would involve great additional weight, steel shields only will be provided for these guns, those between decks having side screens as well, also of steel. A number of machine and other smaller guns will be disposed where convenient. As regards armour, these vessels will carry a belt of compound armour for two-thirds of the length, $8\frac{1}{2}$ ft. broad and 18 in. thick, in the central portion. Above this, for a length of 145 ft., the broadside is to be protected with 5-in. steel plates to a height of $9\frac{1}{2}$ ft. above the water. The barbettes will have compound armour, 18 in. thick, for protecting the machinery employed in the manipulation of the heavy guns. The ends of the vessel have no external armour, but a steel deck will confine any water that may enter, from this portion being penetrated by projectiles, and prevent it from flooding the ship. Even if the spaces at each end were so filled, the trim of the vessel would be little affected.

To drive a floating weight of 14,000 tons through the waters obviously requires powerful machinery, and as it was considered desirable that these vessels should have a speed of 16 knots without pressing the engines, and under ordinary atmospheric draught for the fires, while with forced or artificial draught the speed should be capable of being increased to $17\frac{1}{2}$ knots, boilers and engines are being provided equal to the development under the latter condition of 13,000 horse power. As there will be two sets of engines for revolving twin screws, each set will be of 6500 horse power. When we remember that the 'Warrior' had a single engine of 5000 horse power, which propelled her at 14 knots, it can be realised what a vast increase of power is required to obtain the additional $3\frac{1}{2}$ knots, notwithstanding the great improvements in steam propulsion since that time. In the 'Collingwood,' a vessel of the same displacement as the 'Warrior,' to pass from 14 knots to 17 knots required practically the horse power to be doubled. At moderate speeds modern marine engines are economical in coal consumption, but beyond a certain rate the fuel rapidly disappears. A large supply is therefore essential, and in the new battle ships the amount is fixed at 900 tons.

First class battle ship *Ramillies*, building by Messrs J. and G. Thomson, Clydebank

It is considered that this will enable them to cover 5000 nautical miles at a speed of 10 knots an hour. One matter must be taken into account, and that is the drain on the coal for work unconnected with propelling the ship. Numerous small engines are continually going for driving electric light apparatus, ventilating fans, pumping machinery, and other services, so that practically one boiler is always in use. Coal used in cooking and distilling water swells the total expended in this way, so that even when lying at anchor the stock diminishes at no inconsiderable rate. In time of war, when high speed will have to be maintained, the question of fuel must be a constant anxiety, and I should prefer an addition in this respect at a sacrifice of a few hundred tons of armour in vessels of such dimensions. Nevertheless these eight new first-class battle ships are noble designs, worked out with the ability which has characterised all that has emanated from the brain of Mr White, the present Chief Constructor of the Navy. They will form, as he has said, a squadron of identical character and qualities, capable of proceeding and manœuvring together. As a single group they constitute a naval force which the entire fleets of few other States can equal.

With this unstinted commendation I must at the same time express my preference for a greater number of vessels of smaller size. This is a difficult question, but it has been somewhat obscured by the extreme views of those who advocate vessels of 2000 or 3000 tons for battle ships as a limit. It has been even advanced that a vast number of gunboats is a more advantageous force than a few very large vessels. Those, however, who have practical experience of the sea, and who have endeavoured to benefit by the history of the past, will at once reject such a doctrine. Looking back, I observe in the old days that though four-deckers were to be found in the fleets of our adversaries, we abstained from adding them to our own; that at one time, as a result of war experience, we converted three-deckers into two-deckers; and that this type of vessel was then most largely represented in our fleet. It could cope with the bigger vessel, and if assisted by a companion, with success. On the other hand, it is argued that two frigates never took a line-of-battle ship, and hence one big vessel is better than two small ones; but the argument is fallacious, because frigates were not battle ships, and as a rule did not attempt to attack them. Examples of their doing so and being sunk by a single broadside are to be found in naval history. In the same way we may say now that two cruisers cannot take the place of a battle ship in a sea fight. Yet as actions then were entirely decided by the gun, it might be thought that the greater number of these weapons carried the more efficient the vessel, and such an increase was only effected by adding to the number of decks. Still, we did not do it. And now we have ram and torpedo to contend with, weapons which attack the most vulnerable part of the ship, and which no increase in her dimensions can enable her to withstand. Though a vessel of 20,000 tons could be constructed with armour impervious to the gun, her hull under water could not be made strong enough to resist the shock of a swift ram or the explosion of 200 lbs. of gun cotton, which the latest torpedo carries.

The great argument in favour of the very big ship is that it represents the principle of concentration, and that tactically a small number can be more efficiently handled than a force numerically superior but composed individually of weaker ships. This is true in a general sense, but the principle may be carried too far, and take us on to the 20,000-ton ship alluded to. Admiral Sir Geoffrey Hornby, while endorsing the concentrated strength principle, has also said: 'I think it better that we should have ships of medium size.' Does he look upon 14,000 tons as 'medium size'? My friend Mr White, if he ever reads this work, will probably say here: 'What is the limit you would impose?' and be ready to show that it precludes some important qualification. To this my reply would be that I am prepared to sacrifice some protection, and to risk being struck by the heaviest projectiles, as long as my ship will exclude the remainder. Rapidity of movement and an overwhelming fire from your own guns will probably prove the best defence. There seems to me no reason why a good speed, large supply of coal, and a powerful armament cannot be obtained within a displacement of 10,000 tons. In eight vessels of 14,200 tons we have an aggregate of 113,600 tons of material employed. If we distribute this among twelve vessels, they can be approximately of 9,500 tons. I have asked admirals which of two such squadrons, if pitted one against the other, they would prefer to command. The selection has usually been with the greatest number, for a squadron of twelve ships can be controlled and directed as effectively as one of eight. There are many other points which might be brought forward against the bigger vessel, such as difficulty in harbour accommodation, depth of water, passage through the Suez Canal, individual cost, and time required for completion, but space will not permit my dwelling on them. I am content to rest the argument on the increase of strength given by the additional ram and torpedo power of the numerically superior squadron. These views will not, probably, influence warship construction in the slightest degree. Whether they are sound or not can only be demonstrated by the searching test of war, and all we can say is, that hitherto our experience has been in favour of moderate dimensions for ships and their armament.

CHAPTER VI

COAST DEFENCE—THE RAM

Coast Defence Vessels—Such Constructions of Modern Growth—Erroneous Ideas of Defence—The 'Glatton' and other Coast Service Vessels—Russian Circular Ironclads—Development of the Ram as a Weapon—The 'Rupert' and 'Polyphemus'—Disadvantages of a Vessel for ramming only—Examples of difficulty in ramming.

THE term 'coast defence vessel,' as applied to any craft larger than a gunboat, is, as far as this country is concerned, of modern growth. The principle of building special ships for operations confined to the coast found no favour with our ancestors, taught by the experience of long wars that a seagoing fleet is the best defence against any attempt on the part of an enemy to approach our shores. When, in 1804, Pitt brought forward a motion in the House of Commons condemnatory of the Government's naval policy,—a portion of his indictment was the inadequate provision of gun vessels to act in shallow water against an invading flotilla. Sir Edward Pellew—afterwards Lord Exmouth—then in Parliament, clearly formulated on this occasion the true policy to be pursued. He said: 'I do not really see in the arrangement of our naval defence anything to excite the apprehensions of even the most timid among us. I see a triple naval bulwark, composed of one fleet acting on the enemy's coast; of another, consisting of heavier ships, stationed in the Downs, and ready to act at a moment's notice; and a third, close to the beach, capable of destroying any part of the enemy's flotilla that should escape the vigilance of the other two branches of our defence. As to these gunboats, which have been so strongly recommended, this mosquito fleet, they are the most contemptible force that can be employed. I have lately seen half-a-dozen of them lying wrecked on the rocks. As to the probability of the enemy being able, in a narrow sea, to pass through our blockading squadrons with all that secrecy and dexterity, and by those hidden means that some worthy people expect, I really, from anything I have seen in the course of my professional career, am not disposed to concur in it.' Lord St Vincent was equally emphatic that preparation should be rather directed to keeping the enemy as far from our coasts as possible, and attacking them the moment they come out of their ports, than to awaiting them at home.

It is only when the fleet has been suffered to decline from motives of economy that misdirected attention is turned to some such substitute as elaborate land defences or coast defence ironclads. Such a period was that following the Reform Bill of 1832, until in 1847 an alarm was raised that we were liable to invasion, which, it was stated, had been rendered easy by the introduction of steam. The Duke of Wellington pointed out the defencelessness of the country, and a Royal Commission, in 1859, recommended an expenditure of £10,000,000 on the fixed defences of our naval arsenals. There seemed no one to urge that, if the state of navy was such as to render an attack on any of these places other than a desperate undertaking, the first step should be to strengthen the fleet. But the naval voice was silent, or nearly so. The military element in the country had become predominant, while the words of St Vincent and Pellew were forgotten. We had almost accepted the situation of an inferior naval power. How far we had wandered from the principles that guided us in 1804 can be estimated on reading the debate in the House of Commons, in 1860, on the motion to fortify the ports. Lord Palmerston said on this occasion : ' I am not surprised that the gallant admiral should undervalue the strength of fortifications ; but, nevertheless, I think the history of war shows that they do enable an inferior force to hold out for a certain time against a superior force.' The 'gallant admiral' was Sir Charles Napier, who had said that 'the only sure way to prevent invasion was to have always at hand a superior fleet to the French or any other nation.' He quoted the saying of Mr Tierney, 'give me a well-manned fleet and a full Exchequer and I will defy the world.' But it was of no avail, and we embarked upon a system of elaborate fortification, based upon the assumed defeat, absence, or inferiority of the only line of defence which could not be neglected with impunity.

Tacit acquiescence in a view which apparently contemplates an enemy roaming over the seas without et or hindrance, and his appearance in force without warning on any part of our coast, seems to have led to the construction of vessels with a restricted radius of operation and incapable of service in distant waters. The desire to have within sight, as it were, a portion of the fleet becomes at times exceedingly strong. Each locality demands a squadron for its special protection, and failing to obtain it, urges extensive fortification. The Admiralty, on the other hand, has always had a strong objection to the localisation of any portion of its force. During the Crimean War some uneasiness was felt on the coast of the United Kingdom and India at the absence of British ships. It was then pointed out by the naval authorities that more efficient protection was afforded to this country by confining Russian ships to their own ports than by distributing the British fleet along the east coast of England and Scotland. A similar explanation demonstrated that India was more efficiently protected by our squadron acting in the Chinese Seas than by stationing British ships in the Bay of Bengal. Periodically the same demand is made for local defence, and when ships are denied, an alternative is found in forts and submarine mines, whose principal merit is that they cannot be removed.

It has been asserted that ships being no longer dependent on the wind for propulsion there is an advantage to the side that contemplates attack. Lord

Palmerston, in 1860, said: 'The adoption of steam as a motive power afloat has totally altered the character of naval warfare, and deprived us of much of the advantages of our insular position.' He quoted the opinion of Sir Robert Peel, 'that steam had bridged the Channel, and, for the purposes of aggression, had almost made this country cease to be an island.' It is not difficult to show that such views are entirely erroneous. No change in weapons or method of propulsion can alter the general principles of naval warfare. But this may be fairly advanced, that increased rapidity of movement, improved communications with distant stations, and augmented resources in war material, all tell in the favour of the stronger navy, whether for attack or defence. Squadrons thousands of miles away can now be concentrated at any point, reinforced if threatened, or recalled home, in so many days, while formerly as many months were required. If steam has bridged the Channel, in one sense, it has equally removed the space which intervened between one part of the United Kingdom and another, and has rendered a collection of vessels at any point threatened a matter of a few hours, whereas in former times a contrary wind might delay succour until it was too late. On the whole, therefore, it appears to me that steam would only tell against us in the event of our being completely overmastered at sea, a contingency it seems unnecessary to dwell upon.

In thus dealing generally with the question I by no means preclude the possibility of raids by single vessels that might escape the most complete system of blockade. At no time has it been possible to prevent such attacks by an enterprising enemy, and there is perhaps greater opportunity for them with steam than before. Under such conditions special vessels for coast service have some justification, and confidence is maintained wherever the rest of the fleet is employed. The weak point of the principle is that the best coast defence vessel is a first-class battle ship, especially for an island subject at most periods of the year to weather that is not favourable to any but the most seaworthy craft.

For these reasons the coast defence ironclad, which is largely represented in other navies, is only found to a very limited extent in our own. The first of its kind, built about 1870, was designed with the idea that a type could be produced which might be equally useful for attack within a moderate distance from our shores and for defence in home waters. This was the 'Glatton,' a single-turreted monitor of 5000 tons. Her sides, which are very low, are protected with 12 in. of iron, and a similar thickness was placed on the turret. This is 38 ft. in diameter, and contains two muzzle loading 25-ton guns. When completed in 1872 an experiment was made to test the behaviour of the turret when struck by heavy projectiles. The 'Hotspur,' another vessel with a 25-ton gun, was moored at a convenient distance from the 'Glatton,' and a 600-lb. projectile fired at the turret of the latter. 'It failed to penetrate within or injure the rotating arrangements, the turret being found afterwards to revolve freely, and the guns it con-

THE 'GLATTON.'

tained worked in the most perfect manner. Though a powerful ship in armament and armour, the 'Glatton,' in consequence of her low freeboard, has never been looked upon as capable of more than coast service. Her draught of water, 22 ft., detracts also in some measure from her value in this respect, and consequently in the next vessels designed all considerations but those of pure defence were abandoned. The 'Cyclops,' 'Gorgon,' 'Hecate,' and 'Hydra' were constructed to operate in shallow waters. The displacement was reduced to 3500 tons, armour to 8 in., and draught of water to 15 ft. As some compensation they were given two turrets each, containing a pair of 18-ton guns. The amount of coal carried was 120 tons, while the 'Glatton' stows twice that amount. These vessels, owing to their low freeboard and limited dimensions, were originally unsuited to contend with rough weather, and therefore their seagoing qualities have been improved by building up the sides in the middle portion. This does not diminish the fighting capabilities in the slightest degree, but adds considerably to their seaworthiness.

These vessels were built nearly twenty years ago, and that the principle of their construction is considered erroneous is evident from the fact that no others have been constructed for such special work in this country. Three of somewhat larger dimensions, the 'Cerberus,' 'Magdala,' and 'Abyssinia,' were built here for our colonies. They are also double-turreted vessels, and a useful type for keeping off stray hostile cruisers which might reach our distant possessions with a view to requisitions under threat of bombardment. In the 'Scorpion' and 'Wyvern' we have two small turret vessels of 2500 tons, built by Messrs Laird of Liverpool. They were ordered by the Confederate States during the American Civil War, but were seized by our Government before completion and purchased. They were designed on the ideas of Cowper Coles, and Ericsson, and an interesting account of the history of these vessels until they passed into our hands is contained in a work called *The Secret Service of the Confederate States in Europe*, by James D. Bulloch, their representative over here. Had they crossed the Atlantic under his orders naval events might have run differently. Skilfully handled, they should have made short work of the Northern monitors, to which in all points of construction they were greatly superior.

But if we rightly do not spend money in producing vessels that are unable to accompany a fleet, and take part in any operation it may be required to undertake, other nations have always devoted a considerable portion of their naval estimates to ships for coast defence. In France vessels built under this head have so increased in size that they are quite capable of coping with our battle ships, and hence all comparisons of relative strength are inaccurate which do not take this into account.

Russia was so much impressed with the power displayed by the American monitor that for many years her ironclad navy was principally recruited by similar vessels. With the Crimean War fresh in her memory,

the idea that powerful squadrons could be kept at a
distance by small coast defence monitors was no doubt
hard to resist, however fallacious, and hence the reconstruction of Russia's seagoing ironclad navy is barely
the growth of a decade. Absorbed in this view of a
coast defence which might combine a fort and ship in
one, the head of the Russian navy in 1870, Admiral
Popoff, designed a vessel of which the breadth was

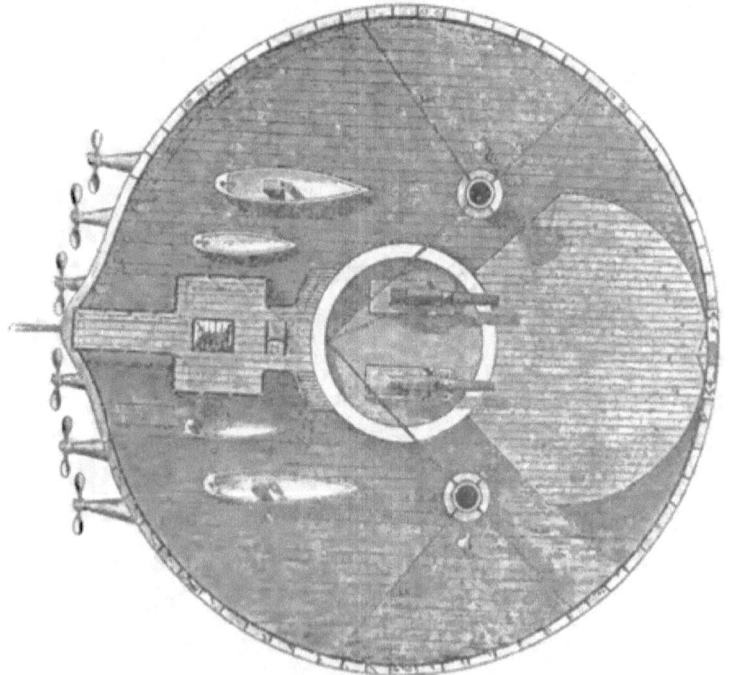

THE DECK OF THE 'NOVGOROD,' CIRCULAR IRONCLAD.

nearly equal to the length. These structures were afterwards more familiarly known as Popoffkas or circular
ironclads. Two were constructed, called the 'Novgorod'

and 'Admiral Popoff.' The latter was the largest. Her dimensions were, length 120 ft., breadth 96 ft., and displacement 3550 tons. Being flat under water she only drew 14 ft. The circular form enabled thick armour to be carried on a comparatively small vessel. On the sides at the water line it was 18 in., and on the deck 2½ in. On the upper deck were two 40-ton guns, mounted *en barbette*. To propel the vessel are four screws side by side, but the speed in favourable weather does not exceed 6 knots. The chief defect is difficulty of keeping them on a straight course. We have found the same in some of our vessels which have great beam in proportion to length, but with the Popoffkas the tendency is to revolve like a saucer on the water. On occasions all directive control over them disappears. As ships, therefore, they were soon discredited, and undiscriminating censure passed on their designer. But they should be regarded as sea forts with the power of shifting their position rather than as portions of the seagoing fleet. A fort rising out of the water, as we see at Spithead, may be regarded as a ship at anchor. It cannot advance to attack, or pursue if passed. Beyond the range of its guns the smallest hostile cruiser may harass with impunity the approaching merchant vessels if opposing war vessels are not at hand. Not possessing the power of concentration at any point threatened, want of mobility in forts must be compensated for by an increase of numbers, until every avenue of approach is covered. If protection is sought by such means against an attack by a powerful ironclad squadron, 500 guns on land are soon absorbed, involving very large garrisons. We may then consider whether the same or better protection could not be afforded by a flotilla. The question is too big to be argued here, and it is only alluded to as some justification for the Russian circular ironclads. Their defective steering could no doubt be improved by building on light ends, so as to give them more resistance to side movement when the rudder is put over, and an armament of two 40-ton guns renders such a type formidable to a battle ship of larger dimensions for ordinary seagoing purposes. Unfortunately, the value of these floating forts was not tested during the Russo-Turkish War. Turkey, though most powerful at sea, abstained from coast attacks, and the circular ironclads were kept in their own waters. They are one of the abnormal growths of peace, and interesting as indicating to what lengths the theory may be carried; but as one ship after another is cast aside, as these vessels have been, we only see more clearly that the vessel which is most efficient for all purposes best answers special requirements

In former days when wooden ships met in combat at sea there was no desire to bring vessels in contact with each other except for the purposes of boarding. However close the action, collision was avoided, as such an incident might cause the loss of masts and yards, placing the vessel at the mercy of her enemy, or allowing the latter to escape if so minded. When two fleets got so mixed up that manœuvring was impossible, the simplest plan was to fall alongside the nearest vessel and secure the two together until one was subdued. At such a time communication from an admiral to his subordinates was impossible, but everyone knew what had to be done. When Nelson had broken the line of the combined fleets at Trafalgar he ran alongside the nearest ship, with the result we all know. He did not attempt to run down any of his opponents, nor can we recall a single incident of one wooden ship deliberately ramming—as we now term it—another. The risk was too great of loss of spars, and the wooden bows were not suited for such an operation. When iron was substituted for wood the latter objection passed away, but the use of the ram as a weapon was chiefly brought about by the same cause that brought the torpedo into prominence. This was the fact that, while every effort had been made to protect ships above water from shot and shell, the most vulnerable part, that below the water line, was more open to attack than ever. Hence the old idea of subduing the fire of ships, and obtaining their surrender by such a disablement of the crew that they were unable any longer to fight their guns, gave place to the modern desire to effect their destruction in a more speedy manner by a blow under water. Should a ship be sunk immediately in this manner, no addition is made to the fleet of the victor, but that of the enemy is effectually reduced. Several incidents have shown this in a striking manner since the introduction of the ironclad. To these allusion will be made later. Hence, from the 'Warrior' to the latest phase of battle ship, the ram has been continually developed in the bows of ships with a view to its use in future actions. In the 'Warrior' this was carried out in an imperfect manner; the stem formed an obtuse angle of large dimensions with the apex or spur, such as it was, at the water line. When the power of the ram had been demonstrated in America, and afterwards at Lissa, we frankly recognised that this weapon was of great importance. All the later vessels had bows which terminated under water in a sharp spur, forming a powerful ram, securely fastened to the ship, and weighing several tons.

While all who were concerned in the construction of vessels in which iron was so largely employed, and those who had to manœuvre them when completed, were soon convinced that the momentum of such a weight brought in contact with another ship must prove irresistible, a few were such enthusiastic champions of the ram as to desire that ships should be constructed specially for this purpose. They went so far as to say that to give guns in addition would diminish the efficiency of the ram by perhaps enshrouding the vessel in smoke at the critical moment. But in France and in England this conception has not been favourably received. Across the Channel small coast defence ironclads were constructed soon after the American Civil War in which the gun equipment was limited to a single turret in the fore part of the ship, and a strong ram added to the bow. The idea was to disconcert an enemy with heavy projectiles just previous to the charge. We carried out the same principle with two vessels, the 'Hotspur' and 'Rupert,' two small but serviceable ironclads, the former completed in 1871, and the latter in 1874. The dimensions of the 'Rupert,' 3200 tons, were such as to ensure handiness in turning, while the vital portions were protected with 12 in. of iron. The gun power was only moderate, consisting of two 18-ton guns in the turret, and two other smaller pieces in the after portion of the ship. It was on the ram that principal reliance was placed.

There being much to commend itself in the 'Rupert' to naval officers, an extension of the same principle was carried out a few years afterwards in the 'Conqueror'

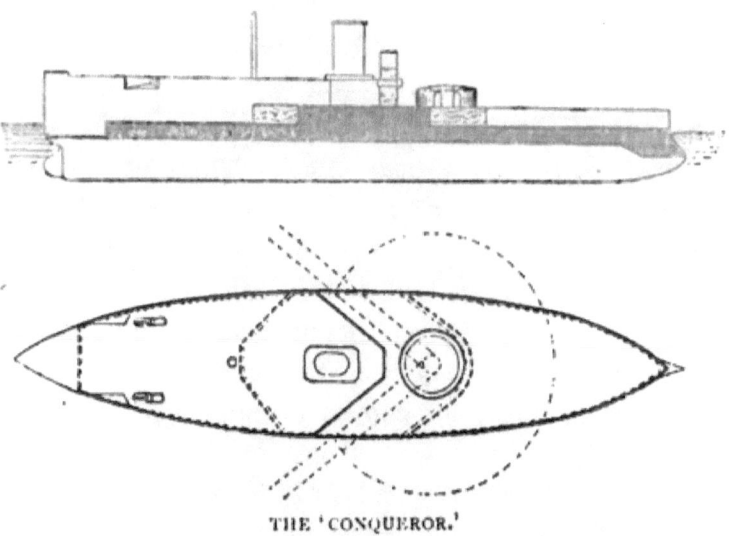

THE 'CONQUEROR.'

and 'Hero.' In order to accommodate more powerful ordnance, and obtain an increased speed, it was necessary to increase the displacement to 6200 tons. This enabled two 43-ton guns to be carried in her single turret, and improved machinery increased the speed to 15 knots. The defect of such vessels is the absence of stern fire, and with 6000 tons a second turret aft seems desirable.

But strong pressure was all the time being put on the Admiralty to build a vessel in which guns should have no place, and the most persistent advocate was Admiral Sir George Sartorius, who appears to have formed an exaggerated view of the ram as a weapon. The result was the construction of the 'Polyphemus.' The leading features of her design were a low hull, exposing but a small mark to an enemy's fire, the portion above water being shaped like a turtle's back, and covered with thin armour to deflect any projectile that might strike it; great speed, by the adoption of special machinery, a powerful ram, and a torpedo equipment. The only ordnance was to consist of a few light guns for repelling boat or torpedo attack. These are mounted on a superstructure necessary for carrying the boats and working the ship at sea. A special point in her design was the formation of the keel as a rectangular groove, in which are placed lengths of cast-iron ballast. This extra weight, amounting to about 300 tons, is not permanently fixed, but can be dropped when required, so as to lighten the vessel if any injury is received reducing the buoyancy. All or portions of it can be released from the conning station. While the vessel is intact the ballast assists in keeping the greater portion of the hull immersed, making a difference of about 12 in. in the draught. Though the 'Polyphemus' was commenced in 1878, difficulties with the boilers delayed her completion till 1882, and several alterations were then made to improve her qualities as a sea-keeping vessel, the original intention being that she should be capable of accompanying a fleet. She has been for some years attached to the Mediterranean Squadron, and though no opportunity has occurred to test her as an engine of war, she has proved quite capable of such service if required. Up to the present she has been without a duplicate in our own or any foreign navy, but the United States are about to construct a vessel on the same principles. It is called a harbour defence ram, and is to be of the following dimensions,—length 250 ft., beam 43 ft., size 2100 tons, and speed 17 knots. The 'Polyphemus' is 2500 tons, and speed 18 knots. The American ram cannot therefore be considered any material advance in this type. I venture to think, moreover, the principle is a mistake, for the following reasons.

When guns were the only weapons to contend with there was some reason to construct a vessel impervious to projectiles and relying solely on the ram. The torpedo alters this condition, as before the ram can be applied such a vessel must come within the radius of the torpedo's range, and though above water she may be invulnerable, below the water line she is as open to attack as any other craft. Then I fail to see the advantage of denying a vessel guns on the plea that their smoke would be an encumbrance when ramming. A captain has the power of withholding his fire at all times, and presumably such an order would be obeyed. Lastly, a vessel without guns disabled in her machinery is at the mercy of any antagonist who can lay off beyond the range of torpedoes, if the ram has these weapons, and use his guns without fear of reply. It appears to me that such an advantage should never be conceded; and for these principal reasons I think the gunless ram is a phase of construction based on erroneous assumptions which have a temporary hold on the imagination, but which disappear under practical consideration of the probabilities in war.

It is, moreover, fallacious to suppose that to ram a vessel under any circumstances is an easy operation even with a superiority of speed. Accidental collisions with disastrous results have, we know, not been unfrequent. The sinking of the 'Vanguard' off the Irish coast by the 'Iron Duke,' and the loss of the 'Grosser Kurfurst' off Folkestone, from being accidentally rammed by a companion, are instances of this and examples of the power of the ram. To strike a ship at anchor as the 'Cumberland' was struck by the 'Merrimac' does not call forth any great exercise of skill. When we examine, however, instances in which it has been desired to ram a ship in movement one is struck by the failures to attain this object which history records. In May 1879, during the war between Chili and Peru, the 'Huascar,' a small turret ship then belonging to the latter power, engaged the Chilian wooden corvette 'Esmeralda.' The latter was, of course, quite overmatched, though it required forty shots from the 'Huascar' before her adversary was disabled. The 'Huascar' then attempted to ram. It was an unnecessary display of power, as the 'Esmeralda' could not escape, and was lying motionless on the water. But these nations are without mercy when at war. Twice the 'Huascar' struck the 'Esmeralda' with her stem, but failed to do serious injury, the captain having stopped the engines too soon. The third attempt was more successful. The 'Esmeralda' was struck on the beam and sunk. Two other ships, the 'Independencia' and 'Covadonga,' were also engaged in the same action, when the former made three ineffective efforts to ram the 'Covadonga,' but failed. At the last attempt she ran ashore and became a wreck.

In the action between the 'Huascar' and the Chilian ironclads 'Blanco Encalada' and 'Almirante Cochrane' several attempts were made to ram the Peruvian vessel, which she evaded, but eventually succumbed to the overwhelming fire of her two opponents. At the battle of Lissa, in 1866, between the Austrian and Italian fleets, there were numerous occasions when ships failed to ram each other. On the other hand, the fact remains that the 'Ré d'Italia' was sunk by the 'Ferdinand Max,' though this was facilitated by injury to the Italian vessel's rudder. A wooden ship, the 'Kaiser,' also rammed the ironclad 'Portogallo,' but sustained more injury herself than she inflicted. In another instance the attempt ended in a graze, the two vessels passing so close to each other that the rammers to the guns could not be used. From such experience we may conclude, and it is capable of mathematical demonstration, that with two ships well handled and free from injury it is only a slight difference of time and movement whether one rams the other or herself sustains the shock; that to bring the stem advantageously in contact with another vessel requires, under any circumstances, considerable skill, but that opportunities may occur in a general action which should be promptly seized. Experience, however, is far from showing that entire reliance should be placed on the ram, to the exclusion of weapons well tried in the past, and which have a much greater radius of action.

CHAPTER VII

ARMOUR—LATER TURRET SHIPS

Early Iron Plates—Increased Thickness—Competition of Guns and Armour—Steel and Compound Plates supersede Iron—Deck and Coal Protection—Progress of Turret Ships 'Nile,' 'Trafalgar' and 'Hood,' 'Victoria' and 'Sanspareil'—Second-Class Battle Ships—Early Types—Latest Development—'Centurion' and 'Barfleur.'

IN describing the 'Inflexible' I have stated that her turrets were protected with compound armour instead of the wrought-iron plates which up to that time had been employed. As the struggle between steel and compound plates has for some years been almost as keen as that between guns and armour, a brief history of this portion of our subject seems here desirable.

I have read that about thirty years ago the present Sir John Brown happened to be at Toulon and saw the new French ironclad 'La Gloire.' Her plates were 5 ft. long, 2 ft. wide, and $4\frac{1}{2}$ in. thick. They had been hammered to these dimensions, as were all the plates of the early American monitors. Mr Brown—as he then was—came to the conclusion that such plates could be rolled, and on his return to England instituted a series of experiments which fully bore out this view. When it was decided to put $4\frac{1}{2}$ in. of iron on the 'Warrior,' rolled plates of this thickness were manufactured without difficulty. In 1861 a target representing a section of the 'Warrior,' and consisting of a 4½-in. iron plate, with 18 in. of teak backing, and an inner iron skin ¾ in. thick, was fired at with a Whitworth rifled gun throwing a flat-headed steel bolt of 80 lbs. The target was indented and cracked, but not perforated.

In 1862 Mr Brown was able to roll at his works at Sheffield, in the presence of Lord Palmerston, an iron plate 18 ft. long, 4 ft. wide, and 5½ in. thick. The following year, when the Lords of the Admiralty visited his works, at the opening of a new rolling mill, the energetic manufacturer showed that plates up to a thickness of 12 in. could be produced.

From that time there was no difficulty in supplying the increased protection demanded for the new ironclad navy, till in the 'Dreadnought' we placed on the hull and turrets plates 14 in. thick. Though the water line amidships of the 'Inflexible' has 24 in. of iron, it is not in one but two plates, each 12 in. thick, with a layer of wood between them.

But already there were indications that no increase in the thickness of wrought-iron plates would suffice to resist the growing energy of the gun. As early as 1869 a Krupp gun of 11 in. calibre had perforated 12 in. of iron and 36 in. of wood. Our own 38-ton gun pierced 19 in. of iron in 1876, and the following year the 80-ton gun sent its projectile through three 8-in. iron plates. In the meantime Mr Schneider had been developing at Creusot, in France, the manufacture of steel plates, and some experiments at Spezzia, in Italy, showed the softness of wrought-iron as compared with steel. The latter resisted penetration to a much greater extent, though it had a tendency to break up when attacked by numerous comparatively light projectiles. From this moment plates composed entirely of wrought-iron were doomed. The manufacturers of them in this country—Messrs Brown and Messrs Cammell—then proposed compound armour. In Cammell's method—which is according to Wilson's patent—a wrought-iron plate is put into a box, placed in a vertical position, and liquid steel poured in between one side of the plate and the side of the box. The composite plate thus made is then rolled, by which process the steel face is hardened and made to adhere rigidly to the wrought-iron foundation. In Brown's method—which is according to Ellis's patent—instead of a box, a thin steel plate is placed at the required distance from the iron plate and the melted steel poured in between the two, making the whole a solid mass. It is then reheated and passed through the rolling mill. In both systems the steel face is about one-third the total thickness. In 1877 experiments with compound armour plates showed their superiority to wrought-iron, and consequently it was decided to place them on the 'Inflexible's' turrets. In 1880 a compound plate made by Messrs Cammell, in which the steel face was 5 in. and the wrought-iron back 13 in. thick, was fired at by the 38-ton gun, with a Palliser chilled shot, the result being that the projectile broke up on impact with the plate, and effected no damage beyond slight indentation and surface cracking. It was then evident that steel projectiles would henceforth be necessary to attack hard armour.

From that time up to the present the competition has been between the compound plates and all-steel plates. The latter resist perforation better, while the harder surface of the former is more effective in breaking projectiles, and causing them to glance off if struck at an angle.[1] For very thick armour we have therefore adhered to compound plates, employing steel plates where only a few inches are required. France has hitherto produced the best all-steel plates, but a demand for such an article could no doubt be met by our own manufacturers. Already Messrs Vickers have made steel plates which have behaved most satisfactorily under severe tests. Steel is continually being improved, and its resistance to perforation increased by the admixture of small quantities of nickel, manganese, or other substance. The original object of armour being to keep out projectiles, I believe we shall soon adopt that material which shows a marked superiority in this respect, and steel plates appear to me to be winning the day. If the projectiles hold together—and those of modern steel make appear to stand impact well—it stands to reason that the medium they have to pass through should, from front to rear, offer a strenuous resistance. When the face of a compound plate is pierced, the remainder is no great obstacle to

---

[1] In the compound plate, owing to the support afforded by the iron back, a harder steel can be used for the face. Unsupported in this way, a steel plate of the same manufacture would be liable to break up under heavy blows, and hence steel armour is made of somewhat softer—or less brittle—though tougher material.

an uninjured projectile having a considerable amount of unexpended energy.

Twenty years ago we commenced experiments against iron plates $1\frac{1}{2}$ in. thick on 6 in. of wood. The target thus formed was placed at a small angle from the horizontal, and fired at with a 9-inch projectile. The protection was insufficient, but succeeding experiments have led to decks of steel 3 in. thick being placed over the submerged portions of vessels. The sides of this armoured deck usually slope down to a short distance below the water line, and are given an additional thickness. This portion of the armoured deck of the 'Blake' and 'Blenheim' is 6 in. thick. Advocates of internal armour urge that, for a given weight, more complete protection can be afforded if disposed in this way than if placed externally on the hull.

Later on experiments were instituted to ascertain what effect masses of coal would have in stopping projectiles, and if it could be ignited by shell. It was found that 20 ft. of coal would stop a 6-in. shot at a short range, and 30 ft. an 8-in. shot, but this would hardly hold good with later guns and steel projectiles. The explosion of common shell did not set the coal on fire.

But this latter result only applies to coal in confined spaces. If placed between decks, it will be more readily ignited. I believe at the battle of Lissa the 'Palestro' was destroyed in this way. Her captain, impressed with the necessity of not running short of fuel, had placed a quantity of coal outside the battery. During the action with the Austrian Squadron a shell exploded in the heap and set it on fire. The occurrence appears to have been unheeded at the time, or the crew were too busy with their guns to be called off. When they did endeavour to extinguish the fire, it had gone too far, and while they were thus employed the ship blew up. Few of the crew escaped, but I have been told by an officer, who took part in the action in another ship, that this mass of coal was over a magazine, and it is believed that the intervening deck was burnt through until suddenly a flaming mass of coal fell into the magazine. This seems a reasonable explanation, as the explosion was unexpected, or preparation would have been made to abandon the ship. This occurrence shows the danger of carrying extra coal about the decks. It appears to me unwise, also, to place reliance on protection from coal when stowed in its proper place. If it is not to be used, why employ it in preference to armour? When consumed in the legitimate way, which circumstances may render necessary, a vulnerable part of the ship may be exposed to an enemy whom this fuel has assisted the ship to overtake, or from whom it has not sufficed to make escape possible.

The disposition of armour and armament adopted in the 'Inflexible' was followed in only four other vessels, the 'Ajax,' 'Agamemnon,' 'Colossus,' and 'Edinburgh.' It was considered that smaller battle ships on the same design would be useful additions to the fleet. The first two named have a displacement of 8700 tons, and carry in each turret two 38-ton guns, while the maximum thickness of their armour is 18 in. Being only 280 ft. long, with a beam of 66 ft., their speed is moderate, and for a long time difficulty was experienced in steering them. The 'Colossus' and 'Edinburgh' were great improvements. By increasing the length to 325 ft., and the displacement to 9500 tons, a speed of over 15 knots was obtained. Their turrets are armed with 45-ton breech-loaders instead of the old guns, and steel instead of iron is mostly used in the construction of the ships.

But naval officers did not approve the departure from the 'Dreadnought' type. The advantages of placing the turrets *en echelon* were more fanciful than real, and consequently, when after a lapse of some years there was a return to double-turret ships, an improved 'Dreadnought' design was decided upon. The 'Trafalgar' and 'Nile' represent this reaction, and as they have not long been completed it is evident the interval was considerable.

These ships are approximately the same size as the 'Inflexible,' viz., 12,000 tons at load draught. They have a central citadel, containing the two turrets, placed on the middle line, as in the 'Dreadnought.' Each turret contains two 67-ton guns. Between the turrets, and above the citadel, are mounted eight 45-pounder guns in a battery, thus giving an auxiliary armament which had not been provided in the earlier turret ships. The length of the 'Nile' and 'Trafalgar' is 340 ft., of which 230 ft. is protected at the water line with compound armour, varying in thickness from 16 to 20 in. The turrets are covered with similar armour, 18 in. thick. Machinery of 12,000 horse power gives these vessels a speed of 16 knots. Compared with the 'Inflexible,' they represent a considerable advance in every detail, and are powerful fighting ships. Their only defect, to my mind—independent of the size and cost—is that the guns are not carried sufficiently high above the water, and for this reason I have always preferred the barbette system. The turret ship 'Hood,' now building, is more than 2000 tons larger than the 'Trafalgar,' and represents what appears to be the final development of this system, which originated in the cupola ship of Captain Coles. The 'Hood' is of similar dimensions to the seven first-class barbette ships of the 'Royal Sovereign' type, and only differs in having her heavy guns mounted in turrets instead of *en barbette*. It remains to be seen which of the two plans will be followed in future designs.

Though the general opinion in the navy has been always in favour of double turrets, especially in vessels of large dimensions, sufficient success in the production of single-turreted ironclads, as exemplified in the 'Rupert' and 'Conqueror,' led to a further extension of this principle in two later ironclads, the 'Victoria' and 'Sanspareil,' now complete. The former was built by Sir William Armstrong's firm at Elswick, and perhaps is the only instance of a first-class battle ship being supplied with the whole of her equipment from a private yard. She has a length of 340 ft., a breadth of 70 ft., and displaces 10,500 tons. In a single turret forward, protected with 18 in. of compound armour, she carries two 110-ton guns. In order to supply the deficiency of stern fire, which the single turret forward entails, the 'Victoria' and her sister have a 29-ton gun mounted aft, working behind a barbette shield. The protection afforded by this arrangement is not great, but considerations of weight doubtless prevented more being done in this respect. To make up for this restriction of the principal armament to three heavy guns, she carries amidships a battery of twelve 6-in. guns and numerous machine guns. Machinery of 14,000 horse power gives these vessels a speed of 16 knots, so that in every respect they show a marked superiority to the 'Conqueror' and 'Hero.' They are the only British ships in which a pair of 110-ton guns are mounted side by side; in the 'Benbow' one of these monsters is placed at each end. The first-class battle ships of to-day thus indicate a variety of ideas concerning offensive and defensive capacity, and a conflict of opinions as to the best disposition of armour and armament. We seem, however, to be approaching the time when experience with these divergent types will enable us to select the best points in each, and combine them in some type which shall finally fill the place of the old three-decker. Whether it will prove equally durable, he who deals with the development of navies half a century hence can alone record.

The two-decker also had her counterpart in the small ironclads built or converted between 1860 and 1870. Those of about 6000 tons and under were usually termed second class. For a country which has im-

The Victoria firing her 110-ton guns.

portant interests in every part of the world, useful service can always be found for vessels of these dimensions.

There were six ships of the same type which for many years carried our flag in the China and Pacific seas. These were the 'Audacious,' 'Invincible,' 'Iron Duke,' 'Swiftsure,' 'Triumph,' and 'Vanguard.' The career of the latter was cut short by sinking, after collision with a consort, in the Irish Channel. None of them exceeded 6500 tons displacement, but they carried a powerful battery of guns and 8 in. of armour at the water line. They were, besides, roomy and comfortable vessels, so that, until left behind by the wonderful advance in engines and armament after their completion, they proved admirably adapted for foreign service. They were succeeded by the armoured cruiser in this duty, and therefore the demand for ironclad battle ships of moderate size diminished.

But under the Naval Defence Act two so-called battle ships of the second class are being constructed, to be named 'Centurion' and 'Barfleur.' The length to which we have gone in adding to the size of all classes is strikingly illustrated in this pair. Their displacement is to be no less than 10,600 tons, which will enable them to combine four 29-ton guns—a pair *en barbette* at each end—ten 45-pounder quick firers, side armour 12 in. thick, and a speed of 18 knots. A certain number of torpedo tubes will also be provided. The 29-ton gun is one that can be worked without the aid of machinery, and hence is not so easily disabled as the larger patterns dependent on hydraulic loading. Its power is about

K

double that of the old 38-ton muzzle-loader, which at one time we considered such an effective weapon. The 45-pounders are to be on the broadside in two tiers, for greater distribution, and to prevent a single shell from disabling two or three of these guns. They will furthermore be screened by stout steel shields. Many are disposed to think that high speed, though essential for a cruiser, is not so requisite in a battle ship. But as vessels like the 'Centurion' and 'Barfleur' will probably take the place, and do the duty, of armoured cruisers, they would be of little value if unable to proceed rapidly from point to point, or to compete in speed with vessels of their own class. For home waters, including the Mediterranean, a moderate speed that can be sustained will suffice.

After dealing with so many ships clad in mail 18 in. thick it may seem that a protection limited to 12 in. is insufficient, but that amount of hard armour will exclude all but the heaviest projectiles, and something must be left to chance. When wrought-iron was succeeded by a less easily perforated substance we might well have retraced some of the steps which culminated in 2 ft. of armour. I should be disposed to say that we should never exceed a maximum thickness of 12 or 14 in., but should offer a high premium on improvements in quality by which greater resistance to projectiles may be attained.

In the 'Centurion' and 'Barfleur' we have a type which will, I believe, be highly commended by naval officers. All the attributes necessary for an efficient fighting ship are present, and the instrument is in due proportion to the human faculty which has to wield it. There must be a point at which this ratio is disturbed. Mechanical science, pushed on by the exertions and talents of a few, may outstrip the capacity of ordinary intelligence, and what is successful experimentally when no disturbing element comes into play may fail under the more searching conditions of war. We, in common with all nations, appear to have gone too far in the production of monster ships and guns, and I trust the reaction that must always follow such excesses will lead to a great increase in the numbers of what, for the moment, we term second-class battle ships.

CHAPTER VIII

CRUISERS

Frigates in Old Time—Speed an Essential—Early Steam Cruisers—'Inconstant' and others—Action between 'Shah' and 'Huascar'—Armoured Cruisers—'Imperieuse' and 'Warspite'—Development of Internally Protected Vessels—'Blake' and 'Blenheim'—'Royal Arthur' Class—Smaller Types—Scouting Duties—Necessity for High Speed.

IN addition to the large vessels which, by the number of their guns, disposed in two, three, or even four tiers, were capable of taking their place in the line of battle, fleets have from very early days contained a number of smaller craft for the duties of scouting, conveying information, and the protection of commerce. We had frigates, corvettes, sloops, and brigs for such work, supplemented by privateers to whom letters of marque were granted. Pepys tells us the first frigate built in England was modelled from a French frigate which Pett the shipwright had seen in the Thames. Attached to a squadron, frigates were relied on to obtain information of an enemy's movements, and being more nimble under sail than the heavier battle ships, could hover round them until their destination seem assured, when they would make off with the intelligence to their own squadron. They were often used also for convoying merchant-ships. The demand for them, therefore, was enormous, and admirals in command could not always obtain an adequate number. Nelson at a critical moment said the want of frigates would be found stamped on his heart, and we shall no doubt suffer from the same deficiency at some future time.

A frigate by itself hardly ever ventured to attack a two-decker except in expectation of the aid of a friendly battle ship, when it would endeavour to delay the enemy until its bigger consort came up. Cases have occurred of a frigate being sunk by a single broadside from a line-of-battle ship. Its most valuable quality was superiority in speed over the more powerful vessel, and as long as the wind remained the only motive power this characteristic was preserved. It even endured for some years after the introduction of steam, but then came a time when, having freely abandoned sail power in battle ships, we endeavoured to combine it with steam in cruisers, the result being that as a rule our small craft were of little value for war purposes. If they met a battle ship at sea they would have been overtaken in flight, while their steam speed was inferior to that of any merchant steamer converted into a commerce destroyer. This dangerous condition of affairs has now passed away. We have frankly recognised that a high speed under steam is the first essential for vessels which have to perform the duties I have mentioned, and it has been secured in those which we have recently built.

There have been fitful periods, however, when we produced steam frigates of high speed. Inspired by the example of the United States, which after the Civil War constructed some fast frigates, we built the 'Inconstant' in 1866, a vessel of nearly 6000 tons, in which the high speed of 16 knots under steam was obtained. She also sailed remarkably well. As the 'Warrior,' the first ironclad, had a speed of 14 knots, it may be considered that the extra 2 knots of the 'Inconstant' fairly maintained the old relative superiority of the class to which she belonged. But this vessel was too large and costly in maintenance to be adopted as a type; so two others, the 'Active' and 'Volage,' of just over 3000 tons and 15 knots speed, were built. We then reverted to the big ship idea, and produced the 'Shah,' of 6200 tons, by which 16 knots were again obtained. Like the 'Inconstant,' she was built of iron cased with wood and coppered. The armament consisted of two 12-ton guns, sixteen $6\frac{1}{2}$-ton guns, and six 64-pounders. Thus the modern frigate, like the battle ship, carried few guns, but of greater power than had hitherto been mounted in this class of ship.

If any supposed that unarmoured frigates of this size could compete with and overcome even the smallest ironclad, the idea was dispelled when the 'Shah' fought and failed to subdue the small Peruvian monitor 'Huascar.' As corroborating my previous remarks on the relative strength of the frigate and the line-of-battle ship, a brief account of this action may here be given.

In the early part of May 1877, during one of the

The *Volage* under sail.
From photograph by Captain C. G. Robinson, R.N.

periodical internal disturbances in Peru, the 'Huascar' was seized by a party of the disaffected, headed by Don Nicolas Pierola. The ship was taken out of Callao Harbour, and proceeded on a cruise to the southward. As she had committed an act of piracy in forcibly removing coal without payment from a British barque, Admiral de Horsey, then flying his flag in the 'Shah,' as Commander-in-Chief of the Pacific Squadron, determined to seize the 'Huascar.' In company with the 'Amethyst,' a corvette of 2000 tons, armed with 64-pounders, the admiral proceeded in chase. On the 29th of May the two ships met the 'Huascar,' and a boat was sent on board demanding her delivery, refusal to be followed by fire being opened upon her by the British vessels. The monitor was only a little over 2000 tons, and her armament consisted of two $12\frac{1}{2}$-ton muzzle-loading guns, in a single turret, and two 40-pounders. But on the water line the ship was protected by $4\frac{1}{2}$-in. iron plates, and the turret by $5\frac{1}{2}$-in. Against this the guns of the 'Amethyst' were of little use, but those of the 'Shah' could, at close quarters and hitting direct, penetrate any portion. On the other hand, the guns of the 'Huascar,' loaded with common shell, would, if they hit, inflict great damage on the 'Shah's' entirely unprotected sides.

With a scratch crew, and against such odds, Pierola might have surrendered his little vessel without any great loss of honour. He preferred to fight, and at three P.M. the action began. A series of broadsides were fired from the 'Shah,' some of which struck the

'Huascar,' but without causing serious damage. The conditions of a sea fight and firing at an armour plate on shore to gauge penetration of projectiles differ widely. A direct blow on the armour of a ship in motion is the exception not the rule, consequently the 'Huascar' was able to endure a severe pounding from the 'Shah' without sustaining fatal injury. On the other hand, her own fire was so slow and inaccurate that the 'Shah' was not struck once. The 'Amethyst' also kept up a smart fire, but without result. The 'Huascar,' except in her gunnery, was well handled, and once or twice tried to ram the 'Shah,' which the superior speed of the latter enabled her to avoid. After a fight of nearly three hours darkness came on and firing ceased. During the night the 'Huascar' got away, and was given up next day by her commander to the Peruvian fleet. She was then uninjured in any vital part, and the water line had not been penetrated although the ship was struck (it was estimated) by about sixty or seventy projectiles. This showed the advantage of even thin armour against guns of moderate power, and tends to confute the opinion that unprotected vessels can under any circumstances take the place of battle ships.

Only a few frigates approaching the dimensions and speed of the 'Shah' were added to the fleet, and then we fell back on a smaller class called corvettes, with less speed but full sail power. For ordinary work in peace time they were well suited, but could not during hostilities have afforded much protection to commerce or been of great service to a squadron seeking intelligence.

The same defect characterised our steam sloops and gun vessels which were distributed in all parts of the world. They were constructed to keep the sea under sail, relying only upon steam when the wind failed. The result was that as sea boats they were admirable, but steaming against a moderate sea they were easily passed by the 8-knot steam collier plodding steadily on for the Suez Canal. But still in a tentative sort of way we recognised the necessity for swift vessels, and while providing those above enumerated, built two vessels, between 1870 and 1880, with a steam speed of 18 knots. These were the 'Iris' and 'Mercury,' remarkable also for being the first vessels built wholly of steel. The hull was not cased in wood and coppered, but simply coated with a composition to prevent fouling and preserve the steel from the action of sea water. Having twin screws, only a light rig was provided, and the armament consisted of ten 64-pounders. The 'Mercury,' attaining on trial a speed of $18\frac{1}{2}$ knots, was the fastest of the two. These ships were called despatch vessels, and for such service are admirably suited. Speed had been made the first consideration, and beyond subdivision of the hull no attempt was made to afford protection, which involved carrying additional weight. The success of the 'Iris' and 'Mercury' led to the construction of others, in which some speed was sacrificed to give a steel deck over the machinery and vital parts, to exclude fragments of shell which might explode within the ship. The displacement was the same, 3750 tons, as also the length, 300 ft., but the armament was made heavier, and hence they were regarded as cruisers. The old subdivision into frigates, corvettes, sloops, and gun vessels was now to pass away and give place to a general nomenclature. The term cruiser covers nearly all classes at the present time, as great and small are built much on the same lines, carrying a heavy gun at the bow and stern, and lighter pieces on the broadside.

A more powerful type has also sprung up called the armoured cruiser. The earliest vessels thus known were the 'Nelson,' 'Northampton,' and 'Shannon,' built between 1870 and 1880. They were of moderate dimensions, well armed, and carried a good supply of coal. Their function in war, as stated by the Controller of the Navy, was not to take their place in the line of battle, but to roam over the seas and drive off any future 'Alabama' acting against our commerce. Unfortunately they failed in the first essential for such work. In none of these ships did the speed exceed 14 knots, and hence they would be quite incapable of overhauling a moderately fast merchant steamer. This defect was remedied in two later vessels, the 'Imperieuse' and 'Warspite,' which combine a speed of 16 knots with a powerful armament and a partial belt of armour 10 in. thick. They carry 900 tons of coal, so are suitable for service in distant seas, and could cope, if occasion required, with any of the smaller ironclads of foreign powers.

To the non-professional mind it may seem that such vessels might also fairly be classed as battle ships of the second or third class, as they carry four

THE 'IMPERIEUSE.'

22-ton guns and thicker armour than any of the early ironclads. It is more the service on which they are to be employed than any special form of construction which has put them in the cruiser category. No more ships of this type have been built. In this country the further development of the cruiser has been in the direction of giving up external armour, and devoting all weight we can give to protection to a steel deck for the whole length of the ship, varying in thickness according to her size. The extreme of this principle is seen in the 'Blake' and 'Blenheim,' our two latest and largest cruisers, each of 9000 tons displacement. The interior is roofed over so as to cover the machinery, magazines, etc., with a steel deck 3 in. thick. The sides of this deck slope down to about 6 ft. below the water line, till they meet the hull, the thickness being double that of the horizontal portion. This disposition of armour does not attempt to exclude hostile shells, but, it is assumed, will prevent their explosion from impairing either the buoyancy or motive power of the vessel. Opinions as to the comparative merit of external and internal armour are divergent, and I offer none of my own. It is one of the many questions which actual conflict can alone decide. But if in the 'Impericuse' and 'Warspite' we marked a considerable increase of speed over the early armoured cruisers, this quality is developed to a still greater extent in the 'Blake' and 'Blenheim.' They are to be provided with machinery of sufficient power to drive them in smooth water at the rate of 22 knots an hour, when pushed to the utmost extent with forced draught. Their ordinary full speed will be 20 knots. Several merchant steamers traverse the ocean at this rate, and in the event of any being converted into hostile cruisers we must have war-ships not inferior in this respect. In all our unarmoured vessels, up to a recent date, the deficiency in speed was in great measure due to their insufficient length. The least sea stopped their progress, while the merchant steamer, being much longer in proportion to beam, was only retarded in the same weather to a very small extent. We have now frankly admitted that length is indispensable for an efficient cruiser. Thus, while the 'Nelson' was 280 and 'Impericuse' 315 ft. long, the extreme length of the 'Blake' and 'Blenheim' will be 400 ft. As their displacement is to be 9000 tons, a powerful armament can be carried. It consists of a 22-ton gun at bow and stern, three 6-in. guns on each side, and a number of machine guns. They will also be fitted to discharge torpedoes from above and below water.

Besides these two, eight others are building, under the Naval Defence Act, of about 7500 tons, in which length and speed are to be somewhat less than in the 'Blake' and 'Blenheim.' The first of these, the 'Royal Arthur,' which was launched by Her Majesty early in the year, is rapidly approaching completion. Her construction is in most respects similar to that of the 'Blake,' but in lieu of a 22-ton gun forward she will carry two additional 6-in. guns further aft, but with command of fire right ahead.

It has always been customary to place a heavier gun than that carried on the broadside as a bow chaser, but the principle is exaggerated when guns of 14 tons and upwards, aggregating with carriage, etc., 20 tons, are placed in the fine bows of vessels not larger than the old frigates. Yet in the Mersey, Severn, Thames, and Forth, modern cruisers of 4000 tons, an 8-in. 14-ton gun has been placed in the bow and stern, the former of which must, with all its appurtenances, be a terrible weight to carry against a head wind or sea. How can we expect speed to be maintained when the vessel is thus handicapped? Such considerations have no doubt led us in the latest cruisers of similar dimensions, of which there are several now building, to limit the guns at the bow and stern to a calibre of 6-in. and a weight of 5 tons. Constructed of the length now necessary to obtain the full energy derived from improved powders, they have a long range for such a gun, and throw a shell capable of dealing terrible havoc to any unarmoured structure. No more need be demanded of vessels not primarily designed to fight ironclads.

The smallest type of cruisers, termed third class, is represented in the 'Medea,' 'Medusa,' 'Marathon,' and 'Melpomene.' Their principal armament consists of six 6-in. guns. They were designed to have an extreme speed of 20 knots, but a sustained speed of about 16 knots an hour on the ocean is probably the most that can be attained. A lighter armament would probably render these vessels more efficient as cruisers. There is no doubt, however, that we are in a better condition for protecting our vast commerce at the present time than we have been during any portion of the last half-century, independent of the aid we should receive from the conversion of some of the fastest merchant steamers into auxiliary cruisers. That other countries contemplate, in the event of war, an attack on our sea-borne trade has been clearly foreshadowed in the writings which have been published abroad, and received with favour by the nations to whom they were addressed. They will not be deterred from this action by the knowledge that the issue of a war cannot depend upon any success obtained in this way unless accompanied by a mastery, more or less complete, over the sea forces of the enemy. We may be harassed but not subdued in this fashion. Knowing the danger, it behoves us, however, to take adequate steps to guard against it, and this we are doing by at last adding to our fleet cruisers from which the modern 'Alabama' will find it difficult to escape. The career of this vessel has often been cited to show the damage that could be inflicted by a single vessel. But considering she was practically unmolested for eighteen months, it is no matter for surprise that the commerce under the stars and stripes, then carried chiefly in sailing ships, should suffer. The number of her captures during this period was under sixty, and only one was a steamer. Semmes was astonished at the absence of method displayed by the North in his pursuit. In his account of the cruise of the 'Alabama,' Semmes, referring to the Secretary of the Navy, said : 'The old gentleman does not seem once to have thought of so simple a policy as *stationing* a ship anywhere.' Vessels were certainly despatched in pursuit of the 'Alabama,' but generally arrived in one sea as she was leaving it for another, her commander calculating pretty accurately how long he could count on undisturbed possession. But her success was of little assistance to the South in delaying its final subjugation.

Vessels for the protection of commerce must not only be swift to run but also long to endure; that is to say, they should carry a large supply of fuel, or much of their time will be taken up in replenishing their stock of coal. I am of opinion that we should make an addition to the proportion of weight now allotted to this important item. Vessels attached to a squadron for scouting or despatch duties need not carry such an amount, or be of such large dimensions. If, as I am inclined to believe, no vessel under 3000 tons can be an efficient cruiser under modern conditions, I think 2000 tons will be sufficient for a despatch vessel or sea scout. A few years ago Messrs Palmer of Jarrow-on-Tyne built for the navy two excellent little ships of 1600 tons, called the 'Surprise' and 'Alacrity,' for this service. They have since done good work in China and the Mediterranean. Their speed is 16 knots, and they carry an armament of four 5-in. guns. For some reason we have built no more vessels like them, but by improving on their design, and increasing the displacement to 2000 tons, an additional ocean speed of 2 knots could be secured. There is a class of vessel, represented by

L

the 'Archer' and a few others, of which the unfortunate 'Serpent' was one, of nearly 1800 tons, which, though designated third-class cruisers, are more suitable for acting with a squadron. They are hampered, however, by carrying six 6-in. guns, too heavy an armament for such craft. Their speed and seaworthiness would be improved by substituting lighter ordnance. We have carried this out in a later class. The 'Barham' and 'Bellona,' of 1830 tons, have a speed of 19 knots and an armament of six 45-pounder quick-firing guns. The projectile of the 6-in. gun weighs 100 lbs.

It will probably strike most people who remember our wooden steam frigates and corvettes how low in the water appear the steel cruisers of to-day. The demand on the naval architect for guns and ammunition, which exceed all former experience, the plea for torpedoes and other new weapons of naval warfare, the advantages of electric lights, the absolute necessity for torpedo nets, all these are impressed upon the constructor by the experts with resistless cogency, so that the vessel becomes like the stage soldier, overladen with weapons. Something must be given up, or dimensions in every class largely increased. A Plimsoll's mark for war vessels is not desirable, but I can conceive that it may become necessary, unless naval officers moderate their demands. Blame is often cast on the naval architect because ships after completion do not realise original expectations. In most cases it should more properly be laid on those who, during construction, have successfully pleaded for a heavier gun, extra torpedoes, and

H.M. Despatch Vessel *Alacrity*, built by Palmer's Shipbuilding Company, Jarrow-on-Tyne.

more numerous crew than the original design contained. This usually accounts for the vessel drawing more water than was intended.

If in a war with a powerful maritime state the patrol of the seas must require a large number of cruisers, the demand for swift vessels for other services will be equally pressing. Endeavours have been made from time to time to lay down the proportion that should exist between such craft and a battle squadron of given strength. Such calculations are futile, because no commander is likely to be satisfied when the time comes with the number allotted to him, in view of demands from all sides which cannot be neglected. Moreover, sufficiency will depend on the work to be done more than on the number of battle ships. But if hostile fleets are to be watched, as they often were of old, by a squadron of frigates, while the main force was out of sight but within speedy communication, the number of vessels required for this work in future will be very great. The coaling question then comes in. Formerly only shortness of fresh water drove ships into port. Their supply was usually sufficient to last for three months. To have some convenient locality where ships could water was an important matter in the old blockading days. Distillation of salt water now renders us independent of this consideration, but it is another demand on the coal supply, which is the measure of a steamer's capacity to remain at sea at the present time. It is difficult to estimate this endurance under the varying conditions of blockade. If position is maintained ordinarily under easy steam, there must be capability of passing to a high rate of speed at short notice, which will be not only a severe trial to the machinery but consume the stock of coal at a rapid rate. Moveable coal depots as close to the scene of operations as possible will be a necessity in cases where no Imperial coaling station is comparatively near, but probably only the experience of a war of some duration can demonstrate the best system for coaling a large fleet operating in all parts of the world.

It is only of late years that the value of scouts to a squadron of battle ships has been recognised, and the method of utilising their services considered. For this and other invaluable experience we are indebted to our annual naval manœuvres. The ubiquity which steam confers in searching the ocean is an advantage which Nelson could not command, but which must in future relieve an admiral from all the anxiety of a foul wind when seeking information of an enemy which has escaped his vigilance. To have in addition one or two fast despatch vessels to warn detached squadrons of such movements, or return home with important intelligence—as Nelson sent a vessel home when he was satisfied that Villeneuve had left the West Indies—will be no less essential on some future occasion. They must be ready to run the gauntlet of the enemy's cruisers, and hence swiftness will be their chief security. They must not stop to fight unless brought to bay, and their armament should be of the lightest description. Up to the present time the development of this type of vessel is incomplete. It took centuries to produce the subdivision—or differentiation, as Admiral Colomb terms it in his *Naval Warfare*—of sailing ships into the several classes suited for the work then imposed on them. We cannot expect that, without the experience of conflict, the immense changes which the last half-century has seen in the composition of fleets will be found to have resulted in a series of types suited in all respects to the novel conditions of the next great naval war.

CHAPTER IX

ORDNANCE

Old Smooth Bore Guns and their Manipulation—Mr Lancaster's System—Introduction of Rifled Guns—Early Inventors—Breech-Loaders introduced and discarded—Woolwich Muzzle-Loaders—Growth of Ordnance to 80-ton Guns—Breech-Loaders again introduced—Increase of Length and Power—Advance to 110-ton Guns—Ammunition—Quick-Firing Guns.

I HAVE indicated, in the first chapter, the description of ordnance used in the navy in 1840. Cast iron guns, with a smooth bore for throwing spherical projectiles, were then employed. Mounted on wooden carriages, with four low, solid wheels — called trucks — of the same material, they were worked by tackles and wooden handspikes. The recoil on discharge was controlled by a stout piece of rope—called a breeching—which passed through a ring at the rear of the gun, the two ends being secured to the side of the ship. Sufficient slack was allowed, so that on discharge the gun would recoil far enough to bring the muzzle just inside the port, where it was in the most convenient position for entering a fresh charge. The decks of a line-of-battle ship were a fine sight when gun drill was taking place. To fire three rounds at an imaginary passing vessel as she quickly shifted her bearing was an exercise calling forth

both skill and physical capacity, in which our sailors excelled. The comparative lightness of the gun, and the simplicity of its mounting, permitted of great variety in the exercise. If a carriage was disabled, the gun could be dismounted without delay. A frequent evolution was to transport a gun from one end of the ship to the other. The sailing trim of a vessel was often altered in this way. The method of giving elevation to the gun was exceedingly crude. Wooden inclined planes called quoins were pushed under the breech, by which the muzzle was elevated or depressed. They were marked in degrees, but were exceedingly likely to be displaced by the movement of the gun. The marking usually took place after the ship was commissioned, and was not unfrequently delayed for a considerable period. It depended on the zeal of the gunner. This recalls to my mind a certain captain, well known for his great faculty of exaggeration, who sent for his gunner some time after commissioning a ship, and said to him : 'Mr Bluelights, are all the quoins marked?' 'Yes, sir,' promptly replied the other. The captain, having good reason to know that this was not the case, merely said, ' I will just go round the gun deck.' Not a single quoin was marked. Turning to his subordinate, he quietly observed, 'Mr Bluelights, you are the biggest liar in this ship.' The other simply looked at him and retorted, no less calmly, 'No, sir, I am not,' with a slight emphasis on the pronoun.

These guns were naturally very inaccurate, and could not be otherwise, independently of the rude methods for directing their fire. In the first place, the bore was considerably larger than the shot, to facilitate loading and the use of red-hot shot. This difference of diameter was called 'windage,' and varied from one-fifth to one-third of an inch. It allowed, therefore, a considerable portion of the gunpowder gas to escape past the projectile, and wasted so much energy. Then, for reasons which would require too technical an explanation for this work, the round shot was subject to special inaccuracies in its flight. These defects were not so manifest at close quarters in action, which officers in command usually sought to attain, and the charge of powder, however reduced in energy by windage, retained sufficient power to penetrate wooden ships. But for some years previous to the substitution of ironclads for the old types of ships the Admiralty of this country had been impressed with the advantages of having the armament of the navy of greatly increased power and weight. This view was confirmed by the introduction of the 68-pounder, which proved a powerful and effective weapon. But when it had been ascertained that this gun was powerless against $4\frac{1}{2}$-in. plates, it was at once evident that some new system of gun construction must be devised. A long series of experiments proved that the old ordnance was exceedingly defective; that every gun, great or small, should be rifled, in order to give long range and precision to the projectile; and that to have the required strength guns must be made of wrought-iron or steel.

The object of a rifled gun is to give to a cylindrical

projectile rotation or spin on its longer axis. The rotatory motion keeps the shot steady during flight, and prevents its being subject to the special influence which caused the inaccuracy of smooth bore guns. A cylindrical projectile is heavier than the round shot of similar diameter. Thus the old 32-pounder was of 6-in. diameter, but the modern 6-in. rifled gun throws a projectile of 100 lbs. weight.

There are other advantages, on which it is unnecessary to dwell, but for many years artillerists had been seeking a satisfactory method of giving rotation to the projectile. One of the earliest inventors in this country was Mr Lancaster, who conceived the idea of making the bore of a gun slightly elliptical or oval, with a twist, so that a projectile of the same shape received a spin during its passage through the bore. Fairly successful experiments resulted in the construction of some of these guns and their employment in the siege of Sebastopol. But they were not reliable, and more than one burst. In the meantime a rifle had been adopted for the army in place of the old smooth bore musket, and it was only a question of working out the principle for larger guns.

In 1846 Major Cavalli, of the Sardinian army, and Baron Wahrendorff, a Swedish noble, had each brought forward a breech-loading rifled gun throwing cylindrical projectiles with pointed heads. Cavalli's gun was of $6\frac{1}{2}$-in. calibre, and had two grooves cut spirally along the bore. The projectiles had two winged projections which travelled in the grooves and caused rotation. The breech was closed by an iron wedge entered from the top of the gun. With the usual interval for improvements, experiments were carried out in Italy with this gun, which showed considerable advance in accuracy over the smooth bores.

Wahrendorff's gun was similar in principle, though the details were different. Trials took place at Shoeburyness in 1850 with both the Wahrendorff and Cavalli gun, but the breech mechanism was defective, and neither was adopted. So matters rested until after the Crimean War, when the question was seriously taken up in this country. Able inventors turned their attention to rifled ordnance, and among the foremost were Messrs Armstrong and Whitworth. In fact Mr Armstrong had made a small rifled gun in 1855, and the principle on which this was constructed was eventually adopted. The first had a steel barrel strengthened externally by wrought-iron, applied in a twisted or spiral form as in a fowling piece. This gives the strength due to the fibre of the material being disposed at right angles to the bore. The gun was rifled with numerous small grooves. The projectiles were cylindrical, of cast-iron, and coated with lead, to take the grooves and so receive rotation. Being pushed in from the rear or breech, allowance for windage was unnecessary, as the projectile was only inserted sufficiently far for the lead coating to abut against the beginning of the rifling, and the action of the powder forced the projectile to take the grooves.

Satisfactory results were obtained, and a larger gun was constructed. The steel barrel was abandoned as being untrustworthy, and difficult to manufacture sound. Coiled wrought-iron was used entirely. The breech-closing arrangement was the same as before. This was arranged as follows. The rear of the gun had a hole through it, forming a prolongation of the bore, and by this aperture powder and shot were entered. Then the bore was closed by an iron plug inserted through an opening on the top of the gun. To press it firmly against the end of the barrel, it was tightened in its place by a screw working in the loading aperture. The Government so highly approved of this gun that Mr Armstrong was knighted and given an official appointment at Woolwich. It was certainly a great improvement both in range and accuracy over any preceding weapon. With one of these guns a range of 9000 yards was obtained.

Between 1860 and 1861 we commenced supplying the navy with 20, 40 and 100-pounder Armstrong guns. My first experience of the sea was leaving England in a 50-gun frigate, towards the close of 1861, with several of these guns for distribution among the ships of the North American Squadron. The arrest of Messrs Slidell and Mason had lately occurred, and relations with the United States were rather strained. But the new guns did not reach their destination, for we encountered a tremendous gale of wind off the banks of Newfoundland, and sustained such damage as to necessitate our return to England. Our cargo assisted the elements in our discomfiture, making the ship roll so heavily, and she had this propensity in a less degree at all times, that much of the damage resulted from this cause. We were not sorry, therefore, to see the guns transferred to another vessel, while we went into dock with all the appearance of having taken part in a severe action.

These Armstrong breech-loaders did not, however, remain long in use in the navy. There was an absence of simplicity for which, coming directly after the old smooth bores, the navy was not yet prepared. The advantages of charging at the breech were not sufficiently apparent. It was formerly difficult to make a mistake in handling a gun, but now more care had to be taken. In one of our periodical small wars, which occurred at that time in Japan, some cases occurred of vent pieces being blown out on firing these guns. This was owing, no doubt, to the plugs not being screwed up tightly, but it created a prejudice against a system in which this might occur. Another objection was that the lead coating on the projectile occasionally stripped off when being forced through the grooves. This affected the land service, as such artillery firing over the heads of troops might give them a leaden shower. Anyhow the fiat was issued that a new gun must be devised which should be rifled and load at the muzzle. Was this a retrogade step taken less that thirty years ago, and at a time when other nations had adopted the breech-loading system? I do not think so. At that time all guns were short, and loading at the muzzle was not ihconvenient. Their handling was equally expeditious, and simplicity was on the side of the muzzle-loader. This advantage would have been

Ordnance.

more apparent in war. Our fault was not in reverting to muzzle loading, but in retaining the system after the introduction of slower burning powder, which required a long gun to utilise all its energy. The new combination gave increased velocity, range, and penetration. As is well known, the path of a shot in the air is a curve, owing to the action of gravity. The quicker it is in travelling the less time there is for gravity to act, and consequently the more nearly does the projectile travel in a horizontal line. One of the great objects in gunnery is to have this path—or trajectory, as it is technically termed—as flat as possible. I have mentioned Mr Whitworth as being early in the field as a designer of rifled guns. His system differed from Mr Armstrong's in important respects. It will be sufficient to allude to his method of rifling and the form of his projectiles. The former consisted of a hexagonal bore with a sharp twist. The projectile had six bearing surfaces and accurately fitted the bore. Mr Whitworth advocated flat-headed steel shot for attacking armour; but a pointed head is less impeded by the wind and better suited for penetrating armour.

Captain Blakeley also put forward rifled guns which did not materially differ from Whitworth's construction. Captain Palliser had already turned his attention to utilising our old smooth bores, by inserting an interior barrel of coiled wrought-iron, the gun being previously bored out for its reception. It was then rifled, and a few heavy rounds fired, which expanded the inner barrel to a tight fit with its cast-iron exterior. A 68-pounder was so converted into a 9-in. muzzle-loading rifled gun and subjected to severe tests in 1863. With a charge of 16 lbs. of powder projectiles up to 680 lbs. weight were fired from it. The recoil was naturally violent under such conditions. It smashed carriages, and then the gun was suspended in iron slings. It broke these, however, and flung itself out of them on to the ground, but did not burst. This eventually occurred with 32 lbs. of powder and a 200-lb. shot. The evidence of increased strength given by a coiled iron barrel led to a number of smooth bores being converted in this way and employed until comparatively recently in the navy. A steel barrel was subsequently used.

When it was decided to revert to muzzle-loading for new guns the Woolwich system was adopted. This consisted of a steel barrel with a series of wrought-iron coils shrunk over it by being put on when heated. They thus tightly gripped the inner tube, and enabled it to sustain the explosion of a heavy charge without rupture. The strength of the gun was considered to lie in the outer coils; the steel tube gave a hard surface to the bore and a homogeneous material for the rifling process. This tube was made from a solid ingot of steel, turned and then bored out to the required diameter. It was thus the most costly part of the gun, while the boring and rifling processes required considerable time before the rest of the parts could be added.

In 1865 we began equipping our ships with guns of this construction. As an advance on the 68-pounder a gun of 7-in. calibre and $6\frac{1}{2}$ tons weight was produced. Its projectile was 115 lbs. weight, while the charge was 30 lbs. of powder. The charge of the old 68-pounder was 16 lbs. At 1000 yards there was sufficient energy to penetrate 7 in. of iron. Had armour not increased in thickness, we might have been satisfied with such a capability. But much stouter plates were now being rolled, and the gun had to grow likewise. Ordnance of 9, 12 and 18 tons, all on the principle described, were successively designed and put afloat. The largest of these was charged with 70 lbs. of powder and a projectile weighing 400 lbs. The 9-in. armour of the 'Hercules' had defied the efforts of a 300-pounder, and Sir William Armstrong, in a letter to the *Times* of June 26th, 1865, said, speaking of a 600-pounder which had then been tried: 'Powerful as this 600-pounder has proved itself to be, I confess I have great doubts of its obtaining the mastery over the "Hercules" target unless the enormous charges already used with that gun be still further increased.' He doubted the possibility of constructing a gun of sufficient strength to penetrate the 'Hercules' target. But hardly had these words been written when heavier guns began to be produced, and we passed on to ordnance of 25 and 35 tons. This was the struggle between guns and armour.

It is not to be supposed that guns of this weight could be carried on board ship without an entire reconstruction of the methods of mounting them. To Captain Scott's iron gun-carriages is due a facility in working these guns which had not in some respects been obtained with the much lighter smooth bore. The same rapidity of loading could not be expected, but a gun could be directed on its object much more expeditiously with cogged wheels and winches than with the old rough method of handspikes and tackles. The gun recoiled up a slide, the extent of the recoil being regulated by friction between carriage and slide. The projectiles, instead of being passed from hand to hand, as in the case of the 32-pounder, were wheeled up in iron trucks to the muzzle and then hoisted by a tackle for insertion. There was still room for the display of strength and activity. We had not arrived at working a lever—as at a railway siding—to actuate a hydraulic ram which would bring up the ammunition, while the movement of another handle ejected a rammer which forced all into its place. By the improved method of mounting already described, and mechanical arrangement for controlling the recoil, we were enabled to work guns weighing 25 tons on the broadside with celerity and safety. Though heavy, such guns were necessarily short. Thus the 12-in. 25-ton gun had a bore only 12 calibres long—the calibre of a piece being the diameter of its bore. As we are now employing ordnance of 25, 30, and 35 calibres, the advance in this respect since 1870 can be realised. But after that date longer and heavier guns were constructed. With the same calibre, 12-in., we proceeded to a 35-ton gun of greater length for the 'Devastation's' turrets. Then a slower burning powder being produced, we found that a 38-ton gun could be made nearly 16 calibres long of

$12\frac{1}{2}$-in. bore, which would speed an 800 lb. projectile with an initial velocity of 1540 ft. per second, an increase of 200 ft. per second over the 25-ton gun, while the charge of powder had advanced from 85 to 200 lbs.

The 38-ton gun was justly considered a great step, but its projectile, weighing 800 lbs. had passed beyond manipulation by hand or tackle. Then the ingenuity of the great Elswick firm provided us with that admirable system by which all the operations of loading, elevating, and training heavy guns are performed by hydraulic machinery. To describe these in detail would require a volume in itself. It will be sufficient to state that, on the principle of the 'Bramah' press, power is transmitted from an engine by water pressure through a small pipe actuating hydraulic rams. Water is contained in a tank and pumped by a steam engine into pressure pipes, by which it passes to the different hydraulic machines and then returns to the tank. One of the advantages of this system is that fewer men are required round the gun. To work a turret by hand originally took fifty men, now it is effected by a third of the number. Then there is no such danger as the bursting of a steam pipe would involve. The gun does not require a high carriage, but rests in a block on the slide. The recoil is controlled by a solid ram fixed to this block, which on discharge of the gun travels in a cylinder full of water. The pressure of the ram or piston forces the water through a number of weighted valves, the resistance of which gradually brings the gun to rest. Then forcing water into the cylinder pushes the piston or ram and the gun out again. The same principle is employed to raise the breech and extract the breech piece when too cumbrous to be withdrawn by hand. Objection has been raised that the system is too complex, and that the gun may be disabled by the rupture of a small pipe. This is true, but the same result may ensue through the destruction of some portion of hand-worked ordnance. It is impossible to have simplicity with any modern gun. It is legitimate, however, to argue that guns should not be mounted afloat which, in the event of anything happening to the hydraulic machinery, cannot be worked by hand.

The 38-ton gun thus loaded and controlled gave great satisfaction. Several of our turret ships are still armed with it, but in time a breech-loading gun will take its place. In 1873 the struggle between guns and armour produced what was then considered likely to prove the climax in each. To equip the 'Inflexible,' carrying 24 in. of armour, with equally powerful ordnance, guns of 80 tons weight were designed. They were originally intended to be of $14\frac{1}{2}$-in. calibre, but were finally bored to 16 in. This gun was given a length of 18 calibres; the charge of powder was 450 lbs. and the projectile weighed 1700 lbs. At 1000 yards it could penetrate 23 in. of wrought-iron, and its initial velocity was 1600 ft. per second.

The following table gives a general idea of the advance made in the size of guns from the time we discarded the 68-pounder smooth bore to the mount-

Sixty-seven-ton guns mounted *en barbette*.

Ordnance.

ing of 80-ton muzzle-loading rifled ordnance in the 'Inflexible':—

Diameter of Bore	Weight of Gun.	Charge of Powder.	Weight of Projectile.	Velocity at Muzzle.	Penetration of Iron at 1000 Yards.
Ins.	Tons.	Lbs.	Lbs.	Ft. per Sec.	Ins.
7	6½	30	110	1500	7
8	9	35	180	1400	8
9	12	50	250	1400	10
10	18	70	400	1380	12
11	25	85	540	1320	13
12	35	140	700	1400	15
12.5	38	200	800	1550	17
16	80	450	1700	1600	23

A few words must now be said about the ammunition. Experiments had shown that against armour cast-iron shot broke up like a snowball, while forged wrought-iron projectiles flattened, as if made of lead, against the hard or comparatively hard surface. In both cases the iron plates suffered little, because the energy was expended in breaking or distorting the missile. In this dilemma Captain Palliser came to the rescue with his ingenious device of hardening the front portion of a shot by chilling. The body is cast in an earthen mould, but the head is formed by a metal mould, which rapidly extracting the heat in this portion gives great hardness to the material. The result is that chilled shot of this nature are able to penetrate wrought-iron plates without breaking up or distortion. They are of cylindrical shape, with a pointed head, which against armour acts like a punch, forced into the plate by the energy of the other portion of the shot behind it. All are cast with a hollow core, which can be utilised for a bursting charge, but the space is so limited that such an addition is of little value. A great merit of these projectiles is their cheapness as compared with those now made of steel, so that they are still largely used for practice, and would be efficient against thinly armoured ships, though unable to cope with the thick steel or compound armour which has superseded wrought-iron for protection.

Other kinds of missiles are common shell and shrapnel shell. The former being required to contain a large bursting charge, have not sufficient strength to pass intact through armour, but are most destructive against any unarmoured portion of a ship. Shrapnel are iron cases containing a great number of small round shot, the case being fractured by a small burster at the required moment. The small shot then spread with the impetus previously acquired in flight. Against boats or bodies of men on shore they are very effective.

It has been mentioned that an improvement in the velocity obtained with the later muzzle-loading guns resulted from modifications in the powder employed. Not in the ingredients, because they had remained unaltered for centuries, and the same may be said of the proportions of the mixture, but by making each individual grain or pellet larger the whole charge took longer to consume. Hence, as the shot travelled down the bore continual increments of gas were generated imparting an augmenting velocity to the projectile, which should reach the muzzle when this was at maximum. If the gun was too short, a large portion of the powder would be blown out unconsumed, and result in wasted energy. Even with considerable addition to the length this occurs in a minor degree, as can be seen by an instantaneous photograph of a gun at the moment of discharge. As guns grew in size so did the grains of explosive composing the charge, first to what was termed pebble powder, and then to cubes of much larger dimensions. At a short distance from the gun unconsumed portions of these are a veritable hail of small projectiles.

In 1880 we appeared to have reached some finality in ordnance. We had advanced from 7 to 80 tons, and found no difficulty in manipulating on board ship the heaviest guns. There had been few accidents of a serious nature. The bursting of a 38-ton gun in the 'Thunderer' owing to the insertion of a double charge was a notable exception. The gun had actually missed fire the previous round without the crew being aware of it. It was then loaded again, and burst with great violence on being discharged. Being one of a pair in a turret, the discharge of the other gun had deceived the crew into a belief that both had gone off. Even spectators watching the target stated that they saw two shot strike the water. Such illusions are not uncommon. When two or more guns are fired at the same instant, and close together, especially if after recoil the gun automatically returns to its place, a single report may cause a doubt as to the discharge of both. This is the converse of the 'Thunderer's' case, but it may apply either way. One thing certainly was evident—such an accident could not occur with a breech-loading gun, because a second charge could not be inserted.

But other causes were at work to bring about once more a complete revolution in our armaments. Foreign powers had in most cases adopted breech-loading guns, and by giving increased length were obtaining higher velocities. This meant increased penetration, in which respect we were being left behind. It became necessary for us to adopt the same principle, because we had arrived at the maximum of length in muzzle-loading ordnance for use in ships. We were undoubtedly slow to appreciate the necessity. There had been no loud demand from the navy for the change, and all ordnance coming to us from Woolwich, which is under the control of another department of the Government, there was naturally no great eagerness in that quarter for a move which would involve an entire change of pattern and construction. This matter belongs to the past, and I am willing to apportion blame to both sides. But when the great Elswick firm produced a 6-in breech-loader, throwing an 80-lb. projectile with a velocity of 1800 ft. per second, it was evident that we must at once discard all idea of adhering to our

The Rodney steaming and firing.

old guns. The Woolwich gun factory, under the able superintendence of Colonel Maitland, promptly grappled with the problem, and from that day we have gradually been overtaking the lost ground. There has been delay, of course, but to entirely rearm the British fleet with a weapon essentially different to all that had gone before in our experience was a stupendous task, and this should be recognised. Mistakes must necessarily occur, and one important change we did not at first make. We adhered to the principle of an inner steel barrel surrounded by wrought-iron coils. There was a distrust of steel, which it took some years to eradicate, though Krupp had always used this material entirely in the construction of his guns. A 6-in. gun on the wrought-iron coil system lately burst with great violence in the 'Cordelia' from some unknown cause.

Since guns of this pattern were made we have discarded the wrought-iron coils, and now strengthen the steel barrel with hoops of the same material. In again taking up breech-loading guns an important matter to decide was the method of closing the breech after insertion of the charge. We could follow the plan adopted by Krupp, of a wedge inserted at the side or a screw plug at the rear, as used in France. The latter was adopted, and with it the ingenious device for saving time of an interrupted screw. The plug is a solid steel block with a screw thread on outer surface. This is divided longitudinally into a certain number of equal parts, and then the screw threads entirely removed from alternate portions. In the screw thread of the gun similar portions are taken away, those remaining being opposite the blank spaces on the block. Consequently the latter can be pushed straight into the gun, and a portion of a turn engages the screw threads on each, so locking the breech without the loss of time involved by screwing the block in the ordinary way. As the cap or tube which ignites the charge is placed in this plug, which has a channel through the centre to allow the flame to pass into the chamber of the gun, there is a mechanical arrangement for preventing the tube being inserted until the breech piece—as this plug is termed—is thus locked. To prevent escape of gas to the rear it is necessary to effectually seal the end of the powder chamber. This is done by securing to the inner end of the breech piece either a thin steel cup, which on discharge of the gun is expanded against the inner sides of the chamber, or a pad of asbestos, which under pressure of the powder gas performs the same function. This, in technical language, is the obturator, and when we consider that the ignited gas exerts a pressure of some 15 tons to the square inch the importance of confining its energy to the base of the projectile may be understood.

As regards method of ignition, we have for some years utilised electricity for this purpose. On an unstable platform, such as a ship presents, it may be readily conceived that any delay in discharging a gun when it bears on an object must result in a miss. The remedy our ancestors had for this was to attain such close proximity to their object that a certain proportion of their projectiles could not fail to hit somewhere. But as close range is not always attainable, and may not be desirable, the delay in igniting the charge by means of a falling hammer or pulling a string should be eliminated. Electricity, being instantaneous, corrects this defect, the only motion required being to press a button. Its advantages are even more apparent when several guns are fired simultaneously and it is desired to lodge their projectiles in one spot. The apparatus simply consists of a galvanic battery, with wires leading to the guns and terminating in a fine filament of platinum silver wire, enclosed in a tube and surrounded by a small quantity of gunpowder. The current, when allowed to pass, heats the filament sufficiently to ignite the powder, and the flame passes on to the charge of the gun.

Having once recognised the advantage of a breech-loader, we proceeded with the design and construction of different patterns suitable for large and small ships. They grew, in fact, similarly to the old muzzle-loaders. We mounted in succession 14, 22, 29, 45 and 67-ton guns, with a length of bore varying from 25 to 30 calibres. By augmenting the powder charges velocities were increased to 2100 ft. per second, the projectiles being over half a ton in weight. No difficulty was experienced by our officers and seamen in becoming proficient with such weapons, though it involved an entirely new procedure in their manipulation. Having been accustomed for years to insert powder first, one can imagine that to reverse the process does not come intuitively. Yet of many changes this is perhaps the simplest. The inevitable was cheerfully accepted. But when these new guns made a jump from 67 to 111 tons, and the number carried by a single ship fell from four to a pair, the policy of thus relying upon such a limited heavy armament, though reinforced by a number of smaller guns, began to be questioned. The case in favour of monster guns is that they represent concentrated power and the ability to do immense mischief if successfully applied. A single projectile from such a piece could disable the stoutest battle ship or penetrate the thickest armour carried. Nor, with the assistance of hydraulic apparatus, is their manipulation more complicated than with guns of half their weight. Though themselves offering a large mark, their very bulk is a protection against light projectiles. As against these points in their favour, three main objections may be stated. First, that the portion of a ship covered by the extremely thick armour is so small that hitting it under the varying conditions of a sea fight must be a chance. Second, it therefore becomes more profitable to attack the larger unarmoured area, or at any rate that area will be struck by the greater number of projectiles. For such work moderate sized guns are sufficient and superior to those throwing enormous bolts, which would pass through thin armour without impediment. Thirdly, there is the risk of half your principal armament being disabled by an accident or by a single lucky shot from your enemy. On the whole, therefore, I think the balance is in favour of smaller guns, and I view monster ordnance as one of the abnormal growths

Turret of *The Victoria*, mounting two 110-ton guns.

of peace which the rough test of war will sweep away. I have not dwelt on the element of time required for construction or cost. They should, however, be taken into consideration.

The projectiles used with our new guns are much the same in shape as before. For receiving rotation they have a copper band, which acts much in the same way as the lead coating in the first breech-loaders without the defect of stripping. Steel shot are, however, necessary to overcome the resistance of steel or compound armour, and to get satisfactory projectiles of this material has long been a difficult matter. France was before us in this respect, but our steel makers when called on rose to the occasion and now produce an efficient article.

Powder has gone through several phases. The ordinary black substance in cubes was replaced by prisms of brown material known as cocoa powder. Then came a demand for something which would give us energy without smoke, and all nations are seeking such an explosive. A propelling agent with this characteristic has been produced in this country by Professor Abel, known as cordite, from its resemblance when manufactured to a grey cord. It is more powerful than ordinary powder, without subjecting guns to an increased pressure, and is comparatively smokeless. One of the chief points to ascertain is whether, under the varying conditions of climate which our vessels experience in all parts of the world, this explosive will remain unaltered after a considerable lapse of time. We must have satisfactory tests in this respect before we can confidently admit it into our ships.

No review of the progress of ordnance would be complete without notice of the great development of what are now called quick-firing guns. They have grown out of the mitrailleuse, first used in the Franco-German War, which consisted in a cluster of rifle barrels automatically fed with cartridges and fired by turning a handle, as sound is produced from a barrel-organ. At first discredited by defective mechanism, which caused stoppage of the action at critical moments, they have since been greatly improved in the systems of Gatling, Gardner, Nordenfelt, and Maxim. The last named has brought to considerable perfection a gun in which the energy of recoil is utilised to perform all the operations of extracting the fired cartridge, reloading, and firing without human interference. Set to operate in this way the gun will continue to fire until its ammunition is exhausted. Against bodies of men the machine rifle—as it might be more fitly termed—can work great execution, but to stop torpedo boats requires a heavier projectile, so that Mr Hotchkiss and Mr Nordenfelt designed a machine gun of larger calibre. In that of the former the barrels revolve, while in Mr Nordenfelt's gun they are stationary. Both are effective weapons. Then came a demand for a single-barrel gun which could throw shot of about 6 lbs. weight and fire several rounds a minute. The ammunition was to be made up like a rifle cartridge instead of, as formerly with small guns,

Six-inch quick-firing gun and shield, designed by Sir W. Armstrong, Mitchell & Co.

having powder and projectile separate.[1] Messrs Hotchkiss and Nordenfelt both complied with the demand, and these were termed quick-firing guns. They are now largely represented in all our ships. An important feature was aiming and firing from the shoulder by means of a wooden shoulder piece attached to the gun, which being accurately balanced could thus be freely moved, horizontally and vertically, with little exertion of the body. The movement of an object could thus be followed almost as easily as the flight of a bird with a fowling piece. These guns have considerable range and penetration; and would be effective against the unarmoured parts of a ship, while the 3-pounder, a smaller piece on the same principle, is specially adapted to meet a torpedo attack.

Observing the success of small quick-firing guns, Sir William Armstrong's firm were not long in extending it to larger ordnance. An increase in the rapidity of fire of all guns is an advantage which every sea fight has endorsed, so a gun having a calibre of 4·7 in. and throwing a projectile of 45 lbs. was designed. The projectile is separate from the powder cartridge, as being more convenient to handle. Very satisfactory results have been obtained with this gun, from which about ten aimed shots a minute can be fired.

The principle, however, has not attained finality, because a 6-in. quick-firing gun has since been constructed, and proved successful. In this gun, also, the projectile is separate from the powder, as it weighs 100 lbs.,

[1] This is the principal cause of obtaining greater rapidity of fire.

and is inserted previous to the cartridge containing the explosive and cap. The case of this is made of brass, and though the construction of this portion is expensive the cartridge cases can be used over again when fired. The rapidity of aimed fire from this gun is about eight rounds a minute. Cordite has been tried with this gun, and it is found that 17 lbs. of this explosive will give the same energy to the projectile as 50 lbs. of ordinary powder, without increased pressure in the chamber.

It is difficult to say what will be the further development of quick-firing guns. One thing seems to me probable, that all charges will be contained in copper cylinders, instead of being enveloped in silk cloth, by which moisture will be excluded, and the explosive guarded against rough usage.[1] Greater rapidity of fire with heavy ordnance then becomes more dependent upon improved training and practice than small details of mechanism in the guns.

[1] Mr Elmore's ingenious process of copper deposition and hardening seems likely to answer this requirement.

CHAPTER X.

TORPEDO WARFARE.

Early Application of the Torpedo in America—The Fish Torpedo—Development by Mr Whitehead—Introduction of Torpedo Boats, and their Progress—Submarine Boats—Protection against Torpedoes—Nets—Electric Search Lights—Torpedo Boat Destroyers—Sinking of 'Blanco Encalada.'

THE torpedo as a weapon of practical utility first came prominently into notice during the American Civil War. To disable a vessel by exploding underneath her a large mass of gunpowder, contained in a water-tight case, had long been a project of enthusiasts, but the difficulty of obtaining an efficient mechanical arrangement for ignition, and keeping the whole apparatus in order when immersed for any length of time, had, up to the period mentioned, prevented any striking success being achieved by this means. Small submarine mines, with a chemical fuse or some clockwork apparatus for their ignition, were laid down in the Baltic during the Russian War, but were in most cases fished up by our ships without exploding. One, however, did explode on the poop of the flagship, after much handling to ascertain the method of ignition; but as the charge was small few of the spectators were injured. When the Southern Confederacy seceded from the United States in 1861, one of the first steps of its naval department was to form a torpedo section to protect approaches to places liable to attack by the Northern fleet. Such energy and ingenuity was shown by this branch of the department, and so little was at first understood of this new mode of warfare by the enemy, that a number of his vessels were sunk by submarine mines. From henceforth it was evident this weapon could not be despised with impunity.

Of course, these mines, being moored or placed on the bottom, only acted if the ship came into their vicinity; and if not covered by guns bearing on the area they protected, could be fished for or destroyed by boats before the vessels advanced. A further development, therefore, was made in taking the mine to the hostile ship by means of a boat. A charge of powder was placed at the end of a long pole, carried in the bows of the boat, which under cover of darkness then sought its victim. On arriving alongside the ship the pole and charge were immersed and the explosive ignited by an electric wire when in contact with the bottom of the vessel. In the confusion that followed the assailant had a fair chance of escape. A most daring, gallant, and successful attack was thus made on the Confederate ship 'Albemarle,' by an officer of the Northern navy named Cushing, in a small steamboat. At the moment of the explosion his own craft sank, but he escaped by swimming, and returned unhurt with the news.

This method of attack then came into favour, but so

great was the risk of discovery when close, and the consequent danger of being sunk by the fire of the ship attacked, that ideas turned in the direction of a torpedo which could be discharged at a vessel from a moderate distance. This resulted in the fish torpedo. The original conception was that of a small sort of boat propelled along the surface and carrying a charge of gunpowder in the bow. An Austrian officer broached this idea to Mr Whitehead, an English civil engineer settled in that country. From this crude proposal he developed the wonderful piece of mechanism now universally known as the Whitehead torpedo. First, he had to fix upon his mode of propulsion. He selected compressed air, working a small engine and a screw in the tail of his fish, as in an ordinary vessel. Steam would condense, and had other disadvantages; gunpowder gas could not be controlled; electricity was not applicable. The result has shown that his choice was a good one. Then he determined that his torpedo should travel under water. An explosion on the surface and against the water line of a ship would have little effect, because most of the gas generated would escape into the air. Immersed, the surrounding water confines the gas and compels it to exert all its energy against the bottom of the ship. If the charge is large enough, this pent-up energy is irresistible. It was desirable, therefore, that the torpedo should strike a ship a certain distance below the water line, keeping this depth during its passage. Now, any vessel containing compressed air has an appreciable weight added to it, but as the air is allowed to escape the vessel is lightened to a corresponding extent. Consequently a torpedo propelled by this motive power would, as the air escaped after doing its work, be continually getting lighter, and if started 10 ft. under water would soon come to the surface and finish its course in this position. This had to be corrected and provided for by special machinery. The torpedo must travel throughout its run in the same horizontal plane. The method by which Mr Whitehead obtains this effectually is the most ingenious part of his invention. It was long kept a secret, but has recently been made public. The general principle is to utilise the pressures due to different depths of water to actuate horizontal rudders, so that the torpedo is steered upwards or downwards as its tendency is to sink or rise.

In the foremost end of the torpedo the explosive is carried, originally gunpowder but now gun cotton, as being so much more powerful, its ignition being effected by the impact of the nose of the torpedo on any hard substance, which forces a pointed striker against a detonating cap.

So constructed, we have an iron or steel fish-shaped body, propelled by air highly compressed, which can be regulated to give a high speed for a short distance or a greater range at a lower rate. By mechanical contrivances the torpedo could be set to run any required distance, and then come to the surface or sink. The firing arrangement was not operative until it had proceeded some way on its course, but for exercise it was necessary that this should be in a condition of safety when the run was finished. As may be imagined, all this required a long period of anxious thought and a series of experiments, but eventually Mr Whitehead brought to the notice of the world what had not often been seen before, an entirely new invention perfect in every detail. Its efficiency was demonstrated on trial, and the weapon adopted by nearly every maritime state. What limited its usefulness was the comparatively low speed, which at first was about 8 knots. Hence, if discharged at a vessel half a mile off, it took a considerable time to traverse the distance, so that any little inaccuracy in its course, currents, or alteration of direction in the vessel aimed at would result in a miss. A great advance was therefore made when the speed was increased to 18 knots by the use of Mr Brotherhood's well-known three-cylinder air engine, a model of compactness, simplicity, and efficiency. When gun cotton was used a less amount of explosive was required for the same result with gunpowder, and hence a smaller torpedo could be employed. The improved weapon was 14 ft. long, with a diameter in its largest part of 14 in. Complete it weighed about 500 lbs. Plant for the manufacture of these torpedoes having been established at Woolwich, a healthy competition arose between our officers and Mr Whitehead's staff, for having started a factory at Fiume in Austria he was now supplying other Governments with torpedoes. Succeeding improvements brought the speed up to 27 knots an hour for a distance of 600 yards. This was the range selected as that at which the torpedo should be discharged at a ship, a maximum distance beyond which the chances of hitting rapidly diminished, while at closer ranges they were increased. In the earlier patterns the head of the torpedo had been made exceedingly sharp, under the idea that this form would give increased speed. But the late Mr Froude's experiments with submerged bodies showed this to be erroneous, and that a better result can be obtained with a bluff head. A further advantage of such a form is that a considerable increase of explosive can be carried without adding to the length of the torpedo. With this modification the later patterns have a charge of 60 lbs. of gun cotton, equivalent, it may be considered approximately, to 200 lbs. of gunpowder. Exploded in contact with the bottom of a ship, the effect must be either to sink or disable, according to the precise locality struck.

This new weapon, directed at the most vulnerable part of a ship, had to be met, and it led to the extension of the double-bottom system. There was an idea that the torpedo might expend its energy on the outer skin, leaving the inner hull intact, and thus save the ship from fatal injury. But as Sir Nathaniel Barnaby truly remarked fifteen years ago: 'I say it is idle to attempt to form the bottom of a ship strong enough to resist a fair blow from a powerful torpedo. The utmost that can be done is to keep the disabled ship afloat after she has received such a blow.' It would be possible to protect the bottoms of ships with armour to withstand the present charges of the Whitehead torpedoes. When this was done, it would only be necessary to increase the charges of the torpedoes and the armour we had applied would become vulnerable.' No more accurate forecast could have been made. The latest development of the Whitehead is a torpedo 18 in. in diameter, with a speed of 30 knots, and carrying 200 lbs. of gun cotton. No modification in construction could render the explosion of such a mass beneath a ship other than irresistible. Should it be otherwise, an addition of 2 in. to the diameter of the torpedo would probably allow the charge to be increased to 500 lbs., and I am quite unable to see how this could be counteracted.

In the successful application of the Whitehead torpedo much depends on the method by which it is launched from the ship or boat. It is now usually discharged, like a projectile from a gun, by means of a small charge of gunpowder, or compressed air, from a tube which it accurately fits. In most cases the tube is a few feet above the water line, and the torpedo is launched at any given moment. But it has always been considered that if it could be projected under water from a ship the apparatus would not be exposed to an enemy's fire, and the torpedo would start under more advantageous circumstances. The preliminary plunge from above water has always been trying to the mechanism contained in the interior. The difficulty under water is to get the torpedo clear of the ship when the latter is proceeding at high speed. An elongated body thrust out of a hole into water rushing past at a rate of 18 knots is naturally subjected to severe strains. It must be supported until the tail is outside, and then the propellers take it onward. After years of research and experiment this has been accomplished, and large ships are now fitted to discharge their torpedoes under water.

When the Whitehead torpedo was introduced it was at once seen that for boat attack it had enormous advantages over the old method of carrying a tin of explosive at the end of a pole. The ship need not be approached within 600 yards, and thus the operation was not one of such great hazard. But any chance of success and escape afterwards would be much increased if it were possible to command in the boat very high speed, so as to reduce the time during which the boat would be under fire in its approach or retreat. Such a consideration led to the development of the high speed torpedo boats which we now see in the hands of nearly every nation. At first it was thought a boat about 80 ft. long would answer all requirements, and Russia in 1877 constructed a hundred boats 75 ft. long and 10 ft. beam. The size was such that they could be transported from the Baltic to the Black Sea by rail. Mr Yarrow, the eminent torpedo boat builder on the Thames, supplied some sets of machinery and drawings from which other sets could be made in Russia. The first of these boats tried on the Neva had a speed of 18 knots. This was a great advance in a boat of such dimensions.

In the meantime Messrs Thornycroft, at Chiswick, had constructed for us the first torpedo boat, which was about 15 ft. longer than the Russian type, and her speed, 19 knots, was considered so remarkable that we

First class torpedo boat, built for the Argentine Government by Messrs. Yarrow & Co.

named her the 'Lightning.' Others were then obtained from both Thornycroft and Yarrow of this type, and in one of the latter's construction a speed of 21 knots was obtained. To attain such a result the best material and workmanship must be combined. Each firm has its special features of construction, and if either is superior in some particular point the other surpasses in another direction.

Having thus a boat of high speed, the equipment was completed by placing a tube in the bow from which a Whitehead torpedo could be ejected. In our boats the tube revolved so as to point on either side as well as ahead. Thus, in attacking a ship the boat could run rapidly past her, and without checking speed discharge the torpedo when in the most convenient position. Other nations fixed the tube in the stem of the boat, so that the torpedo can only be discharged when the bow of the boat is pointed directly to the object. This method is the simplest, as the torpedo is not deflected as on the broadside, for which a special calculation is required. But the disadvantage is that the boat is approaching the enemy, and will continue to do so after discharging her missile until she can turn and retreat. She is thus under fire longer. These boats are from 80 to 90 ft. in length, and in moderate weather are capable of operating a short distance from the coast. Then it was considered they might perform a more ambitious function in keeping the sea independently, or working with a squadron. For this a larger structure was required, and Mr Yarrow provided for Russia a boat

100 ft. long, which steamed out to the Black Sea by herself. This craft was followed by others, for different countries. Some of these, 110 ft. long, crossed the Atlantic under sail temporarily provided.

As demands came for higher speed, so did the length of the boat increase. We ordered a further batch, 125 ft. long, to carry five torpedo tubes, one in the stem and two on each broadside. Then Messrs Thornycroft built two boats for the Spanish and one for the French Government, which, with a length of 147 ft., gave a speed of 26 knots on the measured mile. These boats carry two torpedo tubes fixed in the stem.

Notwithstanding this notable increase of size, it has not been found that these boats can keep the sea for any length of time. The continual motion is so wearing to the crews that in rough weather their physical energy becomes exhausted, and inability to sleep is one of the most trying conditions of such an existence. When attached to a squadron, their presence at sea is a constant source of anxiety, and hence I think it must be recognised that for a craft able to keep the sea much larger dimensions are necessary. The proper function of torpedo boats is to operate from fixed bases on land, to guard the coast, and harass the squadrons or single ships of an enemy that may venture on aggressive action. A blockading fleet would have to be continually on the alert against night attacks by these wasps of the sea.

It has been sometimes asserted that blockade has been rendered impossible by the introduction of steam and the torpedo boat. I am unable to agree to this. There never was a time when blockades were not broken through over and over again. Steam will now enable vessels to remain in positions which dependence on wind in former times prevented them from keeping with certainty. The torpedo boat is a new danger to blockading squadrons, but it can be met by a line of other small craft whose special mission it would be to paralyse the attack before the boats could reach the main body. It has been shown recently that a special vessel of 600 or 800 tons, suitably armed with numerous light guns, forms the most efficient protection to a battle ship, grappling and subduing the small assailants before they can effectually launch their torpedoes. A striking feature of the fleet of 1900 will probably be the great increase in the number of its satellites, as this view receives further confirmation.

Although by adding to the length and displacement of torpedo boats better seagoing qualities have been secured, they have thereby become more conspicuous objects by night or day, whereas formerly, being small, they were not easily seen or hit. The difficulty of getting within range without detection has once more led people to seek a solution in submarine navigation. The idea of travelling under water in an hermetically sealed boat has engaged the attention of many enthusiasts, but hitherto without much practical success. When a submarine boat is in such a state of equilibrium as to freely rise or sink when its buoyancy is increased or diminished, this equilibrium is easily disturbed, and the tendency is then rather to go to the bottom than rise to the surface. At least this appears to have been the habit with most submarine boats since the first tried by Drebell, in the reign of James I., up to the present time. In France and Spain boats capable of acting under water are now under experiment, but in my opinion the chief advantage of a submarine boat is to travel on the surface partially submerged, so that, while the crew can see, the boat itself is almost invisible.

The best protection against torpedoes was at first thought to be in subdividing the ship into numerous small compartments. But it was soon evident that this was not sufficient, and then the system of surrounding a ship with wire netting was devised in order to stop the torpedo before it could come in contact with the hull. The nets are suspended from long booms projecting from the ship's side, and, with the vessel stationary, hang vertically in the water. At sea, or when moving, the nets do not retain this position, and are an awkward appendage not favourably regarded by sailors, who strongly object to anything that may foul the screw. Moreover, torpedoes are now provided with an apparatus in the nose which enables them to cut their way through the netting, and travel on uninjured to the vessel now unguarded. It is probable, therefore, that in the immediate future nets secured to the ships will be discarded, and the torpedo frustrated in some other manner.

Another branch of defence against this attack at night is a powerful light thrown on the advancing

First class torpedo boat, *Ariete*, built for the Spanish Government by Messrs. Thornycroft & Co

object, by which the guns may be directed with accuracy. Among the many uses to which electricity is now applied on board ships of war not the least important is its conversion into a strong beam of light which, when directed from the vessel, illuminates objects within a certain distance. This is universally termed an electric search light. The apparatus consists of a dynamo-electric machine for producing the electricity, a conducting cable for conveying the electricity to the lamp, where it is converted into light by means of two carbon rods, and the rays then concentrated into an intense beam by a reflector.

On a small scale this has been done before, and I believe a search light produced by a voltaic battery and a parabolic reflector was used in the Crimean War. This was little more than a toy, but the dynamo-electric machine, since introduced and perfected, has enabled great advances to be made, while the spherical reflecting mirror, devised by Colonel Mangin, is no less important in utilising the light thus produced. This reflector is of glass, ground so that the circumference is thicker than the central portion. This mirror collects and concentrates all the rays which impinge on it from the carbons in front, and then projects them forward in an intense beam of light. In clear weather small objects can be clearly discerned at upwards of a mile, when the ray is thrown on them, but in fog or mist the light has no penetrative power. There appears to be a deficiency of red rays, which are not absorbed by aqueous vapour to the same extent as the rays of other colour in white light. As also, when these lights are used from a ship, the rest of the horizon is made to seem darker than before, the opinion as to their value is conflicting. They are most efficient when external to the point sought to be protected, and placed so as to illuminate the space that must be traversed before the ships can be reached. I can conceive that, as it is desirable to have special ships to destroy torpedo boats when discovered, other craft might be equally advantageously fitted with powerful lights for this special duty, while the main force remained in darkness.

The electric light detects one colour much better than another. White is most easily distinguished, while a black boat can approach much nearer without being discovered. Steam escaping shows up at a great distance. Torpedo boats, whose period of action is during the hours of darkness, should show as little white as possible.

The want of success which has attended the efforts of those who hoped that torpedo boats could keep the sea led to the demand for a type which is now being largely constructed. This is a vessel of from 400 to 800 tons, which can accompany a squadron and during a naval action dart in under cover of smoke and launch torpedoes at the enemy when he exhibits signs of confusion. The French were the first to carry this idea into practical execution by building the 'Bombe' class, of about 340 tons. They are useful little vessels in some respects, but too small for efficient service in rough weather. We followed with the 'Rattlesnake,' of 550 tons, which has proved an excellent sea boat. But our latest development in this type is a number of vessels of 735 tons. Their armament consists of one 4.7-inch gun at each end and several torpedo tubes. They thus combine a gun and torpedo vessel, which does not appear to me advantageous. A gun of this weight may be useful in the stern if a bigger vessel is pursuing; in the bow it probably reduces her steaming capability against a moderate sea. In the chapter on foreign navies will be found a brief account of what is being done elsewhere in this direction.

It now only remains to consider what the torpedo has done, and whether it is likely to influence still further the course of naval architecture. So far it cannot boast a large score of successes. But when complaint is made that torpedoes do not run straight, and sometimes disappear, it is forgotten how many projectiles lie at the bottom of the sea that never went near the mark aimed at, or how many were fired before such a puny antagonist as the 'Huascar' could be brought to submission. The number of shot and shell fired at Lissa would, if placed against the damage done, afford an instructive lesson. Too much is expected of the torpedo, still only in its infancy. At the same time I would not claim for it equal rank with the gun. We may say, however, that if successfully applied it has the power of doing infinitely greater mischief. An instance of this is to be found in the sinking of the 'Blanco Encalada' in Chili from injuries inflicted by a torpedo, of which the following is a brief account.

When the revolution against the authority of President Balmaceda broke out, the whole of the fleet present joined the insurgents. The latter thus had a free hand on the sea until the arrival at Valparaiso of two swift torpedo vessels, the 'Almirante Lynch' and 'Almirante Condell.' They were built in England, by Messrs Laird, for the Chilian Government, and are of the sharpshooter class. Their dimensions are, length 240 ft., displacement 750 tons, speed 20 knots. The armament consists of two 14-pounder and two 3-pounder quick-firing guns and four torpedo tubes. Having given their adherence to the President, the officers and crew of the two ships were ready for any service against the other side. They were accordingly despatched to attack the enemy's squadron, then lying at Caldera, about 500 miles north of Valparaiso. They arrived off this port just before dawn on April 23d, and observing the 'Blanco Encalada' at anchor, determined to attack at once. The ironclad was taken apparently completely by surprise. If those on board knew of the arrival of the torpedo vessels in Chilian waters, they had not counted on such speedy offensive operations. The ship seems to have been without any net protection. No guard boats patrolled outside the harbour, a portion of the crew was on shore; and it would be impossible to imagine a condition of affairs more favourable to a torpedo attack. It was made with a courage and determination which has always signalised the fierce struggles in this part of the world. Met by a confused and ineffective fire from such guns as could be got into action, the two assailants approached within about 300 yards uninjured, and each discharged two torpedoes, none of which struck the ship. The 'Lynch' then turned, and again passing the 'Encalada' within about 50 yards, discharged a torpedo, which struck the ironclad abreast the engine-room. A tremendous shock was felt on board her. A great many men were killed in the engine-room by fragments of machinery flying in all directions, others on the deck above were thrown down and injured by the concussion. The ship heeled over on being struck, then rolled back, and the water pouring into the interior by the large gap made in her double bottom, she sank in about five minutes. Some of the crew plunged into the sea and escaped to the shore, but a considerable number went down with the vessel. On board the 'Lynch' and 'Condell' the casualties were not numerous or serious. The former vessel suffered most when she passed so close to the 'Encalada,' but both were able to retreat when a large ship was observed approaching the harbour, which was supposed to be the 'Esmeralda,' a cruiser of the enemy, but turned out to be our flagship the 'Warspite.'

It may be observed that the torpedo used on this occasion was one of the latest pattern, of small size, and carrying a charge of about 60 lbs. of gun cotton. From the effect produced some idea may be formed of what 200 lbs. could accomplish. The blow would be resistless in that portion of a ship containing the machinery. The opponent of torpedoes may lay stress on the fact that five had to be fired at close range before one took effect; but the fact remains that a vessel of 3500 tons was sunk in less than half-an-hour by two craft of 750 tons each, and that both were intact after the operation. We have no parallel to this in past naval warfare. It was not possible when the gun alone decided all combats, but now, while we have gone on adding to the dimensions, cost, and power of resisting artillery in our ships of war above the water line, the addition of a few pounds of explosive renders them liable below to the same fate as overtook the 'Blanco Encalada' in Caldera Bay.

CHAPTER XI

STEAM PROPULSION

Steam Navy in 1840—Machinery at that Date—Paddle-Wheel Frigates and Sloops—Horse Power, Nominal and Indicated—Voyage of 'Inflexible'—'Banshee'—Introduction of the Screw Propeller—'Fairy'—'Duke of Wellington'—'Victoria'—Substitution of Iron for Wood—'Warrior' and 'Black Prince'—'Octavia,' 'Arethusa,' and 'Constance'—Progress made up to 1865—Compound Engines—'Pallas'—Increase of Boiler Pressure—Twin Screws—'Inconstant'—Loss of the 'Captain'—'Iris' and 'Mercury'—Steel Protective Decks—'Polyphemus'—Forced Draught—'Lightning'—Yarrow's Boats—'Rattlesnake'—Triple Expansion—'Barham' and 'Bellona'—Decrease in Weight of Machinery—Difference between Men-of-War and Merchant Ships—'Blake' and 'Blenheim'—Large Number of Auxiliary Engines—Supply of Fresh Water—Evaporators—The 'Yaryan'—Growth of Steam in the Navy—Personnel—Probable Approach of Finality in Marine Engineering.

IN the year 1840 steam had already made considerable progress in the Royal Navy since, nineteen years previously, the 'Comet' had made her *début* at Portsmouth. Fifty years ago there were no less than twenty-nine steam vessels whose names appear in the official *Navy List*. Of these the most important were the 'Cyclops,' 300 horse power, 1195 tons; the 'Gorgon,' 320 horse power, 1108 tons; and the 'Salamander,' 220 horse power, 818 tons. The first two of these ships were engaged at the bombardment of Acre, and the 'Salamander' was employed on the coast of Spain during the Carlist War.

At this period all but three of the steam vessels of the navy were fitted with what were then known as 'side-lever' engines. This type was the first ever employed for marine purposes, and it had certain solid advantages which enabled it for a long time to remain the favourite and to resist innovation. So much was it considered to be *par excellence* the engine for ships that,

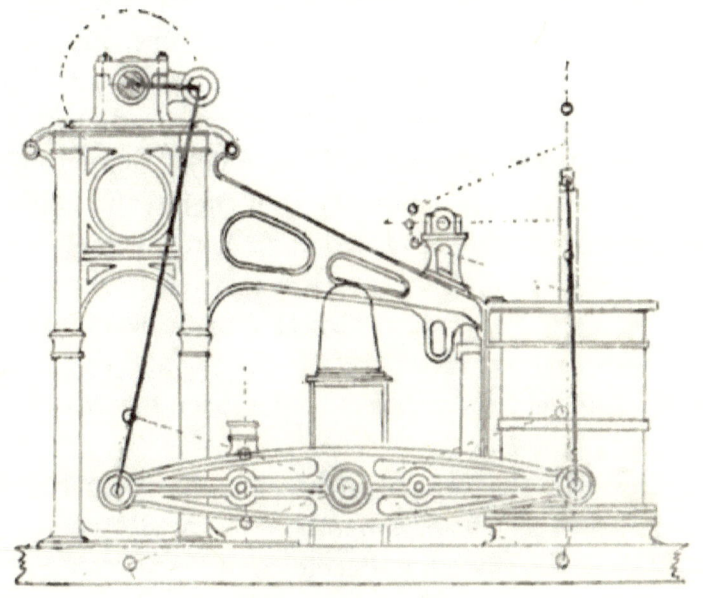

SIDE LEVER ENGINE.

surmounted by a crown, it formed the device for the uniform buttons of the engineers in the Royal Navy; in the merchant service it was similarly worn, but without the crown; and, with a lion over it, the East India Company's engineers adopted it as a distinguishing badge of their class. But in the side-lever engine lightness and compactness were sacrificed to solidity and length of connecting-rod, and as the use of steam gradually spread in the navy, and it became apparent that for every ton saved in the weight of and space occupied by the machinery valuable increase could be effected in the armament and coal capacity of the ship, it was inevitable that the ingenuity of the first engineering country in the world should be directed to the necessity for improvement in marine motive power. Hence we find in 1840 the 'Cyclops,' 'Gorgon,' and 'Prometheus' had been fitted with direct-acting engines[1] by Messrs Seaward, and the total weight of machinery was in their case reduced by about two-fifths. The 'Gorgon' was the first example of the new type of engine, and finished her trials in October 1837, and direct-acting engines soon came into general use in the Royal Navy, although the particular form introduced by Messrs Seaward was by no means that most generally approved or adopted. Still, to them belongs the credit of having been the first in the field.

The year 1843 was a remarkable one as regards the development of steam propulsion in the Royal Navy, for then it was that the 'Penelope,' the first man-of-war supplied with tubular boilers, and the 'Black Eagle,' the first vessel ordered by the Admiralty to be fitted with oscillating cylinders, were added to the list of Queen's ships. The importance at that date of these two enormous strides in marine engineering cannot be over-

[1] 'The distinguishing feature of all direct-acting engines consists in the connecting-rod being led at once from the head of the piston-rod to the crank without the intervention of side-levers.' But this is very ancient history.

estimated. Tubular boilers at once became universal in all ships built for the service, and to this day nobody would dream of applying any but oscillating engines to the driving of paddles. The 'Black Eagle' had side-

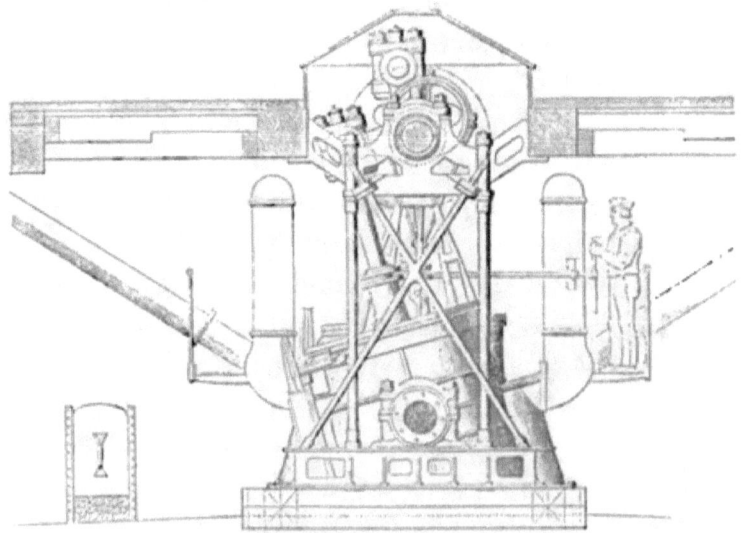

ENGINES OF THE 'BLACK EAGLE.'

lever engines in the first instance, but these were removed and replaced by oscillating ones by Messrs Penn.

In 1846 was commissioned, by Captain William Ramsay, the 'Terrible,' the most powerful steam fighting ship in the world at that date. She was of 1847 tons burthen, carried an armament of twenty-one guns of various calibres, and was fitted with double-cylinder direct-acting engines of 800 horse power by Messrs Maudslay. And here it may be well to digress for a moment to point out to the reader that when speaking of the horse power of the earlier engines 'nominal' is meant.[1] The 'indicated' power developed, that is, the real effective power, varied from about two and a half times the nominal in the case of the 'Gorgon,' in 1837, till it reached more than seven times the nominal in the 'Inconstant,' in 1869. The absurdity and inconvenience of expressing the power of ships' engines by a system of notation absolutely without meaning became so evident that in 1872 the indicated power was ordered to be given in the official *Navy List*.

Exactly contemporaneous with the 'Terrible' was the 'Inflexible,' the first steamship in the navy to make a voyage round the world. No better example can be given of the difference between steam navigation in the Royal Navy at that date and the present than the performance of the 'Inflexible,' which was then considered highly creditable, as indeed it was, to Captain John C. Hoseason, who commanded her and furnished an interesting account of it. She was what in those days was called a sloop, of 1122 tons burthen—not to be confounded with displacement[2]—

---

[1] 'Nominal' horse power was a standard adopted by James Watt for commercial purposes, in which the effective pressure and speed of piston were assumed to be constant quantities in all engines. The rule was well enough when first devised, but the extraordinary thing is that it should have remained in force so long under such entirely different conditions.

[2] 'Tons burthen,' or old measurement as it is often called, was, like 'nominal' horse power, a purely commercial expression. It was obtained by multiplying the 'length for tonnage'—which was found by deducting three-fifths the breadth of the ship from the length, taken at the water line —by the whole breadth and by the half breadth and dividing the product by ninety-four. Displacement tonnage, now in universal use, means the number of tons weight of sea water displaced by a ship floating at her load draught.

and fitted with direct-acting engines by Fawcett capable of working up to 378 nominal horse power. We have no available record of what her real horse power was, but she probably at her best indicated nearly three times her nominal. Her boilers were loaded to what was then considered the ample pressure of 8 lbs. on the square inch. She was in commission from the 9th of August 1846 to the 28th of September 1849. During this time she steamed 64,477 nautical miles, and got over 4392 under sail alone. Her average daily steaming was 186.62 knots, and her fires were alight during 483 days. Her total consumption of coal was 8121 tons, her average distance steamed per ton of coal 7.9 knots, and her average consumption per hour 19.5 cwt. After service in India and China she returned to England by Cape Horn, thus making the circuit of the globe and establishing a 'record' for herself.

A vessel which must not be passed over among the celebrated paddlers is the 'Banshee,' engined by Messrs Penn, which managed to steam from Holyhead to Kingstown, a distance of 55 nautical miles, in three and a half hours on several occasions, this being at the rate of 15.7 knots, then unprecedented. She was afterwards deprived of half her boiler power, to increase her coal carrying capacity, and sent to the Mediterranean to do duty as a despatch vessel, for which service she could always be relied upon as a 12-knot steamer.

Paddle-wheel men-of-war were at one time the most

important factor in our navy—the manufacture of their engines called forth the utmost skill in design, ingenuity of detail, and accuracy of workmanship that were in those days available—but their end was near, and they were soon to become as obsolete and forgotten as though they had never been. Their defects and disadvantages had all along been sufficiently obvious, but nothing better was to hand. Huge outside cumbrous wheels, liable to be utterly disabled by the explosion of a lucky shell, the position of the engines themselves with their most vital parts well above the water line, and the enormous weight of the machinery in proportion to tonnage and horse power, all these objectionable characteristics made it certain that when an alternative method of propulsion was proposed by which these evils would be abrogated, or even sensibly mitigated, it would be welcomed with enthusiasm and eagerly adopted. The enthusiasm and the eagerness were not quite as much to the front as might have been expected, but the conservatism of the navy even now, much more then, may almost be termed bigotry. The screw propeller, however, had in itself such intrinsic merits that, if it did not at first dazzle like a display of fireworks, it soon became as much a national necessity as the breadstuffs it is the instrument of bringing in such quantities to us who would perish without them.

As has so frequently been the case with other inventions, it is not by any means certain to whom the credit of first discovering the screw as a propeller for marine purposes ought to be ascribed, but the matter is not of much importance. As far as the British navy is concerned, Mr F. P. Smith, who succeeded in rousing the Government to action after that splendid inventor Captain Ericsson had failed, is indisputably the father of screw propulsion. Mr Smith brought out with success in 1840 the 'Archimedes,' a vessel of 232 tons and 80 horse power. The Admiralty thereupon ordered the 'Rattler' to be built on the same lines as the paddle-wheel steamer 'Alecto,' with screw engines of the same nominal horse power by Messrs Maudslay, and very soon several more men-of-war were ordered to be fitted with screws. An early example of a successful screw vessel was the Royal yacht 'Fairy,' built of iron in 1845, and engined by Messrs Penn. She had oscillating cylinders driving a cogged wheel geared into a pinion on the screw shaft, so that the screw made five revolutions for every one of the engines. She was kept running for many years between Portsmouth and Cowes, till at last her plating was worn so thin that a bluejacket alongside sent his boathook right through it. She was then replaced by the 'Alberta.'

The 'Duke of Wellington,' Sir Charles Napier's flagship in the Baltic during the Russian War, was probably the last screw ship in the Royal Navy fitted with geared engines. For it was about this time that a change came over the design of machinery for the propulsion of war vessels, so complete and radical as to mark a distinct epoch in its history. When once the fact had been grasped that all men-of-war for the future would be propelled by the screw, the immense advantage realised by the low position of the main shaft, far below the water line, became apparent, as the engines, being horizontal, would be in a great measure protected from the enemy's fire, instead of being, as in paddle-wheel ships, dangerously and unavoidably exposed to it. It was also soon seen what great benefit would be derived if the engines were coupled directly to the main shaft, without the intervention of cogged wheels, to obtain the required number of revolutions of the screw. To ensure this result much higher speed of crank-shaft was necessary, but the engineering skill of the country proved quite equal to the occasion. Messrs Maudslay & Field, and Messrs Penn & Son, now began to almost monopolise the Government orders, as I find that of twenty-six sets of screw engines completed for the Admiralty between the years 1852 and 1860 twenty-one are credited to these two firms. The workmanship of both was admirable, but at that time Messrs Maudslay erred, if anything, rather on the side of strength, and Messrs Penn on that of lightness. The number 'twenty-six' given above is exclusive of a large fleet of high-pressure steam gunboats that were built and engined with unexampled rapidity at the beginning of the Russian War. High-pressure steam was first tried in the navy in September 1853, on board the corvette 'Malacca.' She was fitted with engines working with steam at 60 lbs. pressure by Messrs Penn, but she was not a success; engineers had not yet been educated up to so vast an innovation.

In 1860 was completed for sea a ship remarkable

from a historical point of view as the last three-decker in commission on active service in the British navy. This was the 'Victoria,' of 120 guns and 4403 indicated horse power. She was fitted by Messrs Maudslay with horizontal double piston-rod return connecting-rod engines, a type they had made peculiarly their own, and from which for a great many years they never varied.

The 'Victoria' relieved the 'Marlborough,' a ship of a similar kind, but of only 3054 horse power, as flagship of the Commander-in-Chief on the Mediterranean station. Her engine-room, as compared with the cramped chambers of modern vessels, was of palatial dimensions. The pressure of steam in the boilers was 22 lbs., and at full power the ship attained a speed of over 12 knots. With sail set on her enormous yards, and her progress perhaps helped by her screw, she was a magnificent sight as she made her way in or out of the harbours of Malta or Corfu. But her day had come; she was the last of her race, for it was recognised that in combat with even an ironclad of her day she could have been nothing but a floating shambles. She is, however, worthy of mention here as being probably the finest specimen of a wooden steam man-of-war the world has ever seen. She had but that one commission, and is now for sale to be broken up.

Various causes were now combining to bring about the substitution of iron for wood, but there is no doubt the necessity of providing against the vibration of the screw in high-powered vessels had a great deal to do with it. Iron had been used to a limited extent in the navy, but had not been at all generally approved of. The frigate 'Vulcan' was completed in 1849, and the troopships 'Megæra' and 'Simoom' in the following year, but it was not till June 1859 that the 'Warrior' was ordered as a counterblast to the French 'La Gloire,' then on the point of completion by M. Dupuy de Lôme.

Although this constituted so distinct a landmark in the history of the British navy, it had little or no influence on engineering practice. Engines were made bigger as higher speeds were demanded, but, except in the matter of size, the engines of the 'Warrior' and the 'Agincourt' differed but little from those of the 'Arrogant' and the 'Cossack.' It is true the pressure of steam in the boilers had gradually crept up to 25 lbs. on the square inch, some improvements in detail had also, as was natural, been introduced, but the general principle and arrangement remained unaltered. The engines of the 'Warrior,' however, when she was first commissioned, were considered to involve so vast a responsibility and to require such effective supervision that it was decided to take the unprecedented step of appointing *two* chief engineers to her, whereas to-day the post would unhesitatingly be given to the junior Chief Engineer of the Fleet, if it happened to be vacant and he to be unemployed. Messrs Penn & Son obtained the contract for these engines, as also for those of the sister ship 'Black Prince.' And here a most curious fact may be mentioned which excited a good deal of speculation at the time. The designs for the two ironclads were got out at the Admiralty by Mr Watts, Chief Constructor of the Navy, in consultation with Mr Scott Russell, and identical drawings were sent to the contractors, the Thames Iron Shipbuilding Company and Messrs R. Napier & Sons, of Glasgow, for their information and guidance. The engines were in every way duplicates, of course. And yet the 'Warrior' was, and is to this day, appreciably superior, both in steaming and sailing, to the 'Black Prince.' Many ingenious explanations for this difference were proposed, but none that could in any way be called convincing.

At the latter end of 1860 the Admiralty, being perturbed in their minds at the large amount of the national coal bill, gave *carte blanche* to three eminent engineering firms to construct machinery for three crack sailing frigates of nearly similar tonnage and lines, with the sole view of combining reasonable speed with economy of fuel. The selected frigates were the 'Octavia, 'Arethusa,' and 'Constance,' which were assigned to Messrs Maudslay, Penn, and Randolph & Elder respectively, with no restrictions as to pattern or, it was said, price. Messrs Maudslay elected to supply a three-cylinder engine, working expansively in the ordinary way, with an initial pressure of 30 lbs., which they afterwards reproduced on a larger scale in the 'Lord Warden'; Messrs Penn fitted an exceptionally well executed specimen of their trunk engine, but about neither of these designs was there any decided novelty. The Scotch firm, however, flew at higher game. They had six cylinders to their engines, each triplet consisting of a high-pressure between two low-pressure ones. The initial pressure in the boilers was 60 lbs.; steam was cut off in the middle cylinder of each group at about half-stroke, and exhausted thence into the other two. This deserves notice as being the first instance of the use of the compound engine in the navy, though it was not long after the trials of the 'Constance' that Messrs Humphrys & Tennant employed a simpler form of the same principle in the 'Pallas.' The three ships were sent for a cruise in company to Madeira and back, but no very grand results were obtained. The 'Octavia' became commodore's ship during the Abyssinian War, the 'Constance' went to the West Indies, and the 'Arethusa' to the Mediterranean. After one commission they were never employed again; they were admitted to be failures, and their hulls have long since gone to the shipbreaker, their engines to the scrap heap.

Let us look, then, at the state of steam navigation in the Royal Navy in 1865, the year that marks the close of the first half of the fifty years that this book deals with, and great as the progress made, and radical as the changes introduced in this quarter of a century may seem, they certainly did not surpass in importance either the progress or the changes of the next. In 1865 the paddle-wheel as a mode of propulsion for fighting ships had become entirely obsolete, its place having been taken by the screw. The pressure of the steam in the boilers had increased from 7 lbs. in the

'Rattler' to 30 lbs. in the 'Vestal,' which of itself shows what an advance must have taken place in the art of boiler construction, and every boiler afloat was on the tubular principle. The interposition of gearing between the crank and main shafts had long been abolished, and the number of revolutions of the engines had risen from, say, fourteen to fifty-six. The question of coal consumption was beginning to awaken attention, and as a consequence compound engines and surface condensers were being toyed with tentatively to that end. The 'Warrior,' though completed in 1861, was still the fastest ship we had, with her speed of 14.3 knots, and it was not then considered likely that this speed would be much exceeded in the future except by a few enthusiasts; but the gift of prophecy is rare, and it is possible that a quarter of a century hence the engines of the 'Blake' will be considered as antiquated as those of the 'Warrior' are now. The engine builders of 1865, however, enjoyed advantages of which their successors of to-day may well be envious. The girders of ironclads, the solid oak beams of frigates or converted line-of-battle ships furnished such sound foundations for the bed-plates of the engines, and, above all, the restrictions in the matter of weight were so comparatively benign, that delightful smoothness of working was the rule, and serious accidents were all but unknown.

We now enter on a new era of naval marine engineering. In 1866 was completed the 'Pallas,' a small ironclad designed by Sir E. Reed, and remarkable for having been the first ship successfully fitted with compound engines for the Royal Navy; for though the 'Constance' preceded her, that ship's machinery was a constant source of extreme worry and anxiety to those responsible for the charge of it, while the 'Pallas' in this respect never gave any trouble at all. The 'Pallas' had only two cylinders, instead of six, of unequal volume, one being four times the size of the other. The steam was admitted at high pressure, 60 lbs., into the small cylinder, and thence passed into the larger one, which it of course filled by its expansion. This is the whole principle of compound engines. She had surface condensers, and there is no doubt, for the horse power produced, she was very economical in fuel. The boilers were fitted with superheaters, a series of tubes at the base of the funnel through which the steam passed with the object of drying it and surcharging it with heat—a contrivance that was always looked upon with distrust by naval engineers and has long ago passed into oblivion. Her speed was 13.4 knots, and she was a handy and essentially comfortable little ship.

The compound principle, as introduced by Messrs Humphrys & Tennant for the 'Pallas,' was, but at an interval, adopted for most of the new ships in the navy, until superseded by triple-expansion, to a consideration of which we shall come by-and-by. With compound engines came as a natural consequence surface condensers, and the general use of steam of not less than 60 lbs. pressure. This latter innovation brought about an entire revolution in the shape of ships' boilers.

What was known as the square or 'box' type, that had been in use nearly fifty years, had to be discarded, in view of this increase of pressure, for a circular form, resembling a Gloucester cheese set on edge, with the furnaces on the flat side of it. The thickness of plates had to be greatly increased, the excellence of the metal to be more rigidly insisted on, while the difficulty of manufacture was considerably enhanced. Machines that had been devised for punching out the rivet holes became of no value, as thick plates suffered in strength by the process, and the operation of drilling had to be substituted for it. This was, of course, more expensive, but amply repaid its cost in the long run.

The 'Penelope,' completed in 1868, was the first important ironclad fitted with twin screws, and is noteworthy as having been the forerunner of a long line of twin-screw battleships. When the 'Audacious' class came to be built, immediately following on the 'Penelope,' the twin screw system was not so generally accepted, as two ships of the same type, the 'Swiftsure' and 'Triumph,' were only allowed one screw apiece. Nowadays all vessels we build of any size above second-class gunboats are fitted with two sets of engines. Of the advantages of the plan there can be no doubt, but in this place, where the aim is to be rather historical than critical, any disquisition on the subject would be impertinent—in the original sense of the word.

In August 1869 was commissioned a single-screw frigate that for speed and other good qualities excelled everything the world had hitherto seen, and indeed she has never been beaten in her own line. This was a period of experiment and invention, and the 'Inconstant' was in many ways an example of success in both. She was the first iron ship to be encased in a sheathing of wood, in order that she might be coppered, and so avoid the inconveniences of the fouling which, in spite of so many compositions and nostrums, is still the *bête noire* of all iron and steel hulls. Her engines were supplied by Messrs Penn, and were nominally of 1000 horse power, but when the ship was tried on the measured mile at Stokes Bay they indicated 7360 horse power, and gave the ship, when all her ten boilers were used, a speed of 16.51 knots, which had never hitherto been approached by a fighting ship. With half-boiler power a speed of 13 knots was easily attained, but the 'Inconstant's' weak point was her limited coal endurance. Her supply of fuel was only sufficient for two and a quarter days' steaming at full power, and for nine days at 10 knots an hour. This, of course, is a serious defect, but nevertheless she was a splendid ship in her day. She was remarkable for her speed and handiness under sail alone, and when the squadron was sailing showed herself superior to the 'Bristol,' a wooden frigate of no mean reputation.

But a time came when she was asked to show her speed under circumstances so sad and melancholy as to fill the whole kingdom with grief and mourning. On the night of the 6th of September 1870 the Channel Squadron, under the command of Sir Thomas Symonds, was cruising off Cape Finisterre. The weather after leaving Gibraltar, had been remarkably fine, and the admiral had taken advantage of the smooth water to launch his boat from the 'Minotaur' flagship and inspect the 'Captain.' He did not approve of her, although at that time, because she had made one or two cruises without capsizing, she was supposed to have settled the question beyond dispute as to what should be the type of the British war vessel in the future. There was no particularly bad weather that night; the sea was certainly not exceptionally heavy, nor the wind anything like a real gale, but in an ordinary squall the 'Captain' turned slowly over and 500 precious lives were lost. The 'Inconstant' was the next ship to her, and remarked the disappearance of her lights, but owing to the squall the squadron was more or less scattered, and but little attention was paid to the circumstance. When daylight came next morning the sea was smooth, but there were no signs of the 'Captain,' and at first no alarm was felt about her. The admiral, however, made a general signal, 'Spread in search of "Captain,"' and it was not long before one of her boats was picked up; still nobody suspected the dreadful truth. But later in the day a table known to have formed part of Captain Burgoyne's cabin furniture was found floating, and then there was no room for doubt. Nothing but the capsizing of the 'Captain' could have caused that table to be floating in the Bay of Biscay. A signal was then made for the 'Inconstant' to get up steam for full speed and proceed to England with the terrible news. She had a light fair wind, and from a point just off Corcubion to

Plymouth she averaged 15¾ knots, with one boiler out of her ten held in reserve. This was a fine performance in those days, but she never had the chance of repeating it, for the scare caused by the loss of the 'Captain' resulted in some 300 tons of extra ballast being stowed in her hold, which had the effect of completely ruining her exceptional qualities for speed, whether under steam or sail. She has been employed on various services since then, but is now quite obsolete.

By 1873 the engineer department at the Admiralty finally made up its mind that compound engines were as likely to be profitably employed on board the Queen's ships as they long had been in the mercantile marine. The usual pressure of steam in the boilers of men-of-war had now settled at 60 lbs. on the square inch. Every ship as she was built was being fitted with compound engines, but there was a restless, uneasy feeling among the men who constructed them that they were very far from the end of the journey on which they had started when they first left the 'sweet simplicity' of simple engines and 30 lbs. pressure behind them. They little knew what was in store for them in the future.

Before that time arrived, however, two ships were added to the navy sufficiently remarkable both for hulls and machinery to demand particular notice. These were the 'Iris' and 'Mercury.' Entirely without defensive armour, these ships were intended to rely for safety on their exceptional speed. The 'Iris' was the first ship built in England in which soft steel was employed, and the first vessel of the Royal Navy wholly built of steel. It may be added that she was also the first vessel wherein the construction of her machinery was much hampered by considerations of weight, and as a consequence in her engines were introduced, for the first time, hollow compressed steel shafts, invented by the Whitworth firm. The engines, by Messrs Maudslay, were indeed of a type entirely new to the navy. The firm had obtained considerable credit and renown by the extraordinarily fast passages made by the 'Germanic' and 'Britannic,' Atlantic mail steamers engined by them for the White Star line. The compound engines of the 'Iris' are exactly on the same principle, but horizontal instead of vertical. There are two distinct sets, driving twin screws, and each set has four cylinders, two high-pressure at the back of the two low-pressure ones, arranged in what is known as 'tandem' fashion. 'The narrow beam of the ship, in proportion to the size and power of the engines, rendered it necessary to place the starboard engine in front of the port engine, so that the whole body of the ship is filled with machinery.' So says Lord Brassey, but what was considered an exceptional case in 1876 is now the universal order of things.

The 'Iris' carries 500 tons of coal in the ordinary bunkers, and 250 tons additional in the reserve bunkers. The total weight of the machinery, with water in the boilers and condensers, is about 1000 tons, and the contract price was £93,000. From the *Times* account of her trials we learn that she proved to be not only the quickest ship in the navy but the quickest ship afloat

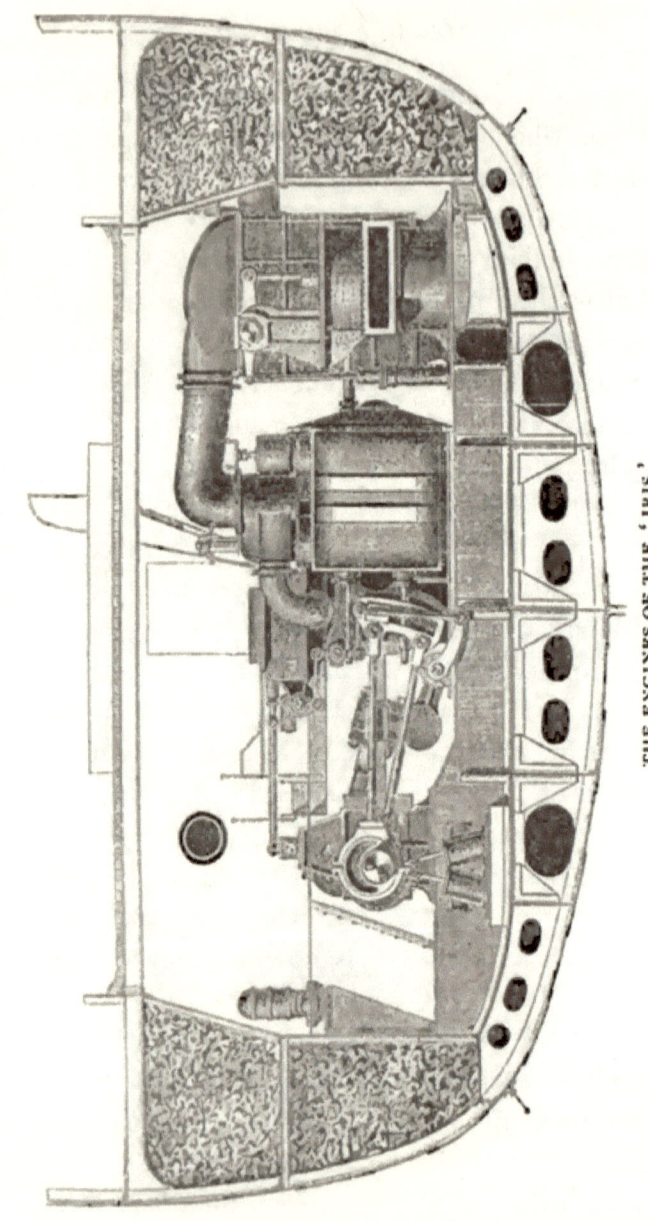

THE ENGINES OF THE 'IRIS.'

having surpassed the highest spead attained by the 'Lightning,' the first torpedo boat supplied to the service—of which craft more by-and-by. There was nothing resembling her in the navy with reference to the proportion of midship section to length, the extreme fineness of her entrance and run, and the ratio of her enormous horse power to displacement. It is doubtful if any trials have been more fraught with valuable instruction to marine engineers than those of the 'Iris.' At first she was a great disappointment to all who had in any way been connected with her. It had been calculated that with 7000 horse power she ought to realise something like a speed of 17.5 knots, but with 7500 horse power she only managed 16.6 knots, the revolutions of the engines being ninety-one.

Space does not permit of any detailed description of the numerous experiments which followed, but it is sufficient to say that the screw propellers were found to be vastly too large in diameter, and their friction in the water was thus excessive, that their pitch was increased, and that the 'Iris,' with 7735 horse power, attained a mean speed of 18.572 knots, fully a knot more than the constructive department at the Admiralty ever expected to get out of her. The 'Mercury,' her sister ship, built on the same lines, under an adjoining shed at the same dockyard, and engined by the same firm, was even more successful, attaining a mean speed of 18.87 knots per hour, and this in 1879. It is hardly to be wondered at that the fame of such unparalleled achievements spread all over Europe and excited the emulation of foreign powers, but at that time they had neither engineers nor shipwrights who could pretend to rival ours.

It has been thought desirable to dwell at some length on the 'Iris' and 'Mercury,' because they undoubtedly indicate an epoch in the history of engineering in the navy and are still very valuable vessels. They have, however, two grave defects, which have prevented any reproduction of their type. They are entirely unprotected, and their coal endurance is very small. More or less provision was made in them to compensate for the absence of armour by water-tight subdivision and by coal protection; still they had to run the risk of being penetrated in a vital part and sent to the bottom by the explosion of a single successful shell.

And here came in one of the most important inventions, suggestions—call it what you will—of the quarter century we are discussing. That was the adoption in otherwise light cruisers of a steel protective deck, which has permitted the grand and beneficial substitution of vertical engines for horizontal ones. And for this idea Rear-Admiral Robert Scott deserves all the credit. The part of a fighting ship that it is most essential to guard from an enemy's fire is the engine-room. In the early days of steam this was naturally accomplished by keeping all the machinery below the water line, but when the idea of a horizontal armoured deck took root engineers were quick to see that they would be comparatively safe under its shelter, and that projectiles would glance off it instead of dropping through to their destruction.

Hence vertical engines, whose height is only limited by that of the protective deck. Every engineer knows that the normal position of a cylinder and piston is perpendicular; circumstances alone have forced him sometimes to be content with the horizontal. At the present time every war vessel of size above a gunboat is supplied with vertical engines. The 'Shannon' and 'Dreadnought,' both built at Pembroke, and the 'Nelson' and 'Northampton,' both hailing from Messrs Elder, of Glasgow, were the first important ships to be so fitted. These four ships were all completed between 1875 and 1878.

In 1881 was launched the 'Polyphemus,' a most remarkable ship, but noteworthy more for her hull, which is fully described elsewhere, than for her machinery. She has twin screws, driven by two pairs of compound horizontal engines constructed by Messrs Humphrys & Tennant, of Deptford, who, it may here be remarked, have latterly built and are building some of the most important engines in the navy. The boilers of the 'Polyphemus,' originally of the locomotive type, gave a great deal of trouble, and new ones were substituted for them with good results. The pressure of steam is 110 lbs. per square inch. It will be observed with what leaps and bounds the pressure of steam advanced in the course of comparatively few years. A quite usual pressure now is 155 lbs., and this will probably be very considerably increased before long.

With the extended application of high-pressure steam came, as a natural corollary, a desire to utilise its advantages to the utmost. To this laudable ambition we owe the introduction of forced draught and triple expansion. The former device, which, for the benefit of lay readers, may be defined as the increase of air pressure in the stokeholds by artificial means, causing the fires to burn more fiercely and to consume more fuel in a given time on the same surface of grate, was, like other new things, only generally adopted in our service after considerable hesitation, and when it had been proved by the French to possess certain advantages too weighty to be overlooked. It may be well here to observe that this is probably the first and only instance of British marine engineers owing anything to any foreign source. Other nations have invariably been content to follow where we led from the very earliest days of steam navigation. In the future it is possible that the restless ingenuity of American mechanicians may produce ideas that we cannot afford to neglect, but at present it may safely be said that the history of English engineering includes all that the rest of the world has hitherto accomplished in that direction.

Forced draught was first employed in the British navy in the 'Lightning,' our earliest torpedo boat, constructed by Messrs Thorneycroft, of Chiswick, in 1877. The system was adopted, primarily if not solely, with the view of obtaining a much greater power with a given weight of boilers than could be obtained with natural draught. Economy of fuel was not the object sought; if it had been, it would not have been found. The 'Lightning,' a boat only 84 ft. long, of 10 ft. 10. in.

beam, and 32 tons displacement, attained a mean speed of over 18 knots. Her engines, supplied by her builders, were compound, driving a single screw. The high-pressure cylinder was 12¾ in. in diameter, the low-pressure 21 in., their stroke was 12 in. She had a steel boiler of the modified locomotive pattern, working at 120 lbs. pressure. Her surface condenser was made of thin sheet copper, and was supplied with a separate engine and centrifugal pump. The machinery of this vessel was very light, steel being largely used, and the workmanship was of the highest class. She was, in her day, a complete novelty, both as regards hull and machinery, and was equally a complete success. She is interesting as the pioneer of a very numerous and important flotilla. By May 1887 Messrs Yarrow, of Poplar, who have always been friendly rivals of Messrs Thorneycroft, had supplied our navy with a torpedo boat, known as 'No. 80,' which illustrates the strides that had been made by both firms in a decade. This vessel has a length of 135 ft., beam of 14 ft., and displacement of about 130 tons. Her triple-expansion engines work up to 1700 indicated horse power, and the trial speed for three hours was 23 knots. She can steam a distance of 2000 knots at 11 knots speed. There is only one locomotive boiler, and it is probable the boilers of this type of boat are the largest ever built on the locomotive principle, but the firm has as yet had no failures with them. Higher speeds with more powerful machinery have been attained in boats built since 'No. 80' by both firms for foreign powers. Messrs Yarrow have recently employed quadruple-expansion engines, with a boiler pressure of 200 lbs., in a boat for the Argentine Government, with the happiest results.

It has been stated that 'No. 80' was supplied with triple-expansion engines, but she was not the first vessel to be so fitted. Here it may be well to mention that whereas in simple engines the whole process of expansion of the steam is carried out in one cylinder, and in compound engines in two, in triple-expansion engines the steam passes through three cylinders, diminishing in pressure at each step before it reaches the condenser. More work is thus got out of the steam for the same expenditure of fuel, and consequently what is known as the 'coal endurance' of ships is considerably increased.

In September 1886 was launched the 'Rattlesnake,' built and engined by Messrs Laird, of Birkenhead, the forerunner of a type of vessel considered by many good judges to be of even more importance in modern naval warfare than the torpedo boats. That the authorities themselves are of this opinion may be seen by the fact that at the present moment there are twenty-two of these vessels, now known as 'sharpshooters,' either completed or in progress. 'In engining these ships the paramount object has been to reduce all weights to a minimum consistent with efficiency,' and in no similar instance has praiseworthy intention been so carried to an extreme as nearly to approach a crime. The propelling machinery of the 'Rattlesnake,' consisting of two sets of vertical triple-expansion three-crank engines, of 2700 horse power at 310 revolutions, was the first of its kind supplied to the navy. The framing is entirely composed of steel, which has also been largely employed in the construction of the machinery throughout. The crank and other shafts are made of Whitworth special steel, and are all hollow. She attained a mean speed of 18.779 knots on the measured mile under unfavourable circumstances as regards weather, and has since then frequently achieved 19 knots on actual service. She has taken an active part in all naval manœuvres of late years, and has been the terror of her imaginary foes, mainly because her engines have never broken down. This is no doubt owing to the fact that the stipulated weight of the machinery was exceeded.

The great difficulty in obtaining and maintaining high speeds in the navy has been the incapacity of boilers to withstand the strain put upon them. For this contracted dimensions have been mainly, and forced draught excessively and injudiciously applied, partly responsible. Forced draught is by no means to be wholly condemned. It is not, as Admiral Mayne called it, purely 'an invention of the Evil One.' But it requires to be used with care and judgment, when it will probably prove as valuable an auxiliary to the steaming power of our warships as it has undoubtedly shown itself to be in the mercantile marine. The 'Barham' and the 'Bellona,' sister ships, deserve a few words as to their machinery, which is very *fin de siècle*. They have each two sets of vertical triple-expansion engines, driving twin screws. The cylinders are 27 in.,

40 in., and 60 in. in diameter, with a stroke of 2 ft. 3 in. The natural draught trial of the 'Bellona' took place in November 1890 in the North Sea, off the mouth of the Tyne, and in a run of six hours she attained a mean speed of 19.46 knots. The mean indicated horse power was 3557. Why could the 'Barham,' fitted with precisely similar engines, only keep up a speed on active service of 2 knots less? In all likelihood it was the human element that came into play and caused the difference. The stokers were not good enough for their work.

Here it may not be inappropriate to call attention to the rapidly diminishing weight of steam machinery for warships in proportion to the power demanded from it. In the year 1853 the 'The Duke of Wellington' was looked upon with pride by the whole country as a magnificent specimen of a steam line-of-battle ship. Her engines were of 1999 indicated horse power; they weighed 400 tons, so that each ton of engines gave 5 horse power, and each horse power was produced by 448 lbs. of machinery. In the 'Bellona' the horse power is 6000—estimated—and the weight of machinery only 270 tons, which gives approximately 100 lb. per horsepower. In torpedo boats the proportion is very much less than this, which all marine engineers have agreed to consider as extravagantly small. 'In the merchant service our tonnage laws encourage the shipowner to build roomy engine-rooms, and consequently the engines are not limited as to space occupied; hence a better design is possible than obtains in the navy. In our mail steamers on the Atlantic 'the weight of machinery per indicated horse power is about 280 lbs.' This shows, says the Liverpool *Journal of Commerce*, how impossible it is to institute comparisons between a merchant vessel and a warship. The question is constantly asked by outsiders why it is that the ships of the Royal Navy cannot make passages equal to those achieved every day by the Atlantic 'greyhounds.' The answer is that they are not built for it. In, say, the 'Teutonic' the propelling machinery is made the great consideration. Everything is, and can be without harm, sacrificed to it. But it is far different in a man-of-war. As was long ago remarked, a fighting ship must always be a compromise. There are three great requisites: offensive power, meaning guns and torpedoes; defensive power, meaning armour, whether applied to sides, turrets, barbettes, or decks; and speed, meaning the most powerful engines, combined with the greatest coal endurance, that it is possible to get a ship of given tonnage to carry. If the tonnage is a fixed quantity, every attempt at extension in the direction of any of these three qualities can only be made at the expense of the other two. Hence the craze for inordinate lightness of machinery.

As the very latest development of extreme steam power, with the view of giving to a warship unprecedented speed, attention must be called to the as yet uncompleted cruisers 'Blake' and 'Blenheim,' engined respectively by Messrs Maudslay and Messrs Humphrys. It is probable that there will be but little difference between them, as far as steaming capabilities are concerned, and so the account, taken from *The Times*, of the 'Blake's' machinery may answer for both vessels, which are, from many points of view, the most important that have been ordered for the Admiralty for many years. The 'Blake' "will be propelled by twin screws, driven by four sets of triple-expansion engines of the inverted vertical cylinder type. Messrs Maudslay, Sons & Field are the makers of these engines and boilers. The collective power they guarantee is 13,000 horse power for twelve hours' steaming at natural draught, and 20,000 horse power for four hours with forced draught; the corresponding maximum speeds are estimated at 20 knots for natural draught and 22 knots for forced draught, when the vessel is run in smooth water with everything at its best. On actual service, judging from past experience, with ordinary conditions of coal and stoking, the engines may be expected to develop about 9000 to 10,000 horse power for long periods of continuous steaming, which would probably give the vessel a continuous speed of 18 to $18\frac{1}{2}$ knots in smooth water. .... Everyone knows, what recent manœuvres have illustrated afresh, that in cruisers of moderate dimensions, capable of attaining high speed in smooth-water trials, the working speeds at sea are limited by other considerations than the power available for propulsion. .... Sailors generally will be sure to welcome the greater length and size of the 'Blake' and 'Blenheim,' because of their capability of maintaining speed in rough water; and their enormous engine power and very high trial speeds give

The Engines of *The Blake*.

them a grand working margin as compared with other cruisers." So far *The Times*, but we do not yet know exactly how these two ships will turn out. Their machinery is, however, our latest and most ambitious effort in the way of naval marine engineering, and forms a remarkable contrast to the engines of fifty years ago.

Perhaps in nothing has the advance of the use of steam on board warships been so extraordinary as in the number of auxiliary engines now considered necessary. And this is a source of danger. The 'Sans Pareil,' for example, has in addition to her main engines no fewer than fifty-eight auxiliary steam engines on board. Some of these are only used occasionally for special purposes, but an enumeration of them will show that many must be constantly in use. They are as follows:—

Main circulating engines,	4	Ventilation exhaust,	2
Auxiliary condenser do.,	2	Forced draught,	8
Main fire engines,	2	Main feed,	4
Auxiliary do.,	2	Auxiliary feed,	4
Bilge engines,	2	Air compressing,	4
Turning engines,	2	Dynamo,	3
Reversing engines,	2	Capstan,	1
Distilled water,	2	Hydraulic pumping,	2
Drain tank,	1	Auxiliary do.,	1
Evaporator feed,	2	Friedman's ejectors,	4
Ventilation supply,	4		

When the ship is at sea it is clear that these engines, many of which are constantly at work, and all of which must be ready to work on an emergency, will consume an appreciable proportion of the coal assumed in the official tables to be available for the purpose of continuous steaming at 10-knot speed, as the consumption for auxiliary purposes varies from about 5 to 8 tons a day.

It will readily be understood that the supply and economy of coal on board a fighting ship are matters of the very utmost importance, and any contrivances tending to facilitate them are of great value, but it is probably less well known that the health and efficiency of modern marine boilers depend very largely on there being no stint in the supply of fresh water for them. Such, however, is the case. Any appreciable admixture of raw sea water is fatal to the delicate constitutions of boilers working at a pressure of 155 lbs. on the square inch. Hence special arrangements have to be fitted for making up the necessary waste of fresh water that must occur during a voyage of very moderate length. Theoretically, if machines were perfect, the fresh water taken in from the shore, converted into steam in the boilers, and reconverted into fresh water by the surface condensers, would not diminish in quantity and might go back to the boilers from week's end to week's end on its round of profitable employment. But, in practice, what with unavoidable leaky joints and occasional escapes of steam at the safety valves, it is found that there is a deficit of hundreds of gallons of water every day, which has to be made up. To this end all ships are now fitted with distilling apparatus, or 'evaporators' as they are generally called, for the purpose of converting salt water into fresh, not only for the use of the boilers but also for the use of the crew. The newest of these, and apparently by a long way the most efficient, is the Yaryan, of American origin, the main principle of which is that the sea water before being evaporated and condensed is pulverised into spray. Professor Lewes, of the Royal Naval College, speaking of most of the other varieties, averred with good reason that the trouble of deposit in the boilers was only transferred to the distillery apparatus; in the Yaryan there has been no trouble at all, because there has been no deposit.

Looking back, then, on the past half century, we find that the whole aspect of marine engineering has changed. And nowhere is this revolution more distinctly marked than in the Royal Navy, where it has produced its most startling effects. In the early days the steam engine was seldom used, and occupied a very minor position in the internal arrangement of a ship, but now it is absolutely requisite for every purpose for which the modern man-of-war exists. Steam machinery now fulfils every function of the latter-day ironclad. Its very air and light, its steering and anchoring, the training and loading of its guns, the motive power of its torpedoes, all these, and many other things, without steam could not be. As a matter of course, as steam machinery became of more and more importance in the navy, so did the position of the officers in charge of it advance. Before 1847 all engineers were warrant officers, but junior of that rank, so that the chief engineer of a paddle-wheel frigate was then, officially, of less account than the carpenter. He is now, as far as rank goes, on the same level as the medical and accountant officers, but his pay is considerably less than theirs, which is a constant occasion of complaint. With regard to the rank and file of the engine-room, the introduction of a class of skilled artificers, which took place in 1869, has proved of very great benefit to the navy, by rendering it possible to reduce very largely the number of highly trained engineer officers, which reduction has, however, been carried too far. The entry and training of stokers—firemen as they are called in the mercantile marine—are in anything but a satisfactory state. As the necessity for increased intelligence among these men becomes more manifest, on account of the number of small yet anything but simple engines that have to be confided to their care, it will probably be found advisable to train them up from boys for their particular duties, in the same way as has long been the practice with seamen. What the future of engineering in the navy may be he would be a bold man who would attempt to prophesy. It is, however, unlikely that in the next decade anything like the same progress will be made as in the past one. There must be a point beyond which, except in matters of detail, improvement of the marine steam engine cannot go. That point has probably very nearly been attained. To the ambitious and sceptical it may be called to mind that, with every inducement to inventors, no substantial difference exists to-day between the best example of a railway locomotive and one of thirty years ago. If any startling revolution in the economy of marine steam propulsion does take place during the lives of the present generation it may possibly be in the direction of the substitution of liquid fuel for coal. But of this there does not seem to be at present any noticeable sign.

CHAPTER XII

FOREIGN NAVIES—EUROPE

Condition of French Navy in 1840—Progress after Franco-German War—Broadside and Barbette Construction—Cruisers—The Russian Flee—Influence of the 'Monitor'—New Departure—Black Sea and Baltic Squadrons—Belted Cruisers—Italy—Creation of a New Fleet after 1870—Monster Ironclads—Cruisers—Germany—Late development of Navy—New Battle Ships and Cruisers—Austria, Spain, Greece, and Turkey.

NOTWITHSTANDING the signal defeats inflicted upon the navy of France at the beginning of this century, she has regained her position as a maritime power, and now possesses a fleet only second to our own. Though in the interval the country has passed through various political phases, involving changes from a monarchy to a republic, the long and glorious traditions of a navy, founded by Richelieu and consolidated by Colbert, have survived, and are the mainspring of that efficiency which we see to-day. Fleets may disappear but traditions survive, and in reconstruction play an important part. How notable this has been in the case of France. Stunned by the blows inflicted on her at sea in all parts of the world, she for some years after the peace of 1815 made no attempt to resuscitate her navy. But in 1820 the country was roused when the Minister of Marine suggested 'to abandon the institution to save the expense, or to increase the expenses to save the institution.' A sum of £20,000,000 sterling was granted, the expenditure of which was to be spread over eleven years. Such progress was made that in 1840, when relations between France and England were strained over the Syrian question, and our fleet had been suffered to fall below its proper strength, eminent French naval officers considered their country fully equal to coping with us at sea. They had in the Mediterranean at this time in Admiral Lalande an officer of great ability and energy, who, it is said, asked permission to attack the British Squadron. But more peaceful counsels prevailed, and we, profiting by the lesson, sent out reinforcements to our undermanned ships. At this time the equipment of French vessels was superior to ours, and their crews were in a high state of efficiency.

When, however, steam superseded sails the position we at once assumed in the construction of steam machinery gave us an advantage, which was apparent at the outbreak of the Crimean War. We had a greater number of steamers, and provided transports to convey French troops for the attack on Bomarsund. France undoubtedly was the first to construct sea-going ironclads, a policy we at first thought folly and then were constrained to follow. Their early ironclads were of the type I have already mentioned, but the expense of such vessels and the time required for their construction prevents the formation of modern fleets in a few years. During the Crimean War a wooden line of-battle ship had been built, equipped, and sent to sea in ninety days. Under the new system a nation cannot thus rapidly reinforce its fleet; and when war broke out in 1870 between France and Germany the fleet of the former was unable to effect any serious diversion in the Baltic. There had been some idea at first of landing a French force in that locality under cover of the fleet, but there was no organisation for such an expedition. The opportunity passed, and the squadron despatched to the Baltic could do little more than blockade the coast until recalled home. The crews then assisted in the defence of Paris, and the naval contingent performed excellent service during the siege.

After this war France steadily set to work to augment her fleet. Between 1872 and 1886 several programmes of shipbuilding were drawn up, and no less than £18,000,000 were devoted to new construction. Practically the French fleet of to-day is the creation of the last twenty years, for nearly all the ships launched previously to 1870 have been removed from the list. Unlike ourselves, the French up to that period adhered to wooden hulls, whose life is limited. One or two remain, and among them the 'Marengo,' which as flagship of the Northern Squadron lately visited our shores.

In 1872 was commenced the first large battle ship built after the war. This was the 'Redoutable.' She was built of iron, with a displacement of 9200 tons. Then followed the 'Devastation' and 'Courbet,' of 10,100 and 9700 tons. The armament in all was disposed in the same way: a central battery, with a

THE 'ADMIRAL DUPERRÉ.'

few heavy guns mounted over it *en barbette*. As with ourselves, guns in France had risen in size to 40 tons weight, and the armour in thickness to 14 in. Then after these ships a new departure was taken—the central battery for the heavy ordnance was abandoned, but instead of adopting the turret, as we had, the barbette system was extended. This was carried out in the 'Admiral Duperré,'[1] begun at the end of 1876. In this vessel the displacement was increased to 11,000 tons, and the armament consisted of four 48-ton guns, placed singly in barbettes, with a number of smaller guns for auxiliary purposes. The complete armour belt had from the first been a special feature of French ships, and in the 'Duperré' it is 21 in. thick at the central portion. A further advance was made in the design of the 'Admiral Baudin' and 'Formidable,' commenced eleven years ago, and now forming part of the Mediterranean Squadron. Their displacement is the greatest yet in the French navy, 11,500 tons. They are armed with three 75-ton guns, mounted in separate barbettes, and have as an auxiliary armament twelve 5.3-in. guns. The armour is similar to that of the 'Duperré.' A special feature in these ships is their lofty freeboard and the height above the water at which the guns are carried. In rough weather this is a great advantage, but of course the target offered to hostile fire is considerable. These two ships are fine specimens of naval architecture.

---

[1] French ironclads no longer carry yards and sails. The illustration shows the 'Duperré' as originally completed.

It will be observed that, whereas we usually mount our heavy guns in pairs, our neighbours prefer to place them singly. By this they gain an additional position at the sacrifice of one gun. The balance between the two systems appears to be equal. Then, from the first, the French have adhered to the complete armour belt, leaving a large area of the side above unprotected. The weak point of this is that shells exploding beneath the platforms on which the heavy guns are mounted would probably put them out of action.

The satisfactory reports of the 'Admiral Baudin' and 'Formidable' have led to three others of similar construction being commenced. They are to be of 12,000 tons displacement, and hence the largest vessels yet designed in France. Whether they will be exceeded remains to be seen. Their names are to be 'Lazare Carnot,' 'Charles Martel,' and 'Jauréguiberry.' Of similar type, but smaller, are the 'Magenta,' 'Marceau,' and 'Neptune.' They carry four 52-ton guns, in separate barbettes.

But though France has been steadily adding to the number and power of her battle ships proper she has been no less assiduous in augmenting the class designed for coast defence. While for such craft we had stopped, in the 'Glatton,' at dimensions within 4000 tons, the French completed several between the years 1860 and 1880 varying from 4000 to 6000 tons. Then came the 'Caiman,' 'Indomptable,' 'Requin,' and 'Terrible,' of 7300 tons, in which the principal armament is a 75-ton gun at each end, and the protection by armour has a maximum thickness on the belt of 17½ in. Such vessels are battle ships to all intents and purposes, though perhaps not suitable for service in distant waters. Three others, of 6600 tons, the 'Tréhouart,' 'Jemmapes,' and 'Valmy' are building. These are to have a 50-ton gun in a turret at each end. We thus see that France has abstained from following the example first set by Italy of building ships of extreme size and equipping them with monster ordnance. The 75-ton gun is the largest she has afloat.

While we had been hampered in the production of fast steam cruisers by the endeavour to give them good sailing qualities as well, the French clearly recognised, twenty years ago, that sail power must be sacrificed and longer vessels built to give speed under steam. This was carried out in two vessels, the 'Sané' and 'Seignelay,' launched respectively in 1870 and 1874, where with a displacement of 1900 tons a speed of 15 knots was obtained. The steam speed of our cruisers of that size rarely exceeded 13 knots.

But after 1880 a great impetus was given to the construction of fast cruisers in France when Admiral Aube was Minister of Marine. He had previously advocated raids on territory and commerce by light forces when at war with a powerful maritime nation whose battle ships were too numerous to cope with. A great number of unarmoured ships were then laid down, several of which are now complete. The 'Tage,' of 7000 tons, is the largest. Her armament consists of sixteen guns, and her speed is 19 knots. The 'Cecille' is another fine vessel, of 5700 tons, with a similar equipment. Neither has external armour, but both have horizontal protection in a steel deck over the machinery and fore and aft the vessel. Then experiments with melinite, an explosive of great power used as the bursting charge of shells, caused ideas to revert to the old system of complete external armour to keep out some of these projectiles, their very destructive effect being clearly demonstrated. The 'Dupuy de Lôme,' named after the eminent naval architect, embodies this principle. Of only 6400 tons, she is coated externally with 4-in. steel plates. This will keep out all small projectiles. A number of other vessels between 2000 and 5000 tons are approaching completion. In all high speed has been considered the chief essential. The armament is usually lighter than that which we give to vessels of similar dimensions, but many of our officers think that in this respect we have gone to an extreme in several instances.

For scouting duties with a fleet France has produced an excellent class of vessel of 19 knots speed and 1850 tons, as in the 'Forbin,' 'Surcouf,' and four others. In the special type of small vessel for counter-attacking torpedo boats that country was first with the 'Bombe' class, of 350 tons. An increased size has, however, been found desirable.

As regards torpedo boats, France possesses a large number, and is steadily adding to it. Their special function is coast defence, and all nations now recognise that squadrons are only impeded if torpedo boats are attached to them. As for the idea that torpedo boats

Gun with shield on *Le Redoutable*.

can be employed in the attack on commerce, this may be dismissed. These craft cannot remain at sea for any time, and their nests will be as well known as the resorts of Jean Bart and Duguay Trouin were in the old corsair days.

The Crimean War found Russia but little advanced in the substitution of steam for sailing ships in her navy, and she was not prepared to meet at sea either the Baltic or Black Sea Squadrons of the allies. At the close of that war efforts were made to recover her old position among the maritime states, and several screw vessels were built. Then when France and England began to produce seagoing ironclads, two Russian wooden ships then building, the 'Sebastopol' and 'Petropaulowski,' were converted into armoured frigates, with $4\frac{1}{2}$-in. iron plates. About this time, however, the naval events of the Civil War in America brought the 'Monitor' type prominently into favour in Russia. Ten monitors, on Ericsson's plans, were ordered in 1863, when Europe seemed inclined to intervene on behalf of Poland. These monitors were built in the Baltic. Then came the Franco-German War and the declaration of Russia in reference to shipbuilding in the Black Sea, but it was some years before Russia was in a position to carry out the construction of battle ships in the southern ports. Moreover, the influence of the monitor was still paramount, and the fleet consisted chiefly of coast defence vessels. Under this influence the circular ironclads, which I have already alluded to, were built. When, therefore, war broke out with Turkey the ironclads of the latter power held a command of the Black Sea which Russia was not in a position to dispute. But in 1880 it was decided to re-create the battle fleet of Russia. A programme was drawn up for a course of shipbuilding in all classes, which was to extend over a period of twenty years. After unavoidable delays a start was made in 1882. As a result we now find in the Black Sea three powerful ironclads completed, named the 'Tchesmé,' 'Sinope,' and 'Catherine II.' They each carry six 50-ton guns, and are fairly well protected with armour; the principle favoured in France of a complete water line belt being adopted. Other battle ships are in course of construction. As Turkey has allowed her former fine fleet to fall into decay, and has added to it no powerful ships, it is evident that as between these two powers command of the Black Sea rests with Russia to-day. This should be clearly recognised, for the condition has now reverted to what it was just previously to Sinope.

In the Baltic several useful types of battle ships have been completed, such as the 'Alexander II.' and 'Nicholas I.,' of 8500 tons, a displacement adapted to the shallow waters of the north. But it is in the construction of cruisers that Russia has shown the greatest ability and energy. The special type favoured is the belted cruiser of between 6000 and 8000 tons for distant stations. Of these there are three, the 'Vladimir-Monomakh,' 'Dimitri-Donskoi,' and 'Admiral Nachimoff,' with a speed of between 15 and 16 knots, of which our 'Imperieuse' and 'Warspite' may be considered the rivals. The latest completed is the 'Pamyat Azova,' of 6000 tons, with a 6-in. belt and a speed of 18 knots. Under construction is a very large vessel of 10,500 tons, to be called the 'Rurik,' with a 10-in. belt, powerful armament, high speed, and large coal supply. Now, when cruisers are built of these dimensions, and carrying such an amount of offensive and defensive equipment, it is evident they are not far removed from battle ships. Our 'Admiral' class, of similar tonnage, may be equally employed as cruisers, and thus the tendency is to jumble all up together until a war demonstrates how the classes should be differentiated—a word I should like to dispense with but cannot find a substitute. It is curious to observe the fidelity with which Russia has adhered to external armour instead of relying upon protective decks, as we have done in the 'Blake' and 'Blenheim.' Of smaller cruisers few lately have been added to her fleet. It is no doubt considered that more effect can be produced by a few vessels of great power than by distributing the force among a larger number of inferior ships.

Russia was one of the earliest states to perceive the valuable assistance that torpedo boats could afford when the coast is menaced by a hostile squadron. In their war against Turkey little was done in this respect, because the Russian torpedo boats were small and inefficiently equipped. As a result of this experience they obtained a boat from Mr Yarrow which was the pioneer of a larger type. This boat, the 'Batoum,'

100 ft. long, steamed out to the Black Sea in 1880 by herself. She has been followed by others of slightly larger dimensions.

In viewing the development of their navies by the different maritime states it is curious to observe how their relative positions have been altered since the beginning of the century. In some instances less than half a century has sufficed to place a country in the foremost rank. Such an example we have in Italy. No country has shown such boldness, originality, and energy in the creation of her fleet. The lesson at Lissa was only an incentive to renewed exertion, and to-day she can justly boast of being able to place in the line of battle a squadron which only two nations of the world can surpass. Yet this has been the work of only twenty years. The earlier ironclads of Italy were those I have enumerated as taking part in the action off Lissa. Then after 1870 two were commenced, the 'Duilio' and 'Dandolo,' similar in design to our 'Inflexible.' They were the first to carry afloat guns of 100 tons, two of which were placed in each of the turrets. They were muzzle-loaders, and made by Armstrong's firm at Elswick. One of these vessels was designed to carry a torpedo boat in a compartment of the stern to which the sea had access. It was a floating boathouse from which the parasite could emerge when desired, and be received back into it when her mission was accomplished. The idea was original but not practical, and it was soon found that at sea getting the boat in and out safely was

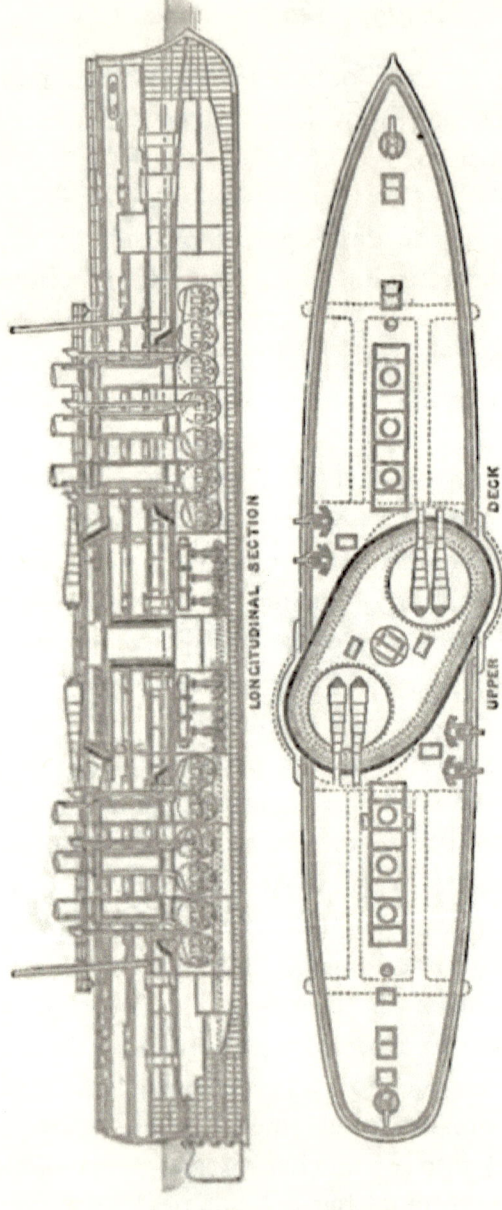

extremely difficult. Eventually the aperture was closed up, and the incident is mentioned as showing that in Italy novel ideas have a chance of being tested.

But in the 'Duilio' and 'Dandolo' Italy did not consider she had reached the maximum of useful efficiency. There was a strong party in favour of individual ships of great power, and their arguments carried the day. The result was an increase to a displacement of 13,800 tons, in two vessels called the 'Italia' and 'Lepanto,' and an entire change in their design. External armour was abandoned, and it was all placed inside the vessel, in a stout deck, round the bases of the funnels, and in a breastwork enclosing the heavy guns. These consisted of four 100-ton breech-loaders, placed in an elongated barbette or redoubt built across the ship, and supported by bulkheads. This structure, with armament, weighs about 2500 tons, and therefore we see a ship not ironclad carrying on her hull the equivalent weight of a cruiser. Machinery of enormous power drives these huge structures at a speed of 18 knots, and they are capable of stowing 1600 tons of coal, which at a speed of 10 knots an hour would enable them to cover about 8000 nautical miles. They are magnificent specimens of naval architecture, but have, in my opinion, a serious defect. This is the absence of external armour, which renders them liable to receive serious damage underneath the structure carrying the heavy guns. The stability of this structure might be compromised by the fire of numerous light guns. Next to these two in size are three vessels of 13,200 tons, the 'Re Umberto,'

'Sardegna,' and 'Sicilia,' which in arrangement are more like our new first-class battle ships. They carry four 67-ton guns, placed in pairs in a barbette at each end of the ship, but the principle of omitting all thick external armour is still adopted. Then there are three others, the 'Andrea Doria,' 'Ruggiero di Lauria,' and 'Francesco Morosini,' of 11,000 tons, somewhat similar to the 'Duilio' and 'Dandolo,' but carrying four 105-ton breech-loading guns in a central redoubt instead of in turrets. Thus Italy possesses ten ironclads of 11,000 tons and upwards, of which all but two are equipped with the most modern artillery and machinery.

She has been equally enterprising with cruisers and smaller vessels. In the 'Piemonte,' built by Sir William Armstrong's firm, she acquired, with the moderate dimensions of 2500 tons, a vessel capable of steaming 20 knots in smooth water without unduly pressing the machinery. This also was associated with a very powerful armament of quick-firing guns. There has been a tendency to overload such vessels with guns, and in the case of the 'Piemonte' my impression on seeing her was that a lighter armament would be more suitable to her dimensions.

Of torpedo-catchers Italy has several of 750 tons and a speed of 20 knots. In this type the experiment was tried of employing three screws to obtain greater speed, for which the 'Tripoli' was selected. But the result was not favourable. It is possible that in a vessel of large size a screw in the centre and one on each side of the stern may answer, but in a small ship they must

Italian cruiser *Piemonte*, built by Sir W. Armstrong, Mitchell & Co.

be so close together that the centre propeller has probably no solid water to work in.

Naturally with such an extent of coast line Italy has a great number of torpedo boats, and the organisation for their use in time of war is very complete. Italy may be justly proud of the navy she has created in twenty years, and her naval officers display a proficiency in handling this *materiel* which is the result of unremitting zeal and industry.

Thirty years ago the navy of the kingdom of Prussia was numerically inferior to that of Austria, but the German Empire is now fast becoming a prominent maritime power. In 1889 a German squadron of ironclads came to England which, though not composed of vessels of large dimensions or latest design, showed in its organisation and the method in which it was handled that the same attention had been given to detail in naval matters as characterises its military department. Up to the present time the largest ironclad is the 'König Wilhelm,' of 9600 tons, of the belt and central battery type, like the 'Hercules' in the British navy. She was launched as far back as 1868, when that system was prominently in favour. Contemporary with this ship are the 'Kaiser' and 'Deutschland,' of 7700 tons, and a few others of smaller dimensions. A later class, composed of the 'Baden,' 'Bayern,' 'Sachsen,' and 'Wurttemberg,' launched between 1877 and 1880, are of 7400 tons, with a central citadel and armament of six 18-ton Krupp guns. The armour on the side only covers the central portion, wherein are located the machinery and heavy guns, but it is 16 in. thick.

For some years after the completion of these vessels no more ironclads were laid down, until the activity of other nations in adding to their fleets spurred Germany to further effort. She could not view with indifference the steps taken by Russia to create a powerful Baltic Squadron. Accordingly, three years ago, a programme of construction was framed, the most important part of which was the completion of four new ironclads of 10,000 tons each. The design selected is somewhat similar to that adopted in late French battle ships— a complete armour belt and three barbettes on the middle line, each containing a pair of 11-in. guns. Between the foremost and middle barbette is the auxiliary broadside battery of light guns. The maximum thickness of belt is 16 in., and it tapers to 11 in. at the ends. These vessels are to have a speed of 16 knots, and all are being built in Germany. Their weak point appears to be the absence of any protection above the belt on the side; but the best distribution of a given weight of armour is a matter about which all experts differ. The distribution of heavy guns in three independent positions seems an excellent one, and provision is made for a high freeboard forward, so that the foremost barbette will have a commanding position. The largest gun mounted afloat in Germany weighs 35 tons, and this pattern is only placed in armoured gunboats. It is considered that for battle ships ordnance of about 25 tons is sufficiently powerful and can be most conveniently handled.

Under the new programme a number of fast cruisers are building, and a few have been completed. The largest type are to be 5500 tons, with a 9-in. bow and stern chaser gun, and eight 6-in. guns on the broadside. They will have a steel protective deck and a speed of 20 knots. The 'Irene,' the first fast cruiser completed, is of 4300 tons, armed with fourteen 6-in. guns, and has a speed of 18 knots. Others are in course of construction. Germany has paid much attention to the organisation of an efficient defence by torpedo boats, and carries out continuous exercise with them in the Baltic and North Sea.

After the Franco-German War two generals in succession were charged with the administration and reorganisation of the German Navy. It was desired that as far as possible the regulations should be assimilated to those of the army, with special regard to the mobilisation of land and sea forces when required. General von Stosch was first selected for Chief of the Admiralty, and on his resignation General von Caprivi was appointed to the post. Both were well known as able organisers, and the result is that all the arrangements for naval mobilisation are as complete as those for the army, and at a word the fleet can be placed on a war footing, ready to perform any service assigned to it. An admiral is now at the head of the Naval Department.

The great advance made by Germany and Italy in

maritime strength has overshadowed the more modest progress in this direction made by Austria. The army has the first claim upon the national purse, and but a small amount can be spared for the fleet. It speaks highly of the management of her naval affairs that, with an annual expenditure of barely £2,000,000 sterling, Austria can show a small but efficient naval force. Her largest ironclad is the 'Tegethoff,' of 7500 tons, launched in 1878. She is of the 'Hercules' type—a broadside battery ship, with recessed sides to give fore and aft fire. Austria has seven others of smaller size, of which the most powerful is the 'Crown Prince Rudolph,' of 7000 tons, launched in 1887, and armed with three 48-ton guns and six $4\frac{1}{2}$-in. guns. The 'Princess Stephanie,' of 5000 tons, also launched in 1887, is similar in design, but less powerfully armed. The largest cruisers are three of 4000 tons of the deck protected type. Two torpedo cruisers, the 'Leopard' and 'Panther,' of 1550 tons, were built for Austria by Sir William Armstrong's firm. They have a speed of 18 knots.

The torpedo flotilla consists of some thirty boats, of which the greater number are of about 80 tons displacement.

Spain, once the great maritime state of Europe, has within recent years begun to rehabilitate her fleet.

In addition to one ironclad—the 'Pelayo,' of 10,000 tons—she has six others building of 7000 tons, and one or two fast cruisers.

Even Greece has been unable to withstand the desire to rank as a naval power, and has lately had three ironclads built in France of about 5000 tons displacement.

Turkey alone seems indifferent to the advantages conferred by an efficient naval force. Under the rule of Abdul Aziz a powerful fleet guarded the Bosphorus and Dardanelles. When invaded by Russia, a supremacy in the Black Sea prevented any transport of troops by that route. But the present Sultan appears to have a greater belief in fixed defences, and his ships lie idly at their moorings, disuse making sad havoc in equipment and machinery. The Black Sea will in future be closed to a Turkish Squadron if hostilities again arise between the two countries, while it is doubtful whether at sea Turkey could now meet Greece. There is, however, still time to do a great deal towards preserving some of the old efficiency—not by tinkering at and altering the older ironclads, as Turkey is ill-advisedly doing, but by keeping what she has got in thorough order, and devoting a small sum annually towards new construction.

CHAPTER XIII

FOREIGN NAVIES—UNITED STATES AND SOUTH AMERICA

Condition of United States Navy before and after Civil War—Apathy in Naval Matters—Change of Feeling in 1880—New Cruisers constructed—Battle Ships decided on and commenced—Special Fast Cruiser—Torpedoes—The Howell Torpedo—Dynamite Gun—Development of Navies of South American States—Chili—Capture of 'Huascar' by 'Blanco Encalada'. and 'Almirante Cochrane'—Peru—The Argentine Republic—Brazil.

IF several of the navies of European states exhibit great progress during the last half century, in the west we observe a fleet practically created in little more than a decade. After a strange apathy of many years, the United States is now fully alive to the necessity of having a fleet commensurate with her position. A few years ago her navy consisted of a number of obsolete monitors and wooden cruisers equally ancient. Such a condition was humiliating, and might be dangerous, seeing that insignificant neighbouring states were in the possession of modern ironclads and swift powerful cruisers. No nation with a long sea frontier and important interests abroad should be without the means of protecting both, and for this an adequate naval force is essential. For the United States this dangerous condition no longer exists. Stirring appeals by successive Secretaries of the Navy have at last roused the nation to action. With a marvellous energy, of which an example was afforded in the last Civil War, America has developed during the last few years everything necessary for the construction and equipment of a modern fleet.

There was no seeking abroad for those appliances which their own country had not hitherto, from want of a demand, produced. The latest ordnance, the best steel armour plates, and marine engines of the most recent design, each requiring special plant for its manufacture were produced on the spot, and warships built which will bear comparison with those of any European state. When we recall the period that has elapsed since we passed from wood to iron in naval construction, and from smooth bore to rifled guns, with the successive phases of improvement in each, none can withhold a tribute of admiration at the manner in which all difficulties in the United States have been surmounted. Defects here and there must occur, but the nation has just cause for pride in the vessels which the Government and private shipbuilding yards have turned out without any abnormal delay in completion.

But brief space need be accorded to a description of the navy previous to and during the Civil War. At the commencement of that struggle America possessed several fine wooden steam frigates of about 3000 tons, and a number of smaller vessels, but the sinking of the Cumberland' by the 'Merrimac' showed that such craft had no chance when opposed to the smallest ironclad. This conclusion was strengthened by the success of the 'Monitor,' and led to a number of similar vessels being constructed with great rapidity. For service in the numerous rivers and inlets of the coast, they had to draw little water. The late Mr Eads designed and constructed several for the Government which only drew 6 ft. Some were propelled by paddle-wheels, and were more like locomotive rafts on which guns were mounted and housed in with iron plates—Captain Cowper Coles's original idea, in fact, carried into practical execution. Then a larger type of monitor was designed by Ericsson as a seagoing ship, and one called the 'Dictator' was completed. Work on another, the 'Puritan,' was suspended in consequence of some error having been made in the calculation of her weights. After a lapse of many years, she is to be now completed with a modern equipment.

At the end of the war it was decided to construct four seagoing turret ships, the 'Miantonomoh,' 'Monadnock,' 'Terror,' and 'Amphitrite.' Only the first named was completed and crossed the Atlantic. She was about 4000 tons and had two turrets. She was of low freeboard, and in a moderate sea her upper deck was swept by the waves.

When the war ceased, retrenchment was the order of the day; the monitors were laid up, where they gradually fell into decay, and only a few wooden ships were annually kept in commission to carry the flag on foreign stations. Though obsolete they were not replaced as long as they were able to perform the ordinary duties of a war vessel in peace time. An effort was made in 1863 to build fast cruisers, and some of 4000 tons and 340 ft. long were designed. But, as we found with the 'Mersey' and 'Orlando,' such dimensions and powerful machinery were incompatible with a wooden hull. The American vessels similarly failed to fulfil expectations, and their existence was a short one. In 1870 Congress decided that the fleet should consist of ten ships, rated first class, of 3500 tons, and twenty of the second class, of 2000 tons. But this abstract resolution was not made concrete by voting the necessary money to carry it into effect, and little was done beyond selling some old vessels. Money received from this source, and a small amount granted by Congress, enabled the naval department to build a few vessels during the next few years which kept the navy going; but in 1876 a fine vessel called the 'Trenton' was launched. Though just under 4000 tons, she had the moderate length of 260 ft., with 45 ft. beam. There was no attempt at high speed, but at full power she could steam 14 knots, and had besides considerable sail area. The armament was composed of eleven 8-in. rifled guns. She was a fine vessel, well suited for cruising in distant seas, but unfortunately was wrecked at Samoa in the hurricane from which the 'Calliope' alone escaped without injury.

In the meantime no new ironclads had been built, and when in 1880 the country was ripe for a considerable augmentation of the fleet, the first want was seen to be that of efficient cruisers. As it was determined not to go abroad for ships and guns, considerable delay was inevitable, so it was not till 1883 that four modern cruisers were commenced, the 'Chicago,' 'Boston,' 'Atlanta,' and 'Dolphin.' The first named is the largest, 4500 tons, with a speed of 15 knots and a mixed armament of four 8-in., eight 6-in., and two 5-in., besides smaller guns. The 8-in. guns are mounted two on a side in sponsons. I think a lighter and more homogenous armament would have been better, but the 'Chicago' is undeniably a very powerful vessel. The 'Atlanta' and 'Boston' are similar in design, but smaller, while the 'Dolphin' is a despatch vessel of 1500 tons. All have been completed, and proved successful, a matter highly creditable to all concerned.

The country was now willing, and even eager, to show what could be done in the New World with ship construction. Five more cruisers, the 'Newark,' 'San Francisco,' 'Charlestown,' 'Baltimore,' and 'Philadelphia,' were commenced in 1887, of approximately the same size as the 'Chicago,' but with a considerably higher speed. All have a protective deck, with sloping sides, on which the armour is 4 in. thick, while on the horizontal portion it is $2\frac{1}{2}$ in. The armament of three of these ships consists of twelve 6-in. guns, but two, the 'Charlestown' and 'Philadelphia,' have a pair of 8-in. and only six 6-in. guns. Their full speed varies from 18 to 20 knots. The 'Baltimore' steamed from Copenhagen to Lisbon in just over five days, averaging 17 knots, an excellent performance.

A fleet of cruisers only cannot, however, safeguard

THE UNITED STATES CRUISER 'CHARLESTOWN.'

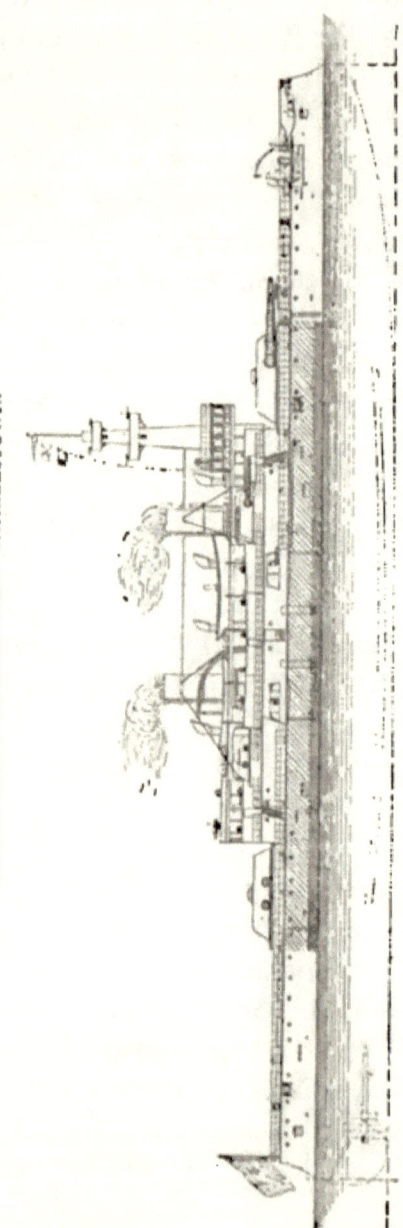

THE UNITED STATES COAST LINE BATTLE SHIP 'INDIANA.'

all the interests of a great nationality. More powerful vessels may at any moment be necessary, and the United States is now wisely constructing battle ships. The first begun is the 'Texas,' the design of which originated in this country. With an imposed limitation of 6000 tons great power of offence and defence cannot be provided, but the accepted design embodies a partial belt, 12 in. thick; two turrets, placed diagonally in a central citadel, each containing a single 12-in. gun; and an auxiliary armament of six 6-in. guns. The armour on the turrets is 12 in. thick, and the ends of the vessel are protected with a 3-in. steel deck. The 'Texas' is to have a speed of 16 knots. This design does not commend itself to me. Too much is aimed at. The freeboard forward should be higher and lighter guns mounted. In our service the preference is given to turrets on the centre line. The position *en echelon* does not give the advantages it was at first thought to have.

A somewhat larger vessel, also under construction, the 'Maine,' has likewise two turrets, one on the bow and the other on the quarter, each containing a pair of 10-in. guns. She has an auxiliary armament of six 6-in. guns, and also carries a partial belt of armour 11 in. thick. The 'Maine' is termed an armoured cruiser, and the design included sail power, but it is doubtful whether this will be eventually provided.

Towards the close of 1889 it was decided to construct three larger vessels, termed coast line battle ships. Presumably the name was given to calm any suspicion that the country was about to embark on an active foreign policy, but it is quite obvious that a vessel which can only operate in sight of land has but a limited use. These vessels, the 'Indiana,' 'Massachusetts,' and 'Oregon' will, however, be quite capable of proceeding to any part of the world should the honour of the country demand this service. They are to have a displacement of 10,300 tons, and will be 350 ft. long and 69 ft. broad. Of this length 190 ft. of the water line will be protected by an armour belt having a maximum thickness of 18 in. There will be a turret at each end containing a pair of 13-in. guns, four smaller turrets in addition will each carry two 8-in. guns, and there will also be four 6·in. guns, besides machine guns. It is difficult to state any great advantage attached to such an armament. On the other hand, the complication of having so many different kinds of ammunition may prove most inconvenient, besides demanding great space for its stowage. Simplicity in ordnance as regards the number of sizes for naval purposes is urgently needed in these days. It may be essential to supplement the few heavy guns which a modern battle ship can carry with a number of lighter pieces, but there is no necessity for an intermediate grade. I even venture to suggest that about four different calibres would answer all requirements, and naval officers would welcome such a limitation. But to return to the American ships. In all other respects the design seems excellent, and in keeping within 10,500 tons the temptation to build monster vessels has been avoided. The view of the naval department at Washington is that 'the lack of important naval battles in recent years stands in marked contrast to the desperate efforts of European powers to equip extraordinary vessels designed to combine the invulnerable and the irresistible. A war of moderate duration between first-class naval powers would prove that a balance of advantages, unsuspected by many, rests with that vessel which has comparative simplicity, even though it be concomitant with a greater exposure of life, a lower speed, and reduced powers of offence.' This seems to me admirably put, but I think the argument for simplicity applies also to the armament.

Two of these battle ships are to be built by Messrs Cramp, of Philadelphia, and the third at the Union Iron Works, San Francisco. At both yards cruisers have been completed in which the workmanship has proved to be excellent.

In addition to the cruisers already mentioned, some others have been, or shortly will be, commenced. The most powerful is the 'New York,' a vessel of about 8000 tons, combining external and internal armour. The former consists of a 5-in. belt opposite the machinery, while the interior of the ship has a protective deck running the whole length, with sloping sides, which portion will be 6 in. thick, while the remainder will be 3 in. There will be a barbette forward and aft, also on each broadside. Two 8-in. guns will be mounted in the bow and stern barbettes, and a single gun of the same calibre in the broadside barbettes. There will also be an auxiliary armament of twelve 4-in.

quick-firing guns. Her sea speed is to be 20 knots, and she will carry sufficient coal to steam 13,000 miles at 10 knots. Though terming this vessel an armoured cruiser, she may be equally considered a second-class battle ship capable of engaging with many ironclads of foreign powers or vessels of similar design, such as the 'Warspite' in our own and the 'Admiral Nachimoff' in the Russian navy.

Perhaps it is the fact that in America there are few large merchant steamers of great speed—such as we possess in the 'Teutonic' and others capable of being converted into commerce protectors—which has led that country to design a warship, at present known as 'No. 12,' of equal speed and greater offensive power than any merchant vessel, to specially act against the commerce of a hostile state. Her principal characteristics are to be: great length, 410 ft., which is 35 ft. more than the 'Blake' and 'Blenheim;' a speed of 22 knots; great coal capacity, 1500 tons; and a protective deck with 4 in. armour on slopes and 2½ in. on the horizontal portion. Her armament will be composed of one 8-in., two 6-in., and twelve 4-in. guns, in addition to a number of small rapid fire guns. The design appears to me well conceived for the object in view, especially as regards the armament, and restricting the heaviest gun to a calibre of 8 in. Her success or failure will depend on whether the expectations as to speed are realised. A special point in connection with the machinery is that she is to have three screws. It is considered that with such a displacement, 7500 tons, the extra propeller will give additional power, though in a small vessel this is not found to be the case. For the slower speeds, the centre screw alone working should prove sufficient, while those on each side would be disconnected and freely revolve with the progress of the vessel. Time can alone show whether this assumption is correct.

As regards torpedo boats, up to a very recent date none existed in America; but one has now been completed, 138 ft. long, which attained a speed of 23 knots, and others no doubt will follow.[1]

It is curious that up to the present no American war vessel has carried a locomotive torpedo. The Whitehead was not adopted when taken up by other nations, and efforts have for some time been directed to obtain a torpedo of native origin. Several have been put forward, but the most promising is one invented by Captain Howell of the American navy. It is similar in shape to the Whitehead, but instead of being driven by compressed air the Howell torpedo is propelled by two screws actuated by the rapid rotation of a heavy steel flywheel. This is fixed inside the torpedo, and spun to a great velocity, before the torpedo is launched, by an independent motor on board the ship, worked by steam or electricity. The axes of the wheel are connected to the screw shafts, by which power is transmitted to the propellers. This flywheel also acts as a

---

[1] For the particulars of all this modern construction I am much indebted to the excellent paper on the subject read by Mr Biles at the meeting of the Society of Naval Architects in the spring of 1891.

gyroscope, in keeping the torpedo on a straight course, so that any deviation and consequent inclination of the torpedo is at once corrected by the gyroscopic pull in the opposite direction. Hence the torpedo travels in the line of projection, and is not deflected by the passing water when launched from the deck of a vessel proceeding at any rate of speed. This is the most valuable quality of the torpedo, as it obviates the necessity of calculating deflection due to different speeds of ship, which with the Whitehead torpedo have to be carefully verified and collated. On the other hand, the latter has a considerably higher speed, which, moreover, is uniform throughout the run, the engines being governed to work at a set pressure from first to last. But in the Howell the flywheel, having when spun up the enormous velocity of 9000 revolutions a minute, has throughout the run a continually decreasing velocity, diminishing the speed of the torpedo until it stops altogether. It is easy to understand that a subaqueous missile which reaches a vessel with sluggish movement has no chance of penetrating a net, and is more liable to be diverted from the object. If this defect can be remedied, and the speed increased, there is a simplicity about the Howell torpedo which to me is very attractive. The absence of an air chamber much reduces the length, which is important on board ship, and in proportion to the amount of explosive the total weight of the torpedo is considerably less than the Whitehead. The present efficiency of the latter has been the work of some years, and I understand it is at last to be adopted in America;

but should the Howell exhibit decided improvement it may eventually take the other's place.

Compressed air is a convenient force, and for propelling a projectile has the great advantage of not varying in its action. Two charges of gunpowder of equal weight may, from variation in manufacture, or a slight difference in moisture, or climatic influence, throw two projectiles in succession from the same gun to widely distant spots. The atmosphere when compressed is not subject to such influences or variations, and has a less violent action than gunpowder. These characteristics have led to its employment to propel large charges of high explosive from a long tube, more commonly known as the dynamite gun. This originated in America, where a successful application of the principle has led to the construction of a small vessel called the 'Vesuvius' with three of these guns, from which 500 lbs. of dynamite or gun cotton can be thrown to the distance of a mile with great accuracy. The velocity being low, considerable elevation has to be given, as in mortar fire, and hence against a moving object a successful shot is most uncertain. But against an object whose position does not alter, when the range is ascertained, great destruction could be accomplished with such projectiles.

In the armament of their new fleet the United States has been able to commence at a period when the experience of other nations in breech-loading rifled guns can be utilised. But plant and machinery for construction had to be provided as well as the heavy steel forgings from which the modern gun is made. Under the energetic initiative of a most able Bureau of Ordnance all this has sprung up, and guns are now constructed equal in power to any produced in Europe. For seagoing purposes it is not intended to exceed 50 tons in weight. They have already a 10-inch gun, under 30 tons weight, which throws a 500-lb. projectile with a velocity of 2000 feet per second. Taking all things into consideration, I do not think that a more cumbrous weapon, in fewer numbers, is any advantage afloat.

It is evident that before the century closes the United States will probably possess a fleet recalling the old days when her wooden walls were to be seen in every sea, easy of recognition by their lofty spars, and noted for the smartness of their exercises.

A review of foreign navies would be incomplete without a word on those which have sprung up in South America. Chili, Peru, and the Argentine Republic, as well as Brazil, have each come to European shipyards for this portion of their armed strength. In the 'Esmeralda' Chili purchased one of the swiftest and most powerful cruisers of moderate dimensions. She was designed by Mr White and built at Elswick. The war with Peru added the 'Huascar' to her fleet. A brief account of this incident will be interesting as the only conflict between ironclads since Lissa.

The 'Huascar,' already described in the account of her action with the 'Shah,' had been doing considerable damage on the Chilian coast, so that it was determined to put a stop to her depredations. Chili therefore despatched the 'Almirante Cochrane' and 'Blanco Encalada' in pursuit. These were small ironclads, of 3500 tons, then armed with muzzle-loading rifled guns, in a central battery protected by 8 in. of iron, while the armour belt was 9 in. thick. As the 'Huascar' had only 5-in. armour, and was 1400 tons smaller, she would have been overmatched by either of her opponents. Early one day in October 1879 the two Chilian vessels sighted the 'Huascar,' and giving chase, the 'Cochrane,' about 9.30 A.M. arrived within 3000 yards of the enemy, her consort being some 3 or 4 miles astern. The 'Huascar' was the first to open fire, but without result. The ships continued to close, as the 'Cochrane' was slightly the faster of the two, and at 1500 yards poured in a hot fire upon the 'Huascar.' Several shell penetrated the thin armour of the Peruvian vessel. One burst inside the conning tower and killed the captain. Another exploded inside the turret and did considerable execution, while others disabled the steering gear and apparatus for working the turret. The 'Huascar's' return fire had little effect. One of her shots struck the 'Cochrane's' armour and glanced off, another entered the ship, but did little damage.

In less than three-quarters of an hour it was evident the 'Huascar' could not avoid capture. She had fought pluckily, but escape was impossible, because she had not the speed, and the 'Encalada' had now come up. The latter at once joined the fray, tried to ram the 'Huascar,' but failed, and nearly collided with her consort. A shell which about this time passed through the 'Cochrane's' battery, killing two men, is believed to have been fired from the 'Encalada.' Soon after the 'Huascar's' turret was again penetrated, and nearly all those inside were killed. Her flag was hauled down after a fight of an hour and a half, in which she had about seventy men killed and wounded out of 220.

Her own fire had been very inaccurate. Out of about forty shots fired from her guns only two or three struck the enemy. This shows the danger of limiting the armament to so few guns, especially when gunners are unskilful. In the attack of one ship by a pair the rapid motion which steam gives renders it difficult to keep clear of each other's ram and projectiles when at close quarters.

It is noteworthy that the machinery of the 'Huascar' was not materially damaged and that few shots struck in the vicinity of the water line. There was no danger of the ship sinking when she surrendered. This was brought about mainly by the disabling of her armament and loss of men. A fact to be remembered when we accumulate armour to protect the vitals and lay bare other portions of the ship.

Thus Chili added a useful little vessel to her naval force, but the late civil war has deprived her of the 'Blanco Encalada,' under circumstances lately familiar to us. Two more cruisers, built in France, the 'Errazuriz' and 'Pinto,' are on their way out. They are of about 2500 tons, high speed, and moderate armament.

Peru, since her crushing defeat by Chili, has been

practically without any navy, and seems unable to find funds to recreate one.

The Argentine Republic may take some pride in possessing one of the fastest cruisers in the world. This vessel, designed by Mr Watts, Chief Constructor at Elswick, and built by that firm, was sold to the Argentine Government, and is now known by the somewhat inconvenient name of '25 de Mayo.' On her trial she attained a speed of over 22 knots an hour. Whether in the hands of her present possessors she will ever again accomplish such a result may well be doubted.

Brazil has two ironclads of moderate size — late acquisitions — in the 'Riachuelo,' and 'Aquidaban,' but no cruisers over 17 knots speed.

From this review it may be gathered that the number of states which aspire to own a war navy has very largely increased. In Europe, Belgium alone of states which have a sea coast is without ships of war. Even Roumania boasts a cruiser. New navies are springing up also in the far East. At present, however, the old balance of power on the sea seems undisturbed.

INDEX

A.

'ABYSSINIA,' The, 123.
'Achilles,' The, 56.
Acre, bombardment of, 15-22.
'Active,' The, a frigate fitted with paddles worked by the capstan, 13.
'Active,' The, a steam cruiser, 150.
'Admiral Baudin,' The, of the French Navy, 253-4.
'Admiral' class, The, 105, 108, 259.
'Admiral Duperré,' The, of the French Navy, 253.
'Admiral Nachimoff,' The, of the Russian Navy, 258, 280.
'Agamemnon,' The, first two-decker, designed for the screw, 24, 33.
'Agamemnon,' The, turret ship, 141.
'Agincourt,' The, 56, 221.
'Ajax,' The, turret ship, 141.
'Alabama,' The, action between 'Kearsage' and, 67-70; career of, 160-1.
'Alacrity,' The, 161.
'Albemarle,' The, a Confederate ship, 194.
'Albion,' The, 24, 33.
Alexander, Fort, at Sebastopol, 32.
'Alexander II.,' The, of the Russian Navy, 258.
'Alexandra,' The, 63-4, 67, 89; at bombardment of Alexandria, 91.
Alexandria, bombardment of, 90-92.
Algiers, capture of, 15.
'Almirante Cochrane,' The, of the navy of Chili, captures the 'Huascar,' 285-6.
'Almirante Condell,' The, torpedo vessel, belonging to Chili, contest with the 'Encalada,' 208-9.
'Almirante Lynch,' The, torpedo vessel, belonging to Chili, sinks the 'Encalada, 208-9.
'Amethyst,' The, action between 'Huascar' and, 151-2.
'Amphitrite,' The, of the United States Navy, 272.
'Andrea Doria,' The, of the Italian Navy, 264.
'Aquidaban,' The, of the Brazilian Navy, 287.
Arabat, bombardment of, 36.
'Archer,' The, 162.
'Arethusa,' The, 222-3.
Argentine Republic, The, **ship of, 287**.
Armaments, 2, 6, 25, 256, 283.
Armstrong, Sir William, hydraulic power applied to rotating turrets, 87; builds the 'Victoria,' 143; Armstrong breech-loader guns, 172-4, 177; hydraulic machinery for guns, 179; 6-in. breech-loader, 184; quick-firing gun, 191; guns of the 'Duilio' and 'Dandolo' made by, 260; 'Piemonte' built by, 264; 'Leopard' and 'Panther' built by, 268; 'Esmeralda' built by, 284; '25 de Mayo' built by, 287.
'Atlanta,' The, of the **United States Navy, 274**.
'Audacious,' The, 145, 226.
Austria, navy of, 267-8.
Azof, Sea of, expedition to, 35, 36.

B.

'BADEN,' **The,** of the German Navy, **265**.
Balaclava, operations at, 29, 30.
Baltic Squadron, The, in the Crimean **War,** 11, 37-41.
'Baltimore,' **The, of the United States Navy,** 274.
'Banshee,' **The,** 216.
Barbette system, The, 102-110.
'Barfleur,' The, 145-6.
'Barham,' The, 162, 239-40.
Barnaby, Sir Nathaniel, Chief Constructor of the Navy, the 'Inflexible' designed by, 85, 198.
'Batoum,' The, Russian torpedo boat, 259.
Batteries, 16, 34, 38, 40-1.
'Bayern,' The, of the German Navy, 265.
'Bellerophon,' The, at the bombardment **of** Acre, 18.
'Bellerophon,' The, of 1863, 62.
'Bellona,' The, 162, 239-40.
'Benbow,' The, at the bombardment of Acre, 18, 20-1.
'Benbow,' The, of the 'Admiralty' class, 106-7, 144.
Berdiansk, operations at, 36.
'Birkenhead,' The, 43.

T

'Black Prince,' The, 56, 221-2.
'Blake,' The, 157-8, 224, 241-3, 259, **280**.
Blakeley's, Captain, rifled gun, 175.
'Blanco Encalada,' The, sunk by a torpedo, 207-10; capture of the 'Huascar' by the 'Almirante Cochrane' and, 285-6.
'Blenheim,' The, 157-8, 241-3, 259, **280**.
Blockade, effect of introduction of **steam and** torpedoes on, 203.
Bomarsund, bombardment of, 39, 249.
'Boston,' The, of the United States Navy, 274.
Bow chaser, 159.
Brazil, ironclads belonging to, 287.
Brotherhood, Mr, three-cylinder **air engine, 197.**
Brown, Sir John, rolled plates, 136-7; compound armour, 138.
Burgoyne, Captain, 36; lost in the 'Captain,' 80.

C.

'CALEDONIA, The, 60.
'Cambridge,' The, formerly the 'Edinburgh,' 10.
Cammell's, Messrs, compound armour, 138.
'Captain,' The, 80-1, 227-9.
Carronades, 7.
Cartridges, paper, 9.
'Carysfort,' The, 18.
Castor,' The, 18.
'Catherine II.,' The, of the Russian **Navy,** 258.
Cavalli's, Major, breech-loading **rifled gun,** 171-2.
'Cecille,' The, of the French Navy, **255-6.**
Cellular sub-division of the double **bottom of** ships, 88.
'Centurion,' The, 145-7.
'Cerberus,' The, 123.
'Charles Martel,' The, of the French Navy, 254.
'Charlestown,' The, of the United States Navy, **274.**
Charnock, **upon French and English ships,** 3.
'Chicago,' **The, of the United States Navy, 274.**
Chili, The navy of, 284-6.
Coal, power of, to stop projectiles, and danger of, **140-1**; question of supplying steamers with, 163; national bill for, 222, 224; 'coal endurance' of ships, 238; amount used for auxiliary engines, 243.
Coast defence vessels, 115-27; coast defence ironclad only found to a very limited extent in our navy, 120; Popoffkas or circular ironclads of the Russian Navy, 125-7.
Cockburn, Sir George, First Naval Lord of the Admiralty, **23.**
Coles, Captain Cowper, in the expedition **to** the Sea of Azof, 36, invention of 'cupola' or turret ships, 71-2; 'Royal Sovereign' and Prince Albert constructed for home service, from his designs, 79; designs the 'Captain,' and is lost in her, 80; 'Scorpion' and 'Wyvern' designed **on** the ideas of, 124, **143, 272.**

'Collingwood,' The, 106, 110.
'Colossus,' The, 141-2.
Commerell, in the expedition to the Sea of Azof, 36.
'Congress,' The, engagement with the 'Merrimac' in the American Civil War, 75-6.
Congreve, Sir William, rockets introduced by, 26.
'Conqueror,' The, 130, 143-4.
'Constance,' The, 222-3, 225.
Constantine, Fort, in the harbour of Sebastopol, 32, 34.
Cordite, 189, 192.
Corvettes, 152-4.
'Courbet,' The, of the French Navy, 250.
Crimean War, The, manning of the fleet for, 11; the 'Terrible' in the, 15; bombardment of batteries in, 16; Transport Department during, 27; operations in the Black Sea, 28-36; in the Baltic, 36-42; floating batteries in, 46-48.
Cronstadt, attack on abandoned, 38-9, 46-7.
'Crown Prince Rudolph,' The, of the Austrian Navy, 268.
'Cumberland,' The, sunk by the 'Merrimac' in the American Civil War, 75, 133, 271.
Cupolas, or turrets, Captain Coles' scheme for, 72.
'Cyclops,' The, 123.

D.

'DANDOLO,' The, of the Italian Navy, 260, 264.
Deck, steel protective, invented by Rear-Admiral Robert Scott, 234; in the French Navy, 256; not adopted in the Russian Navy, 259; in the German Navy, 267.
'Dee,' The, 14.
'Defence,' The, 56.
'Deutschland,' The, of the German Navy, 265.
'Devastation,' The, 82-3, 178.
'Devastation,' The, of the French Navy, 250-1.
'Dictator,' The, of the United States Navy, 272.
'Dimitri-Donskoi,' The, of the Russian Navy **258.**
Distilling apparatus, or evaporators, 244.
'Dolphin,' The, of the United States Navy, 274.
Double bottom, for iron ships, 87-8.
Douglas, Sir Howard, on the expense of shells, 8.
'Dreadnought,' The, 84, 137, 142, 235.
'Duilio,' The, of the Italian Navy, 260, 264.
'Duke of Wellington,' The, 218, 240.
Dundas, Admiral Deans, in command of the Mediterranean Squadron in the Crimean War, 28; reluctant to join in the attack on Sebastopol, 31-2; returns home, 35.
Dundas, Rear-Admiral the Hon. R., sent to the Baltic in the place of Sir Charles Napier 40-1.
Dunsany, Lord, on mastless ships, 52.

Index.

'Dupuy de Lôme, M., at the head of the French naval constructive department, produces the first seagoing ironclad 'La Gloire,' 49.
'Dupuy de Lôme,' The, of the French Navy, 256.
Dynamite gun, The, originated in America, 283.

E.

'EDINBURGH,' The, a turret ship, 141-2.
'Edinburgh,' The, in the bombardment of Acre, 18-21.
'Edinburgh,' The, now known as the 'Cambridge,' 10.
Electric search light, The, 205-6.
Elmore's, Mr, process, 192, *note*.
'Emerald,' The, 24.
'Empress of India,' The, 109.
Engines, side-lever, 212; direct acting, 213; tubular boilers and oscillating cylinders, 213-14; compound, 223, 225, 229; vertical, 235; auxiliary, 243.
'Erebus,' The, an ironclad, 46.
'Erebus,' The, Sir John Franklin's ship, 23.
Ericsson's revolving turrets, 71; builds the 'Monitor,' 76-7; his screw propeller, 77; 'Scorpion' and 'Wyvern' designed on the ideas of, 124, 218; ten monitors on plans of, ordered for Russia, 257; larger type of monitor as seagoing ship designed by, 272.
'Esmeralda,' The, of the Chilian Navy, 284.
'Excellent,' The, 9.
Exmouth, Lord, reduces Algiers, 15-16.
Experiments for testing behaviour of iron under shot, 43-4.

F.

'FERDINAND MAX,' The, Austrian ironclad engaged in the battle of Lissa, 95; Admiral Tegethoff leads the attack in her, 98; sinks the 'Ré d'Italia,' 100, 134.
Floating batteries proposed by the Emperor Napoleon, 46; constructed for the Crimean War and employed in the Black Sea, 46-8; Popoffkas, 125-7.
'Forbin,' The, of the French Navy, 256.
Forced draught, 236, 239.
'Formidable,' The, of the French Navy, 253-4.
'Forth,' The, 159.
France, Colbert's Maritime Inscription, 11; navy of, 248-257.
'Francesco Morosini,' The, of the Italian Navy, 264.
Franklin's, Sir John, expedition to the Arctic, 23.
Frigates, 2; Jackass, 6; steam, 14; early, 148-9; high speed, 149-50; relative strength of line-of-battle ship and, 150-52; name passed away, 154.

G.

'GALATEA,' The, 14.
Gardner quick-firing gun, The, 190.
Gatling gun, The, 190.
German Empire, navy of the, 265-7; four new ironclads ordered, 266.
'Glatton,' The, 120-3, 254.
'Gloire, La,' of the French Navy, first seagoing ironclad, 49, 50, 52, 55; her plates, 136, 221.
'Gorgon,' The, coast defence ironclad, 123.
'Gorgon,' The, paddle steamer employed in the bombardment of Acre, 18.
Graham, Sir James, the 'Excellent' established for training seamen in gunnery, improved by, 9.
Greece, navy of, 269.
Guns, 32-pounders used in 1838, 42-pounders discarded, 68-pounder introduced in 1840, 7, 170; 29-ton, 145; rifled, 170, etc.; breechloaders, 171, 174; Woolwich system muzzleloading, 176; Captain Scott's iron gun carriages, 177; 35-ton, 38-ton, 178-9; 80-ton, 180; bursting of a 38-ton in the 'Thunderer,' 183; 6-in. breech-loader, 184; steel barrel with hoops, the interrupted screw, 185; 111-ton, 188; objections to monster, 188; quick-firing, 190; 4.7-in. calibre and 6-in. quick-firing, 191.

H.

HALE'S, Mr, improved rocket, 26.
Hamley, Sir Edward, on Sir Edmund Lyons in the Crimean War, 30. *note*.
Hastings, Captain Sir Thomas, placed over the 'Excellent,' 9.
'Hazard,' The, 18.
'Hecate,' The, 123.
'Hector,' The, 56.
'Hercules,' The, 62-3, 177, 265, 268.
'Hero,' The, 130, 144.
Hewett, in the expedition to the Sea of Azof, 36.
'Hood,' The, 143.
Hornby, Sir Geoffrey, on size of ships, 113.
Hotchkiss', Mr, machine gun of large calibre, 190; single-barrel quick-firing gun, 191.
'Hotspur,' The, 120, 130.
'Howe,' The, a screw three-decker, 24.
'Howe,' The, of the 'Admiral' class, 106.
Howell torpedo, The, 281-2.
'Huascar,' The, turret ship belonging to Peru, sinks the 'Esmeralda' with her ram, 133-4; engaged by the British ships 'Shah' and 'Amethyst,' 150-2, 207; captured by Chili, 284-6.
'Hydra,' The, 123.
Hydraulic machinery for guns invented by the Elswick firm, 179-80, 188.

I.

IGNITION by electricity, 186-7.
'Imperieuse,' The, 154-8, 259.

'Inconstant,' The, 150, 227-9.
'Indiana,' The, **of the** United **States Navy,** 278.
'Indomtable,' The, **of the French Navy,** 254.
'Inflexible,' The, 85-9, 105, 136-8, 141-3, 180-1, 260.
'Inflexible,' The, first steamship of the navy to circumnavigate the world, 1846-9, **215-16.**
'Invincible,' The, 145.
'Irene,' The, of the German Navy, **267.**
'Iris,' The, 153, 229-34.
'Iron Duke,' The, 133, 145.
Iron, the use of, for **construction of ships,** 43, etc.
'Italia,' The, of the Italian Navy, 263.
Italy, navy of, 260-5.

J.

'JAURÉGUIBERRY,' The, **of the French Navy,** 254.
'Jemmapes,' The, of the French Navy, 255.

K.

'KAISER,' The, ironclad of the German Navy, 265.
'Kaiser,' The, wooden screw line-of-battle ship in the Austrian Navy, 95, ; engaged at Lissa, 99-101, 134.
'Kearsage,' The, United States sloop, sinks the 'Alabama,' 67-70.
Kertch, Fort of, on the Sea of Azof, captured in the Crimean War, 35-6.
Kinburn in the Black Sea, bombardment of, 47-8.
Kinglake, on the capture of Kertch, 35, 42.
'König Wilhelm,' The, of the German Navy, 265.

L.

LAIRD, Messrs, the 'Birkenhead' built by, 1845, 43; the 'Captain' built by, 80; 'Scorpion' and 'Wyvern,' for the Confederate States, built by, 124; two torpedo vessels, for Chili, built by, 208; 'Rattlesnake' built by, 238.
Lancaster's, Mr, gun, 171.
'Lazare Carnot,' The, **of the French Navy,** 254.
'Leopard,' The, of the Austrian Navy, 268.
'Lepanto,' The, of the Italian Navy, 263.
'Lightning,' The, 201, 233, 236.
Line-of-battle ships, 2.
Lissa, battle of, 93-102, 129, 134, 140, 207, 260.
Locks, flint and percussion, 9.
'Lord Clyde,' The, 60.
'Lord Warden,' The, 60, 222.
Lyons, Captain E. M., son of Sir Edmund, in the expedition to the Sea of Azof, 36.

Lyons, Sir Edmund, second in command of the Mediterranean Squadron at the beginning of the Crimean War, 28; at the bombardment of Fort Constantine, 33; in chief command of the Black Sea fleet, expedition to the Sea of Azof, 35, 36; Sir E. Hamley on, 30, *note.*

M.

'MAGDALA,' The, 123.
'Maine,' The, **of the United States Navy,** 277.
Malmesbury, Lord, on the **manning** of our ships for the Crimean War, 11.
Mangin's, Colonel, spherical reflecting mirror, 205.
Manning of ships, The, 10-12.
'Marathon,' The, 159.
Maritime alliance, in, there must be one head, 34.
Maritime Inscription, established by Colbert, 11.
'Massachusetts,' **The,** of the United States Navy, 278.
Maxim gun, The, 190.
'Mayo, 25 de,' The, **of** the Argentine Republic's navy, 287.
'Medea,' The, paddle-wheel vessel, 14.
'Medea,' The, third-class cruiser, 159.
Medium-sized ships, reasons for, 113.
'Medusa,' The, 159.
Mehemet Ali, operations against, 17.
'Melpomene,' The, 159.
Melville, Lord, established the 'Excellent' for training seamen in gunnery, 9.
Merchant **vessel** and a warship, comparison between, 241.
'Mercury,' The, 153, 229-34.
'Merrimac, The,** of the Southern States, action with the 'Cumberland' and 'Congress,' 75-6; with the 'Monitor,' 78, 103, 133, 271.
'Mersey,' **The, cruiser of** 4000 tons, 159.
'Mersey,' **The, wooden** frigate launched in 1858, 25, 50, **273.**
'Miantonomoh,' **The,** of the United States Navy, 272.
Milne, Sir **Alexander, on the percussion** lock, 9.
'Minotaur,' The, 56, 59, 63, 228.
M'Killop, in the expedition to the Sea of Azof, 36.
Models, ships built from foreign, 3.
'Monadnock,' The, of the United States Navy, 272.
'Monarch,' The, 80-1, 83, 85.
'Monitor,' The, designed by Ericsson for the Northern States, 71, 76-7; action with the 'Merrimac,' **77-79,** 103, 272.
Monk, Mr, designer of ordnance, 7.
Mortars, 8.
Mullens, an Irishman who drew plans for the Spanish Government, 4.

Index. 293

N.

NAPIER, Sir Charles, 10; on steam in the navy, 13; fits the 'Galatea' with paddles actuated by winches inboard, 14; second in command at the bombardment of Acre, 18-20; in command in the Baltic during the Crimean War, 37-40; on fleets v. fortifications, 117.
Napoleon I. on the English fleet, 1-2.
Napoleon III. proposes floating batteries, 46.
Naval architecture, few changes in during first half of the century, 2; School of, 3; time for a new system, 49.
Naval brigade at the siege of Sebastopol, 31.
Naval estimates for 1832 and 1834, 2.
Nelson, Lord, 5.
'Nelson,' The, 16.
'Nelson,' The, armoured cruiser, 154, 158, 235.
'Newark,' The, of the United States Navy, 274.
'New York,' The, of the United States Navy, 279.
'Niagara,' The, of the United States Navy, 24.
'Nicholas I.,' The, of the Russian Navy, 258.
'Nile,' The, 142.
'No. 12,' of the United States Navy, 280.
'No. 80,' torpedo boat, of the British Navy, 237-8.
Nordenfelt's, Mr, machine gun, 190.
'Northampton,' The, 154, 235.
Northcote, Sir Stafford, on the Crimean War, 27.
'Northumberland,' The, 56.
'Novgorod,' The, Russian circular **ironclad**, 125.

O.

'OBTURATOR,' 186.
'Ocean,' The, 60.
'Octavia,' The, 222-3.
Ordnance, smooth bore universally employed before 1840, 6, 166; rifled gun, 170, etc.
'Oregon,' The, of the United States Navy, 278.
'Orlando,' The, 25, 50, 273.
Osborn, Sherard, in the expedition to the Sea of Azof, 36.
Oscillating cylinders, 213-14.

P.

PADDLE-WHEEL **steamer, 12, 13, 14, 214,** 216-17, 223.
Paixhans, Colonel, horizontal shell fire in place of shot, proposes to armour ships, 1825, 45-6.
'Palestro,' The, Italian ironclad, 95; blown up in the battle of Lissa, 100-1, 140-1.
'Pallas,' The, 223-5.
Palliser's, Captain, gun, 175-6; device for hardening the front portion of shot.
Palmerston, Lord, on fortifications v. **fleets,** 117, 119.

'Pamyat Azova,' The, of the Russian Navy, 259.
'Panther,' The, of the Austrian Navy, 268.
'Pelayo,' The, of the Spanish Navy, 268.
Pellew, Sir Edward, afterwards Lord Exmouth, on fleets as defence against invasion, 115-17.
Persano, Admiral, Italian commander in the battle of Lissa, 94; false strategy, 96; attack on San Giorgio, 96-7; the action, 98-101.
'Philadelphia,' The, of the United States Navy, 274.
'Phœnix,' The, 14, 18.
'Piemonte,' The, of the Italian Navy, **264.**
'Pique,' The, 4-5, 18.
Plates, wrought-iron, **136**; steel, **137,** 139; compound, 138-9.
'Polyphemus,' The, 131-2, 235.
Popoff, Admiral, of the Russian Navy, designs circular ironclads, **125**; the 'Admiral Popoff,' 126.
Powder, 182; **pebble, 183**; cocoa, 189; cordite, 189, 192.
'Powerful,' The, 10, 18, **20.**
'Prince Albert,' The, 79.
'Prince Consort,' The, 60.
'Princess Charlotte,' The, 18.
'Princess Stephanie,' The, of the **Austrian** Navy, 268.
Prizes, French, always 'took the lead,' 3.
Projectiles, spherical, always employed before 1840, 6, 166; cylindrical, 171.
'Puritan,' The, of the United States Navy, 272.

Q.

QUADRUPLE expansion, engines, **238.**
'Queen,' The, 5-6, 24, 33.
Quoins, 169.

R.

RAGLAN, Lord, 29, Sir Edmund **Lyon's** influence over, 30, *note.*
Ram, use of the, 128-135.
'Ramillies,' The, 109.
'Rattler,' The, 218, 224.
'Rattlesnake,' The, 206-7, 238.
Razées, two-deckers cut down to 50-gun frigates, 6.
'Ré d'Italia,' The, Italian ironclad in the battle of Lissa, 95, 99; sunk by the 'Ferdinand Max,' 100-1, 134.
'Redoubtable,' The, of the French Navy, 250.
Reed, Sir E., Chief Constructor of the Navy, 61-2.
Rendel, **Mr** G., hydraulic **power for rotating** turrets devised by, 87.
'Repulse,' The, 109.
'Requin,' The, of the French Navy, 254.
'Resistance,' The, 56.
'Resolution,' The, 109.
'Ré Umberto,' The, of the Italian **Navy, 63.**
'Revenge,' The, 109.

Index.

'Revenge,' The, in the bombardment of Acre, 18, 20.
'Rhadamanthus,' The, 14.
'Riachuelo,' The, of the navy of Brazil, 287.
Robinson, Sir Spencer, Controller of the Navy, 60.
Rockets, 25-6.
Rous, Captain the Hon. H., of the 'Pique,' 4-5.
'Royal Alfred,' The, 60.
'Royal Arthur,' The, 158.
'Royal Oak,' The, 109.
'Royal Oak,' The, wooden ship cut down and armoured, 60.
'Royal Sovereign,' The, barbette ship, 109, 143.
'Royal Sovereign,' The, wooden ship cut down and armoured, 79.
'Ruggiero di Lauria,' The, of the Italian Navy, 264.
'Rupert,' The, 130, 143.
'Rurik,' The, of the Russian Navy, 259.
Russell Scott, Mr, naval architect, co-designer of the 'Warrior,' 50, 222.
Russia, navy of, 257-60.

S.

'SACHSEN,' The, of the German Navy, 265.
'Salamander,' The, 14.
Samuda, Messrs, build the 'Prince Albert,' 79.
'Sané,' The, of the French Navy, 255.
'San Francisco,' The, of the United States Navy, 274.
San Giorgio, port of Lissa, 96; attack upon by the Italian fleet, 97, 100-1.
'San Josef,' The, Spanish ship taken by Lord Nelson, 4.
'San Nicolas,' The, Spanish ship taken by Nelson, 4.
'Sanspareil,' The, 143-4, 243.
'Sardegna,' The, of the Italian Navy, 264.
Schneider's, Mr, steel plates, 137.
Schultz, Colonel, Polish officer, defends Acre, 17, 22.
'Scorpion,' The, 124.
Scott's, Captain, iron gun carriages, 177.
Scott's, Rear-Admiral Robert, steel protective deck, 234.
Scouts, value of, 164.
Screw propeller, 12; Sir W. Symonds on, 23; question of inventor of, 217; first employed in the British navy, 218; vibration of caused substitution of iron for wood, 220; paddle-wheel entirely superseded by, 223; twin, 226; three, 264, 280.
Sebastopol, bombardment of, 16, 29-34; Mr Lancaster's guns, employment in siege of, 171.
'Seignelay,' The, of the French Navy, 255.
Semmes, Captain, of the 'Alabama,' action with the 'Kearsage,' 67-70, 160.
Seppings, Sir Robert, Surveyor of the Navy, introduces round sterns, 2.
'Serpent,' The, 162.
'Severn,' The, 159.

'Shah,' The, 150; action with the 'Huascar,' 151-2.
'Shannon,' The, 154, 235.
Shells, 8; common and shrapnel, 182.
Shot, double, 7; red-hot, 25, 170.
'Sicilia,' The, of the Italian Navy, 264.
'Sidon,' The, 15.
'Simoom,' The, 43, 221.
Sinope, effect of shell on wooden ships, 8, 25.
'Sinope,' The, of the Russian Navy, 258.
Sloops, steam, 14.
Smith, Sir Sydney, defence of Acre, 17.
Spain, fleet of, 268.
Steam propulsion, 211-47.
Sterns, square and round, 2; elliptical, 6.
Stewart, Captain, in the bombardment of Acre, 21.
Stopford, Admiral the Hon. Sir Robert, commander-in-chief at the bombardment of Acre, 18-22.
Stores, ships', 5.
'Stromboli,' The, 18.
Submarine boats, 203-4.
Suez Canal, 64.
'Surcouf,' The, of the French Navy, 256.
'Surprise,' The, 161.
Sveaborg, 38-9; bombardment of, 40-1.
'Swiftsure,' The, 145, 226.
Symonds, Sir William, Surveyor of the Navy, 3; improvements, 4; designs for the 'Vanguard,' 5; the 'Queen,' 6; dislike for steamers, 22.

T.

'TAGE,' The, of the French Navy, 255.
'Talbot,' The, 18.
'Tchesmé,' The, of the Russian Navy, 258.
Tegethoff, Admiral, Austrian commander in the battle of Lissa, 95-102.
'Tegethoff,' The, of the Austrian Navy, 268.
'Temeraire,' The, 104.
'Terrible,' The, commissioned in 1846, 214.
'Terrible,' The, of the French Navy, 254.
'Terrible,' The, steam frigate in the Crimean War, 15.
'Terror,' The, floating battery, 46.
'Terror,' The, of the United States Navy, 272.
'Terror,' The, Sir John Franklin's ship, 23.
'Texas,' The, of the United States Navy, 277.
'Thames,' The, 159.
Thames Iron Works, The, the 'Warrior' built at, 55, 222.
Thornycroft, Messrs, 'Lightning' torpedo boat built by, 200-1, 236.
'Thunderbolt,' The, 46.
'Thunderer,' The, 18.
Torpedo boats, 200-10; French, 256; Russian, 259; Italian, 265; German, 267; Austrian, 268; American, 281; catchers, 264.
Torpedoes, 193-210; Howell, 281.
'Trafalgar,' The, 142.
Transport department in the Crimean War, 27.
'Trehouart,' The, of the French Navy, 255

Index. 295

'Trenton,' The, of the United States Navy, 273.
Triple expansion, 236-38.
'Tripoli,' The, of the Italian **Navy, 264.**
'Triumph,' The, 145, 226.
Tubular boilers, 213, 224.
Turkey, navy of, 269.

U.

UNITED STATES, navy of, 270-84.

V.

'VALIANT,' The, 56.
'Valmy,' The, of the French Navy, 255.
'Vanguard,' The, ironclad sunk by the 'Iron Duke,' 133, 145.
'Vanguard,' The, launched in 1835, **5.**
'Vernon,' The, 4, 24.
'Vesuvius,' The, 18.
'Vesuvius,' The, American ship with three dynamite guns, 283.
Vickers', Messrs, steel plates, 139.
'Victoria,' The, ironclad, 143-4.
'Victoria,' The, last three-decker, 24, 220.
'Vladimir-Monomakh,' The, of the Russian Navy, 258.
'Volage,' The, **150.**

W.

WAHRENDORFF'S, Baron, **breech-loading rifle** gun, 171-2.
'Warrior,' The, 50-6, **63, 67, 88, 110, 128-9,** 136-7, 150, 221-2, 224.
'Warspite,' The, 154, 157, **209, 259, 280.**
'Wasp,' The, 18.
Watts, Isaac, Chief Constructor of the Navy, co-designer of the 'Warrior,' 50; and 'Black Prince,' 222.
White, Mr, Chief Constructor of the **Navy,** eight first-class battleships, 111, 113.
Whitehead torpedo, The, 195-200, 281-2.
Whitworth's, Mr, rifled gun, 172, 175.
Wire netting round a ship to stop torpedoes, 204.
Woolwich system, The, muzzle-loading guns, 176.
Wrangel, Baron, Russian **general in command** at Kertch, 35.
'Wurttemberg,' The, of the **German Navy, 265.**
'Wyvern,' The, 124.

Y.

YARROW, Mr, torpedo boat builder, boats for Russia, 200-1; 'No. 80' for the British **navy,** 237; the 'Batoum' for Russia, 259-60.

THE END.

COLSTON AND COMPANY, PRINTERS, **EDINBURGH.**

EVENTS OF OUR OWN TIME.

A Series of Volumes on the most Important Events of the last Half Century, each containing 300 *pages or more, in large* 8vo, *with Plans, Portraits, or other Illustrations, to be issued at intervals, cloth, price* 5s.

Large paper *copies* (250 *only*), *with* Proofs of the Plates, cloth, 10s. 6d.

READY.

THE WAR IN THE CRIMEA. By General Sir EDWARD HAMLEY, K.C.B. With Five Maps and Plans, and Four Portraits on Copper, namely:—
- THE EMPEROR NICHOLAS.
- GENERAL TODLEBEN.
- LORD RAGLAN.
- COUNCIL OF WAR.

THE INDIAN MUTINY OF 1857. By Colonel MALLESON, C.S.I. With Three Plans, and Four Portraits on Copper, namely:—
- LORD CLYDE.
- GENERAL HAVELOCK.
- SIR HENRY LAWRENCE.
- SIR JAMES OUTRAM.

ACHIEVEMENTS IN ENGINEERING. By Professor VERNON HARCOURT. With Portrait of R. STEPHENSON, and many Illustrations.

IN PREPARATION.

THE AFGHAN WARS. By ARCHIBALD FORBES. With Four Portraits, and several Plans.

THE DEVELOPMENT OF NAVIES. By Captain EARDLEY WILMOT, R.N. With many Illustrations.

THE LIBERATION OF ITALY. By EDWARD DICEY. With Portraits on Copper.

THE REFOUNDING OF THE GERMAN EMPIRE. With Portraits on Copper.

THE EXPLORATION OF AFRICA. With Portraits on Copper.

THE CIVIL WAR IN AMERICA. With Portraits on Copper.

THE OPENING OF JAPAN. With Illustrations.

Other Volumes will follow.

LONDON: SEELEY & CO., LIMITED, ESSEX STREET, STRAND.

PICTURESQUE PARTS OF ENGLAND.

THE PEAK OF DERBYSHIRE. By J. LEYLAND. With Etchings and other Illustrations by HERBERT RAILTON and ALFRED DAWSON. Cloth, 7s. 6d. Large-Paper Copies (250 only), 12s. 6d.

'When Mr Leyland throws in Haddon Hall and Chatsworth, Ashbourne, and the Dove, his "Peak" has elements of interest sufficient for three or four ordinary books. . . . Altogether Mr Leyland has produced a delightful book on a delightful subject, and it is impossible to lay it down without regret.'—*Saturday Review.*

AN EXPLORATION OF EXMOOR. By J. LL. W. PAGE. With Map, Etchings, and other Illustrations. Second Edition. Cloth, 7s. 6d.

AN EXPLORATION OF DARTMOOR. By J. LL. W. PAGE. With Map, Etchings, and other Illustrations. Second Edition. Cloth, 7s. 6d.

NEW AND CHEAPER EDITION OF

WESTMINSTER ABBEY. By W. J. LOFTIE. With 74 Illustrations by HERBERT RAILTON. Cloth, 7s. 6d. An Edition is published, with 12 Copper-Plates, at 21s.

'Though a dozen books have been written on Westminster Abbey, we know of none at once more complete and admirable, both from a literary and an artistic point of view, than the volume before us.'—*Publishers' Circular.*

LADY MARY WORTLEY MONTAGU. By ARTHUR R. ROPES, M.A. With 9 Portraits after Sir GODFREY KNELLER, &c. 7s. 6d. Large-Paper Copies (150 only), 21s. nett.

PREVIOUS VOLUMES OF THE SAME SERIES.

MRS THRALE, afterwards Mrs Piozzi. By L. B. SEELEY, M.A. With 9 Illustrations after HOGARTH, REYNOLDS, ZOFFANY, and Others. Cloth, 7s. 6d.

FANNEY BURNEY. By L. B. SEELEY, M.A. With 9 Illustrations after REYNOLDS, GAINSBOROUGH, COPLEY, and WEST. Cloth, 7s. 6d.

HORACE WALPOLE. By L. B. SEELEY, M.A. With 8 Illustrations after Sir JOSHUA REYNOLDS and Sir THOMAS LAWRENCE. Cloth, 7s. 6d.

LONDON: SEELEY AND CO., LIMITED, ESSEX ST., STRAND.

RECENTLY PUBLISHED.

THE RUINED ABBEYS OF YORKSHIRE. By W. CHAMBERS LEFROY. With many Illustrations, by A. BRUNET-DEBAINES and H. TOUSSAINT. New Edition, Price 6s., cloth.

OXFORD. Chapters by A. LANG. With many Illustrations, by A. BRUNET-DEBAINES, H. TOUSSAINT, and R. KENT THOMAS. 6s., cloth.

CAMBRIDGE. By J. W. CLARK, M.A. With many Illustrations by A. BRUNET-DEBAINES and H. TOUSSAINT. 6s., cloth.

WINDSOR. By W. J. LOFTIE. Dedicated by permission to Her Majesty the Queen. With many Illustrations. Price 6s.

STRATFORD-ON-AVON. In the Middle Ages and the time of the Shakespeares. By S. L. LEE. With many Illustrations. 6s., cloth.

EDINBURGH. Picturesque Notes. By ROBERT LOUIS STEVENSON. With many Illustrations. 3s. 6d., Cloth. 5s. Roxburgh.

AN EXPLORATION OF EXMOOR. By J. LL. W. PAGE. With Map, Etchings, and other Illustrations. Second Edition. Cloth, 7s. 6d.

AN EXPLORATION OF DARTMOOR. By J. LL. W. PAGE. With Map, Etchings, and other Illustrations. Second Edition. Cloth, 7s. 6d.

LONDON: SEELEY AND CO., LIMITED, ESSEX ST., STRAND.

WORKS BY MRS MARSHALL.

JUST PUBLISHED.

WINCHESTER MEADS IN THE DAYS OF BISHOP KEN: a Story. By Mrs MARSHALL. With Eight Illustrations. Price 5s., cloth.

'Mrs Marshall has done her work well, and produced an excellent book.'—*Church Bells.*

'Mrs Marshall has produced another of her pleasant stories of old times.'—*Saturday Review.*

UNDER SALISBURY SPIRE. A Tale of the Times of George Herbert. With Illustrations. Sixth Thousand. Price 5s., cloth.

'One of the best works which have ever come from Mrs Marshall's pen.'—*Athenæum.*

IN THE CITY OF FLOWERS; or, Adelaide's Awakening. With Illustrations. Price 5s., cloth.

'Very wholesome reading. . . Altogether the story is excellent.'—*Guardian.*

ON THE BANKS OF THE OUSE; or, Life in Olney a Hundred Years Ago. With Illustrations. Fourth Thousand. Price 5s., cloth.

'No better story than this has been written by Mrs Marshall. To any admirer of Cowper, the woodcuts representing the old haunts of the poet will be of much interest.'—*Guardian.*

IN FOUR REIGNS. The Recollections of Althea Allingham, 1785-1842. With Illustrations. Fifth Thousand. Price 5s., cloth.

'The reader will close the volume of Mrs Allingham's recollections with regret. Seldom does one meet with a book of such a sympathetic and touching character. . . . The particulars which it affords of the earlier life of our beloved sovereign are of unusual interest, and will be eagerly received by all who unite in doing honour to the revered name of Victoria.'—*Morning Post.*

UNDER THE MENDIPS. With Illustrations. Fifth Thousand. Price 5s., cloth.

THE MISTRESS OF TAYNE COURT. With Illustrations. Third Thousand. Price 5s., cloth.

IN THE EAST COUNTRY. With Illustrations. Fourth Thousand. Price 5s., cloth.

IN COLSTON'S DAYS. With Illustrations. Fifth Thousand. Price 5s., cloth.

LONDON: SEELEY AND CO., LIMITED, ESSEX ST., STRAND.

A NEW AND CHEAPER EDITION OF

Mrs Marshall's Earlier Works.

PRICE 3s. 6d.

VIOLET DOUGLAS.

CHRISTABEL KINGSCOTE.

HELEN'S DIARY; or, Thirty Years Ago.

HEIGHTS AND VALLEYS.

LADY ALICE.

MRS MAINWARING'S JOURNAL.

Other Volumes will follow.

Mrs Marshall's Popular Series.

1s. Sewed; 1s. 6d., Cloth.

THE TOWER ON THE CLIFF. Ninth Thousand.

THE TWO SWORDS. Ninth Thousand.

BRISTOL DIAMONDS. Ninth Thousand.

HER SEASON IN BATH. Tenth Thousand.

UP AND DOWN THE PANTILES. Ninth Thousand.

THE OLD GATEWAY. Fourteenth Thousand.

ROMANCE OF THE UNDERCLIFF. Sixth Thousand.

LONDON: SEELEY AND CO., LIMITED, ESSEX ST., STRAND.

WORKS BY PROFESSOR CHURCH.

THE HAMMER: A Story of the Maccabees. With Eight Illustrations. 5s., cloth.

A YOUNG MACEDONIAN. In the Army of Alexander the Great. With Sixteen Coloured Illustrations. 5s., cloth.

STORIES FROM HOMER. Twenty-first Thousand. With Coloured Illustrations. 5s., cloth.

'A book which ought to become an English classic. It is full of the pure Homeric flavour.'—*Spectator.*

STORIES FROM VIRGIL. Fifteenth Thousand. With Coloured Illustrations. 5s., cloth.

'Superior to his "Stories from Homer," good as they were, and perhaps as perfect a specimen of that peculiar form of translation as could be.'—*Times.*

STORIES FROM THE GREEK TRAGEDIANS. Tenth Thousand. With Coloured Illustrations. 5s., cloth.

'Not only a pleasant and entertaining book for the fireside, but a storehouse of facts from history to be of real service to them when they come to read a Greek play for themselves.'—*Standard.*

STORIES OF THE EAST FROM HERODOTUS. Eighth Thousand. With Coloured Illustrations. 5s., cloth.

'For a school prize a more suitable book will hardly be found.'—*Literary Churchman.*
'A very quaint and delightful book.'—*Spectator.*

THE STORY OF THE PERSIAN WAR FROM HERODOTUS. Fifth Thousand. With Coloured Illustrations. 5s., cloth.

'We are inclined to think this is the best volume of Professor Church's series since the excellent "Stories from Homer."'—*Athenæum.*

STORIES FROM LIVY. Sixth Thousand. With Coloured Illustrations. 5s., cloth.

'The lad who gets this book for a present will have got a genuine classical treasure.'—*Scotsman.*

ROMAN LIFE IN THE DAYS OF CICERO. Fifth Thousand. With Coloured Illustrations. 5s., cloth.

'The best prize-book of the season.'—*Journal of Education.*

LONDON: SEELEY AND CO., LIMITED, ESSEX ST., STRAND.

WORKS BY PROFESSOR CHURCH.

THE STORY OF THE LAST DAYS OF JERUSALEM, FROM JOSEPHUS. With Coloured Illustrations. Sixth Thousand. 3s. 6d., cloth.

'The execution of this work has been performed with that judiciousness of selection and felicity of language which have combined to raise Professor Church far above the fear of rivalry.'—*Academy.*

A TRAVELLER'S TRUE TALE FROM LUCIAN. With Coloured Illustrations. Third Thousand. 3s. 6d., cloth.

'There can hardly be a more amusing book of marvels for young people than this.'—*Saturday Review.*

HEROES AND KINGS. Stories from the Greek. Sixth Thousand. 1s. 6d., cloth.

'This volume is quite a little triumph of neatness and taste.'—*Saturday Review.*

THE STORIES OF THE ILIAD AND THE ÆNEID. With Illustrations. 1s., sewed, or 1s. 6d., cloth.

'The attractive and scholar-like rendering of the story cannot fail, we feel sure, to make it a favourite at home as well as at school.'—*Educational Times.*

THE CHANTRY PRIEST OF BARNET A Tale of the Two Roses. With Coloured Illustrations. Fourth Thousand. Price 5s.

'This is likely to be a very useful book, as it is certainly very interesting and well got up.'—*Saturday Review.*

WITH THE KING AT OXFORD. A Story of the Great Rebellion. With Coloured Illustrations. Fourth Thousand. 5s.

'Excellent sketches of the times.'—*Athenæum.*

THE COUNT OF THE SAXON SHORE. A Tale of the Departure of the Romans from Britain. With Sixteen Illustrations. Third Thousand. 5s.

'A good stirring tale.'—*Daily News.*

STORIES OF THE MAGICIANS: THALABA; RUSTEM; THE CURSE OF KEHAMA. With Coloured Illustrations. 5s.

'Worthy of all praise.'—*Pall Mall Gazette.*

THREE GREEK CHILDREN. A Story of Home in Old Time. With Twelve Illustrations. Third Thousand. 3s. 6d.

'This is a very fascinating little book.'—*Spectator.*

TO THE LIONS! A Tale of the Early Christians. With Sixteen Illustrations. Third Thousand. 3s. 6d., cloth.

'The picture of the life of the early Christians is drawn with admirable simplicity and distinctness.'—*Guardian.*

LONDON: SEELEY AND CO., LIMITED, ESSEX ST., STRAND.

RECENTLY PUBLISHED.

BORDER LANCES: A Romance of the Northern Marches. By the Author of "Belt and Spur." With Coloured Illustrations. Price 6s.

THE CITY IN THE SEA: Stories of the Old Venetians. By the Author of "Belt and Spur." With Coloured Illustrations. Third Thousand. Cloth, price 5s.

BELT AND SPUR: Stories of the Knights of Old. With Coloured Illustrations. Fifth Thousand. Price 5s., cloth.

'A very high-class gift-book of the spirit-stirring kind.'—*Spectator.*
'A sort of boy's Froissart, with admirable illustrations.'—*Pall Mall Gazette.*

THE PHARAOHS AND THEIR LAND: Scenes of Old Egyptian Life and History. By E. BERKELEY. With Coloured Illustrations. Cloth, price 5s.

CHAPTER ON ANIMALS. By P. G. HAMERTON. Fifth Edition, with Eight Etchings. Cloth, price 5s.
Also a larger Edition, with Twenty Etchings. Price 12s. 6d.

THE SYLVAN YEAR. By P. G. HAMERTON. Third Edition, with Eight Etchings. Cloth, price 5s.
Also a larger Edition, with Twenty Etchings. Price 12s. 6d.

SUN, MOON, AND STARS. A Book on Astronomy for Beginners. By AGNES GIBERNE. With Coloured Illustrations. Eighteenth Thousand. 8vo, price 5s., cloth.

'Welcome as a prize-book.'—*Pall Mall Gazette.*
'An excellent little book of astronomy without Mathematics.'—*Spectator.*

THE WORLD'S FOUNDATIONS. Geology for Beginners. By AGNES GIBERNE. With Illustrations. Sixth Thousand. Price 5s., cloth.

'The exposition is clear, the style simple and attractive.'—*Spectator.*
'One of the most useful books that can be given to young persons.'—*Scotsman.*

THE OCEAN OF AIR. Meteorology for Beginners. By AGNES GIBERNE. With Sixteen Illustrations. Fourth Thousand. Price 5s., cloth.

FATHER ALDUR. The Story of a River. With Illustrations. By AGNES GIBERNE. Price 5s., cloth.

AMONG THE STARS; or, Wonderful Things in the Sky. By AGNES GIBERNE. With Coloured Illustrations. Fifth Thousand. Price 5s.

LONDON: SEELEY & CO., LIMITED, ESSEX ST., STRAND.

www.ingramcontent.com/pod-product-compliance
Lightning Source LLC
Chambersburg PA
CBHW030310240426
43673CB00040B/1121